# CARESSES
Sergi Belbel

# THE SCORCHED GARDEN
Juan Mayorga

# BAZAAR
David Planell

# BLEEDING HEART
Antonio Onetti

# ROUNDABOUT
Lluïsa Cunillé

# WOLF KISSES
Paloma Pedrero

## Other Volumes in the International Collection

# SPANISH PLAYS

## New Spanish and Catalan Drama

Edited by Elyse Dodgson and Mary Peate

SERGI BELBEL ■ CARESSES
Translated by John London

JUAN MAYORGA ■ THE SCORCHED GARDEN
Translated by Nick Drake

DAVID PLANELL ■ BAZAAR
Translated by John Clifford

ANTONIO ONETTI ■ BLEEDING HEART
Translated by Oscar Ceballos and Mary Peate

LLUÏSA CUNILLÉ ■ ROUNDABOUT
Translated by Oscar Ceballos and Mary Peate

PALOMA PEDRERO ■ WOLF KISSES
Translated by Roxana Silbert

THE INTERNATIONAL COLLECTION

## NICK HERN BOOKS

London

*in association with*

**A Nick Hern Book**

*Spanish Plays* first published in Great Britain in 1999
as an original paperback by Nick Hern Books Limited,
14 Larden Road, London W3 7ST

Typeset by Country Setting, Kingsdown, Kent CT14 8ES

Printed and bound in Great Britain by Athenaeum Press Ltd,
Gateshead, Tyne and Wear

A CIP catalogue record for this book is available from
the British Library

ISBN 185459 418 4

# Contents

# Foreword

The Royal Court Theatre has been involved in an exchange
with new writers in Spain over the last six years. In 1993,
Andalusian playwright Antonio Onetti took part in the Royal
Court International Summer School, our annual residency for
emerging playwrights and directors from all parts of the world.
He worked on the translation of his new play with directors
Roxana Silbert and Mary Peate. In 1995 David Planell and
Antonio Álamo joined this new wave of young Spanish
playwrights. As Álamo said at the time, 'The word is
becoming respectable again.'

In March 1996, the Spanish newspaper *El País* published a
leading article about the new playwrights proclaiming a new
found energy and enthusiasm among young theatre writers.
The British Council then funded a research trip for the Royal
Court to explore a creative exchange between playwrights in
Spain and Britain. Playwrights, directors and artistic directors
in Madrid, Barcelona and Seville convinced us we were at the
beginning of an important and innovative dialogue about new
writing for the theatre.

We returned with over a hundred plays from Spain and formed
a reading committee at the Royal Court. We then selected six
plays for a week of rehearsed readings of new plays from
Spain and commissioned translations of the plays into English
from Spanish and Catalan. The plays in this volume were chosen
for the 'Voices from Spain' week of rehearsed readings at the
Royal Court in April 1997. We were looking for new plays
from Spain which were original, contemporary, challenging
and diverse. Each writer travelled to London for the rehearsal
of their play. The translator attended rehearsals with the
playwright to work with actors and the director on the first
reading of their play in another language.

This project was jointly funded by the European Commission
Kaleidoscope Programme and the British Council. The British

Council also enabled playwrights and directors from Spain to travel to London for the reading week. The enthusiasm and commitment of all the Spanish practitioners involved made it possible for the reciprocal exchange of British writers in December 1997. *Nueva Dramaturgia Britànica* was produced at the Sala Beckett in Barcelona, at the Cuarta Pared in Madrid and at the Centro Andaluz de Teatro in Seville with plays by nine Royal Court playwrights translated into Spanish and Catalan:

* Sarah Kane            *Reventado* (*Blasted*)

* Phyllis Nagy          *Desaparecida* (*Disappeared*)

* Rebecca Prichard      *Essex Girls*

* David Greig           *Europa* (*Europe*)

* Jim Cartwright        *Yo Lamí el Desodorante de una Furcia* (*I Licked a Slag's Deodorant*)

* Meredith Oakes        *Fe* (*Faith*)

* Stephen Jeffreys      *El Llibertí* (*The Libertine*)

* Kevin Elyot           *Aquella Noche con Luis* (*My Night with Reg*)

* Jez Butterworth       *Mojo*

All the writers were invited to Spain to attend the rehearsed readings of their play in either Spanish (Castilian) or Catalan.

The Royal Court Theatre has been the home of new theatre writing in Britain since the English Stage Company under George Devine took up residence there in 1956. The Royal Court's impressive international repertoire included new plays by writers such as Samuel Beckett, Bertolt Brecht, Max Frisch, Jean Genet, Eugene Ionesco, Arthur Miller and Wole Soyinka. Since 1993 the Royal Court has placed a renewed emphasis on the development of new international work and partnerships now exist between innovative theatre writers and practitioners in many different parts of the world. Spain is the most comprehensive programme because it embraces both senior writers emerging through exchange and the development of young playwrights. Enthusiasm from our Spanish partners has allowed many ideas to flourish.

Onetti, Álamo and Planell showed there is energy among new writers in Spain. We are delighted that since they first attended the Royal Court International Residency, other playwrights and directors have taken part: Chiqui Carabante, Beth Escudé i Gallès, Borja Ortiz de Gondra, Mercè Sarrias, Juan Mayorga, José Ortuño, Andrés Lima and Carlota Subirós Bosch.

This initiative has also inspired a new generation of Spanish translators of new British plays. Playwright Antonio Onetti translated Meredith Oakes' *Faith*, Antonio Álamo translated Sarah Kane's *Blasted*, David Planell translated Rebecca Prichard's *Essex Girls* and Borja Ortiz de Gondra translated Phyllis Nagy's *Disappeared*.

I am thrilled at how much has been achieved since the project began. The Royal Court produced the English premiere of David Planell's *Bazaar* in the Theatre Upstairs in November 1997. In Spain, Phyllis Nagy's *Disappeared* opened at Cuarta Pared in Madrid in April 1998 and *My Night with Reg* opened in Valencia in November 1998. The Royal Court and the British Council are planning a future programme in Spain of some of the Royal Court plays in Spanish and Catalan and the next `New Voices from Spain' is scheduled for 2000 in London.

In autumn 1998, playwright Sarah Kane, director Mary Peate and I had the opportunity to work with some of the most promising new playwrights in Spain, finalists in the recently created Miguel Romero Esteo Prize for young Andalusian playwrights. The young writers were particularly inspired by working with Sarah Kane. Tragically, Sarah Kane died on 20 February 1999. The following month the group presented readings of the plays they began with her as a special tribute. They continue to work together.

Young playwrights in Spain have been very impressed by the new British plays they have read in the Spanish translations. We hope the plays in this volume will be treated with similar enthusiasm.

Elyse Dodgson
*Royal Court Theatre, London*

## Introduction

The six playwrights in this volume contributed to a resurgence of new writing for the theatre in Spain from the mid 1980s onwards. The previous generation had championed physical theatre and visual spectacle, but by the late 1980s there was a renewed interest in plays, both twentieth-century Spanish classics and plays by living writers. By the mid 1990s, there was enough interest in new plays for a new generation of playwrights to have emerged across Spain, produced mostly in smaller theatres.

Spain produced more new plays in the 1990s than in previous decades. The first reason for this was a reaction against pioneering physical theatre companies who had dominated the Spanish theatre scene in the late eighties. Second, there was a reaction against *auteur* directors which was happening across Europe. Third, there was exposure to innovative European playwrights through international festivals. Finally, there was simply curiosity about what a new text-based theatre might be; Ernesto Caballero, playwright and teacher, expressed this as 'a need to discover what is theatrical in the word'. In 1993 playwright José Sanchis Sinisterra (then artistic director of La Sala Beckett in Barcelona) stated: 'It seems to me that theatre writing is going through an interesting, hopeful time. After the imperialism of directors and the apogee of gesture, image and group theatre, we're going through a period of questioning theatricality through writing. Today it is the author who is beginning to show the way ahead in theatre'.*

Incentives to young playwrights included prizes for new writers, such as the prestigious Marqués de Bradomín, set up

---

* Me parece que la escritura teatral atraviesa un momento interesante, esperanzador. Después del imperialismo de los directores de escena, y el apogeo del teatro de grupo, de gesto, de imagen, estamos en una etapa de cuestionamiento de la teatralidad desde la escritura. Hoy comienza a ser el autor el que señala la linea de evolución de teatro.' (From an interview with Juan Joaquín Vizcaíno in El País, quoted in Teatro Español Contemporáneo, by Wilfred Floeck and Alfonso de Toro, 1995.)

in 1985 (first won by Sergi Belbel), and the Calderón de la Barca prize. Artistic directors started to produce new plays despite a perceived financial risk. José Sanchis Sinisterra at La Sala Beckett in Barcelona and Guillermo Heras of Centro Nacional de Nuevas Tendencias in Madrid produced new plays by young playwrights and both set up writers' groups to help develop their work. Through the 1990s playwrights placed themselves at the centre of theatre production. Some writers began to direct or produce their own plays. Of the writers in this volume, Antonio Onetti, Sergi Belbel and Paloma Pedrero are also directors, and there are other examples of writers who directed their own work in the face of a lack of interest from directors. Playwright Juan Mayorga is a member of El Astillero, a group of four writers who help each other develop, produce and publish their own plays.

These plays were selected by a group of readers on behalf of the Royal Court Theatre to reflect something of the diversity of contemporary theatre writing in Spain but from the perspective of British theatre. We searched for plays by men and women from different parts of the country. We were looking for the best and most diverse group of young writers emerging in Spain.

Sergi Belbel (born 1963, Barcelona) is a Catalan playwright, translator, director and lecturer who writes in Castilian Spanish and Catalan. In his *Caresses* (*Carícies*, 1991) he draws on the structure of Schnitzler's *La Ronde*: a chain of duologues, where each character appears in two consecutive scenes in a different relationship. Belbel creates an overview of society through a range of ages, professions and attitudes. He presents recognisable characters and relationships and then overturns our assumptions about them. Relationships are often ambiguous: the characters avoid the issue or play out different roles. A little boy is merciless, streetwise and ready to mug a destitute old man, but then naive and sympathetic. This reversal of perspective on character unsettles and surprises, evoking a precarious world of unstable identity, random relationships and lack of social structure. Belbel creates a cold and cruel world. Relationships breed resentment and hatred, people are ruthless, almost savage. Characters feel pain and inflict pain: they long for a gentle world but lack understanding, love or the ability to communicate. A fragmented society leaves everyone exposed, raw and isolated. With Belbel, the world is brutal, but the tone is ironic. *Caresses* is surprising and witty, and the language is vivid, playful and rhythmic.

Lluïsa Cunillé (born 1961, Badalona) writes in her mother tongue, Catalan, although she too has written in Castilian Spanish. In *Roundabout* (*Rodeo*, 1992), Cunillé abstracts character into archetype. Characters are nameless and described only by their relationship to the protagonist: friend, brother, father, client, woman and other client. Cunillé drains this world of colour: local reference and idiom are almost entirely absent, the setting is a featureless office. Social interaction is mundane: a pointless existence which stirs an aching desire to break out. 'She' is cool and taciturn, which provokes nervous chatter in others. There is only one scene in which she speaks inconsequentially and at length: with 'Woman', who unnerves and distresses her. For Cunillé, minimal language is a protest against fiction, rhetoric and self-deception. With precise and patterned language, any deviation, detail or generalised emotion becomes charged with significance.

Paloma Pedrero (born 1957, Madrid) is a playwright, director and actress. Her early play *Wolf Kisses* (*Besos de Lobo*, 1987) is set in an imaginary village in central Spain in the early 1970s. Romantic love, a rural setting and a classical narrative infuse the play with a fairy-tale quality. Ana returns home from boarding school in the city. In conflict with herself and her environment, she searches for identity and love. She overcomes resentment of her father, finds friendship with Luciano, a homosexual local boy who is treated like a village idiot, and waits to be rescued by her lover. She struggles against her family and a claustrophobic, narrow society but achieves a degree of self-knowledge and liberation. Pedrero creates a gentle, poetic tone for this modern fairy-tale, which offers some glimmer of hope despite the fleeting nature of love.

Antonio Onetti (born 1962, Seville) is a playwright, teacher, screenwriter, actor and director. Onetti's *Bleeding Heart* (*La*

*Puñalá*, 1991) shows two characters on the edge: Lady Marlboro (La Winston), a transvestite who runs a sweet and cigarette stall, and Malacara, a homeless pickpocket. The setting is specific: a small square in Seville, during the early hours of Wednesday of Easter Week. La Winston is a social outcast because of her homosexuality and her transvestism, and yet she is a devotee of one of Seville's adored Virgins, La Puñalá. By setting the play during Easter, Onetti throws into relief the contradictions of a traditional Catholic society which at once includes and excludes its misfits. Onetti highlights the conflict between Lady Marlboro's fervent spirituality and her mercenary sexual dealings with Malacara. As a petty criminal, Malacara still loves Easter Week with equal passion, but his concerns are material: the street festival offers excellent pick pocketing. When the Virgin of La Puñalá's jewels are stolen, he responds with a combination of greed, residual Christianity and pagan superstition. Onetti's language is inspired by the accent and idiom of the streets of Seville, but it is an invented language which emphasises the contradictory needs, desires and attitudes of his characters.

David Planell (born 1967, Madrid) is a playwright and screenwriter. *Bazaar* (*Bazar*, 1996), is more overtly socio-political than the other plays in this volume. It shows a first generation Moroccan settler, Hassan, and his nephew, Rashid, in their new country, and explores the social conditions which affect and drive them. Hassan is a striving businessman who has tried hard to assimilate himself into Spanish culture; he rarely visits Morocco and prefers to speak Spanish. Rashid is interested in learning about his roots, has a number of friends of Moroccan descent and, much to Hassan's disgust, smokes dope. Planell analyses the situation of the two men through the structure of a highly entertaining farce. Hassan makes a '*You-Have-Been-Framed*' style video of a local chancer called Anton who falls off his bike and crashes into a flower stall. Increasingly desperate attempts to refilm the accident create conflict between Hassan and Rashid, bring danger in their reliance on Rashid's racist friend, and ultimately end in reconciliation. Through the antics of the day, Hassan and Rashid come to a greater understanding of each other and of their position in relation to their two cultures.

Juan Mayorga (born 1965, Madrid) is a playwright and teacher.
*The Scorched Garden* (El Jardín Quemado, 1994) deals with
real history in its concern with the Spanish Civil War but is set
in a psychiatric hospital on an imaginary island off Spain.
Doctor Garay, the director of the hospital, is investigated by a
young man, Benet, who says he is a medical student studying
the methods of the famous doctor, but then claims he is taking
over as a result of Garay's malpractice. Benet disapproves of
Garay's refusal either to treat his patients, who are left to live
out their fantasies and delusions with no attempt to cure them,
or to impose any structure on their day. Garay is also suspected
of killing twelve republican poets who disappeared on a boat
during the civil war, and it is part of Benet's mission to solve
the mystery of how they died. Benet tries to disprove Garay's
theories about treating patients, and to understand what
happened to the poets, but is left frustrated and unsure what to
make of his experience on San Miguel. *The Scorched Garden*
is intriguing and elliptical, and explores the instability of
reality, and the impossibility of finding an objective version of
the past.

There are a number of characteristics which are common to all
six plays: they all make use of naturalism, they explore social
concerns but avoid ideological solutions, they often portray
characters with little influence. But there is a diversity of style
which reflects the search for a new aesthetic to express new
ideas, and which indicates the vibrancy of new playwriting in a
country which is turning to its young playwrights to reflect its
concerns. At the end of the nineties young Spanish playwrights
are beginning to see more of their work produced in larger
theatres and this increasing prominence looks set to continue.

Mary Peate
*Royal Court Theatre, London*

## Acknowledgements

The editors would like to thank the following for their
commitment to this project: the writers, translators, readers,
directors and actors who took part in the 1997 *New Voices from
Spain* season at the Royal Court Theatre.

This project was supported by the Kaleidoscope Programme
of the European Commission and the British Council. The
Royal Court is also grateful to the Instituto Cervantes, COPEC,
Culture from Catalonia, and the Cultural Office, Spanish
Embassy, UK for their additional support.

We are grateful to the following individuals for making *New
Voices from Spain* possible: Antonio Álamo, Michael
Billington, Carmen Brieva, Madeline Conway, Maria Delgado,
Rafael Fente, Simon Gammell, Laia Gasch, David George,
Emilio Hernández, Louise Higham, Glòria Illas, Lina Lambert,
Keith Lawrence, Dr. Dámaso de Lario, Francesc Marieges,
Aurélie Mérel, Domènec Reixach, Juan Toledo, Judith Wilcock
and Graham Whybrow.

*Voices from Spain* was developed in association with the
British Council. We owe a particular debt to David Codling
and Ann Bateson of the British Council Madrid who began this
project with us.

# CARESSES

*Ten Scenes and an Epilogue*

*by*

SERGI BELBEL

*translated from the Catalan by John London*

Sergi Belbel (born Terrassa, Barcelona 1963) is a leading playwright, director and translator. He is a founder member of the Theatre School of the Universitat Autónoma de Barcelona and has been Lecturer in Dramaturgy at the Institut del Teatr, Barcelona, since 1988. He has written 17 plays, many of which have won prizes, which include: *Calidoscopios y faros de hoy* (1985), *Elsa Schneider* (1987), *En companyia d'abisme* (1988), *Tàlem* (1989), *Carícies* (1991), *Després de la pluja* (1994), *Morir* (1994), *La Sang* (1998). He has also written screen plays for drama serials for Televisió de Cataluñya. Some of his plays (particularly *Carícies*, *Després de la Pluja* and *Morir*) have been translated and produced in several countries in Europe and South America. *Després de la Pluja* (*After the Rain*) was performed in English at the Gate Theatre, London in the spring of 1996.

*Caresses* (*Carícies*) was first performed in English as a rehearsed reading in the *Voices from Spain* season in the Theatre Upstairs on 8 April 1997 with the following cast.

| | |
|---|---|
| MIDDLE AGED MAN | Bruce Alexander |
| MIDDLE AGED WOMAN | Amelda Brown |
| WOMAN | Doña Croll |
| OLD WOMAN | Freda Dowie |
| MAN | Neil Dudgeon |
| BOY | Danny Dyer |
| YOUNG WOMAN | Alexandra Gilbreath |
| GIRL | Samantha Morton |
| LITTLE BOY | Daniel Newman |
| OLD MAN | Jeff Nuttall |
| YOUNG MAN | Shaun Parkes |

*Director*   Mary Peate
*Translator*   John London

*Translator's Note*

The punctuation of this translation follows that of the author.

**Characters**

YOUNG MAN

YOUNG WOMAN

MIDDLE-AGED WOMAN

OLD WOMAN

OLD MAN

LITTLE BOY

MAN

GIRL

MIDDLE-AGED MAN

BOY

WOMAN

*Places:* different spaces in a city.

*Period:* the nineties.

## Scene One

*Living room of a flat in the city centre. Armchairs.* YOUNG MAN *and* YOUNG WOMAN.

YOUNG MAN. It's strange.

YOUNG WOMAN. What?

YOUNG MAN. All this.

YOUNG WOMAN. What do you mean?

YOUNG MAN. I don't know if you've noticed.

YOUNG WOMAN. No. Noticed what?

YOUNG MAN. I've got this feeling that . . .

YOUNG WOMAN. Go on.

YOUNG MAN. This strange feeling . . .

YOUNG WOMAN. What's wrong?

YOUNG MAN. It's as if . . .

YOUNG WOMAN. As if what?

YOUNG MAN. As if we . . .

YOUNG WOMAN. We, what?

YOUNG MAN. As if we didn't have . . .

   *Pause.*

YOUNG WOMAN. What?

YOUNG MAN. Anything to say to each other any more.

   *Pause.*

YOUNG WOMAN. Yes.

YOUNG MAN. Yes, what?

YOUNG WOMAN. Yes we do have something to say to each
other.

YOUNG MAN. Oh yes?

YOUNG WOMAN. Yes.

YOUNG MAN. What?

*Pause.*

YOUNG MAN. Go on, what?

YOUNG WOMAN. I can't think of anything, now.

YOUNG MAN. You see?

YOUNG WOMAN. No. I don't see.

YOUNG MAN. You don't want to see.

YOUNG WOMAN. But, see what? What? Come on: would
you be so good as to tell me what the bloody hell I should
see?

YOUNG MAN. Do you want me to tell you again?

YOUNG WOMAN. No. If you're only going to repeat what
you've already said, you'd better shut up.

YOUNG MAN. Okay, then, if I'd better shut up, I'll shut up.

*Pause.*

YOUNG WOMAN. We have plenty of things to say to each
other, even now, you know very well. I know there are
things you think and keep quiet because you don't want to
say them, or you don't want to say them to me, yes, say
them to me, to me, because of some problem of yours I
don't know about, which even you yourself don't know
about, and that hurts me, you know?, it hurts me, it upsets
me, and it upsets me to see you like this, to see me like this,
to see us like this, filling all these idle moments of silence
with idle words, and with insults, your insults, because what
you've just said is an insult, you're insulting me, you're

insulting me when you say you don't have anything to say to me any more.

YOUNG MAN. Excuse me. Just a minute.

YOUNG WOMAN. Why are you interrupting me!! You always interrupt me when I start . . . start building up a . . . a coherent argument which goes beyond the . . . the monosyllables which are so characteristic of our daily conversation!! You're just like my mother, and if I left home it wasn't exactly to go and live with somebody identical to her or even worse!! None of this excuse me just a minute!! I was the one who was speaking and I'm the one who'll carry on speaking!! And we'll see if things don't start changing in this shit-hole, at least in this one!

*He slaps her violently in the face.*

YOUNG MAN. When somebody says 'Excuse me' you react, you shut up and you listen, do you understand? And I said 'Excuse me' to make a passing comment within your . . . marvellous, ever-so coherent and ever-so explicit argument, and I intend doing so, do you hear?, I intend doing so, I intend doing so, I intend doing so!!

*He slaps her again in the face, even more strongly.*

I didn't say *I* don't have anything to say to you any more, do you hear?

*He slaps her for the third time, savagely.*

I said we don't have anything to say to each other any more. Not me. Not you. I said we.

*Silence.*

YOUNG WOMAN. What do you want for dinner?

YOUNG MAN. I don't know. What is there?

YOUNG WOMAN. There's meat, eggs, salad. I can do you spaghetti if you want.

YOUNG MAN. No, no, pasta at night, no, afterwards I get heartburn. One of those salads with lots of different things and a good pudding.

YOUNG WOMAN. We've got lettuce, tomatoes, carrots, sweet corn, olives, celery, onions.

YOUNG MAN. No, no, onions, no, it repeats on me afterwards.

YOUNG WOMAN. Yes, and what's more your breath stinks and afterwards there's an unbearable stench in the bed.

YOUNG MAN. We could mix in bits of apple and pineapple, if we've got any, of course.

YOUNG WOMAN. Ooh, yes. A tropical salad. That would be lovely. There's only tinned pineapple, I'm afraid.

YOUNG MAN. That's okay.

YOUNG WOMAN. Good. Come on, then. Ooh! I don't know if there's anything for pudding.

YOUNG MAN. Isn't there any crème caramel?

YOUNG WOMAN. Oh, yes, I forgot. How silly of me. I bought a couple of tubs at lunchtime. Oh, and we've got yoghourts as well.

YOUNG MAN. I'd prefer crème caramel.

YOUNG WOMAN. Well I'll have a yoghourt.

YOUNG MAN. I'll have a crème caramel.

YOUNG WOMAN. Okay then, you have a crème caramel and I'll have a yoghourt, there's no problem.

YOUNG MAN. There's no problem. Shall I help you make the salad?

YOUNG WOMAN. Yes. We'll be quicker together. Shall we go into the kitchen?

YOUNG MAN. Yes.

*They make as if to exit. She stops.*

YOUNG WOMAN. Excuse me. Just a minute.

YOUNG MAN. What?

*She punches him in the stomach and knees him in the groin. He falls to the ground.*

YOUNG WOMAN. We've run out of oil.

YOUNG MAN. Oh.

YOUNG WOMAN. You'll have to ask the neighbour for some.

YOUNG MAN. Oh, I can't brea . . .

YOUNG WOMAN. Come on, get up, we mustn't waste time.

YOUNG MAN. Oh. Oh.

YOUNG WOMAN. Come on, hurry up, get up, grab a glass
and while I soak the lettuce, go and ask the neighbour to fill
it up with olive oil. But make sure it's olive oil, okay?,
I can't stand salads with sunflower oil or corn oil, they're
tasteless.

YOUNG MAN. You nasty snake.

YOUNG WOMAN. Get up and come to the kitchen.

YOUNG MAN. You're repulsive.

*She kicks him in the face.*

YOUNG WOMAN. Are you getting up or aren't you getting
up?!

*She kicks him again right in the face.*

Are you coming to the kitchen or aren't you coming to the
kitchen?!!

*She kicks him in the face again.*

Are you going to ask the neighbour for oil or aren't you
going to ask the neighbour for oil?!!!

*Another kick in the face, this time much stronger.*

Do you want a tropical salad . . . or don't you want a
tropical salad?!

*Silence.*

YOUNG MAN. Oh.

YOUNG WOMAN. What?

YOUNG MAN. Ooh.

YOUNG WOMAN. Oh dear, I can't understand you.

YOUNG MAN. Oooh.

YOUNG WOMAN. I'm sorry, if you can't articulate more
clearly . . .

YOUNG MAN. Ooooh.

YOUNG WOMAN. Do you, perhaps, want to say something
to me?

YOUNG MAN. Mmm . . . yes . . .

YOUNG WOMAN. You see? You see how you've still got
something to say to me?


**Scene Two**

*A park. A stone bench.* YOUNG WOMAN *and* MIDDLE-
AGED WOMAN.

YOUNG WOMAN. What do you want?

MIDDLE-AGED WOMAN. Listen to this.

YOUNG WOMAN. What are you going on about? Listen to
what?

MIDDLE-AGED WOMAN. Just let me read it out. You
know . . . it's very difficult for me to speak. And what I
want to tell you . . . but no. Listen carefully.

YOUNG WOMAN. What is it?

MIDDLE-AGED WOMAN. It doesn't matter. It doesn't matter
who wrote it. It doesn't matter how it's written. The words
are what matter to me. It's meant for you and for me. I hope
you understand it. I'm doing this so you understand me.

*She picks up the book on her lap and reads:*

'Now that night is coming, silence is frightened away,
because it is not true that silence is night. It's one of those
clichés: thinking that everything stops when everybody

stops, and then everybody thinks . . . eventually stopping after all that routine, means stopping time and entering into rest, and they think that is night: a soldier's rest, a boring piece of theatre, a prelude to sleep, a hollow interval, a much needed nothingness. Now that night is coming, a new time denies time; fuels desire, fosters excess: moments become eternal, unconfessable secrets are . . . brutally revealed, pretences collapse, some mad gesture can make everything explode, unusual passions, unsuspected desires . . . Night is the engine of eloquent silence, where time is not time, where place is no place at all, where darkness is radiant and nothingness is impossible . . . '

YOUNG WOMAN. That's enough, mother, put a sock in it!

MIDDLE-AGED WOMAN. What?

YOUNG WOMAN. Just fucking well shut up. Shit what a pain! What the bloody hell are you trying to tell me, if you're trying to tell me anything? You haven't made me come so far so late to give this lecture full of nonsense, to spew up, just because, as casual as you like, this load of still births and pedantic sentences, sublime pieces of pretentiousness written by an idiot for a bunch of morons who don't know what they really are?! As if I didn't know you . . . Stop all this rubbish. Tell me quickly what you want, I don't have much time, I'm having dinner with somebody. I can't waste time like a crazy old woman . . .

MIDDLE-AGED WOMAN. Go, then.

YOUNG WOMAN. Don't start!

MIDDLE-AGED WOMAN. I'm just asking for a short moment, that's all. I'm so lonely, my child, and I think so many things. Since you left, the place isn't what it used to be. Before it was hell, a constant battle: rows, sour faces, shouting, worrying, nerves, stress. I know, I admit it: per-haps it was my fault, war had broken out between us, a little hostile war made up of the slightest gestures and slightest words and eternal silences. The cruellest war is war between women, and it's crueller still if it's between mother and daughter. But now that you're not there I need it so much . . .

YOUNG WOMAN. Have you gone mad?

MIDDLE-AGED WOMAN. Yes.

YOUNG WOMAN. You admit it?

MIDDLE-AGED WOMAN. Yes.

YOUNG WOMAN. Is that why you made me come here? Is that why you've bothered me and begged me to come and see you and listen to you? To tell me what I already know? To tell me you're mad?

MIDDLE-AGED WOMAN. No. To tell you the time has finally come.

YOUNG WOMAN. Which time?

MIDDLE-AGED WOMAN. The time.

YOUNG WOMAN. To put you in a home?

MIDDLE-AGED WOMAN. To tell you the truth.

YOUNG WOMAN. If you feel so lonely living on your own, if you're frightened of growing old and not having anyone whose head you can fill with your stories, with your obsessions, you can live in a home, there are some very good ones now.

MIDDLE-AGED WOMAN. It wasn't my fault.

YOUNG WOMAN. You'd get to know people, somebody would take notice of you, you'd enjoy it, they'd listen to you there. I've been told they're beautiful, apparently they're not prisons any more, they're more like . . . a kind of hotel, for old people but really clean, you can go and come back when you want to and they do outings.

MIDDLE-AGED WOMAN. I'm sorry I waited so long.

YOUNG WOMAN. I've been telling you for some time now and you won't take any notice of me.

MIDDLE-AGED WOMAN. I'm not your mother.

YOUNG WOMAN. It's a good place for you, the home.

*Silence.*

MIDDLE-AGED WOMAN. What time is it?

YOUNG WOMAN. It's very late.

MIDDLE-AGED WOMAN. Daughter.

YOUNG WOMAN. What?

MIDDLE-AGED WOMAN. I thought this was the best place to tell you that I've finally taken a decision about this obsession of yours for getting rid of me and stop being a burden for you and the world. I know I'm still young, but I'm aware of my illness and I'm aware that I can't live alone and I'm aware that everything chokes me and that I tell lies, I tell you lies, I tell myself lies to kill time or to make up for it, and that's why I'm asking you . . .

YOUNG WOMAN. You're speaking like a book.

MIDDLE-AGED WOMAN. . . . . I'm asking you to take all the steps and spare me problems and paperwork and legal hassle and phone calls and visits and don't pay any attention to what I say, to what I've said to you.

YOUNG WOMAN. Yes, you're right. It's the best place. It's such a peaceful park. So secluded, mother. So secluded.

MIDDLE-AGED WOMAN. I don't understand you.

YOUNG WOMAN. Don't worry. I'll take care of everything.

MIDDLE-AGED WOMAN. Thanks.

YOUNG WOMAN. Mother.

MIDDLE-AGED WOMAN. What?

YOUNG WOMAN. You should have had an abortion.

MIDDLE-AGED WOMAN. I'll like it, I'm sure. I'll like the home.

YOUNG WOMAN. Goodbye. And stop reading those things. They'll drive you more insane.

MIDDLE-AGED WOMAN. Call me.

YOUNG WOMAN. Even more.

**Scene Three**

*Lounge in an old people's home. A sofa.* MIDDLE-AGED
WOMAN *and* OLD WOMAN.

OLD WOMAN. I used to like dancing the tango.

*Pause.*

MIDDLE-AGED WOMAN. I liked rock-and-roll.

*Pause.*

MIDDLE-AGED WOMAN. I always danced rock-and-roll,
every Saturday, every Sunday, and I sneaked out through the
courtyard window, my parents didn't know, and he used to
wait for me in the back alley, behind the courtyard, it was at
the back of the house, and we grabbed each other's hand;
his hand was always warm, mine was cold, and he warmed
mine up, and we used to run off to the north of the city.
There, you could already hear the music from the main
street: real rock-and-roll, and we danced like mad, and it
was like that for a whole year, maybe longer, our hands
stuck together and our bodies stuck together, each weekend
until . . . until . . . that little girl came along, that stupid little
girl, you can't imagine how much I hated her, my disgusting
daughter: she stopped me from dancing!, and my parents
had put bars on the back window and I sat rotting inside and
my stomach got more and more swollen every day; but one
day, to get it all out of my system, I was so frantic I escaped
and went there all by myself, to the main street, to the
dance-hall on the main street, all by myself, he wasn't there
any more and he never came back and I never saw him
and I still remember him, muscular arms and strong legs, a
bronze stomach and burning hands, he ran away, but that
night I danced like never before, it was a drug, I couldn't
stop and everybody looked at me and I danced by myself,
the stupid thing had already spent seven months of lethargy
rotting inside me, sucking my blood, the food of my insides,
here inside me, implausibly inside this belly which is now
flabby, and she bounced up and down, she must have been
bumping against my intestines, into my stomach, into my

bones, into my liver and kidneys; I wanted to shake her, make her dizzy, puke her up; my revenge: almost six months, since the first bouts of nausea, six months that she'd stopped me from dancing rock-and-roll, that moron, that untimely monstrous creature! Because you need two to dance to rock-and-roll and he ran away and they shut me up; but that evening I danced by myself like a mad woman in front of everybody and when my favourite song was played the blood flowed right down to my ankles . . .

*Pause.*

OLD WOMAN. I liked dancing the tango because I hate men as well, I hate them as well; and when we danced, that little idiot didn't even notice. And he was happy, the poor wretch, thinking that he was controlling me . . . they always say . . . men are in control with the tango . . . and I knew that wasn't right, and there and then I chucked him, in the dance-hall, when he wanted to put his hand in between my legs after we'd danced his favourite tango (which was the one I liked least). Poor boy, I can't even remember his face, only his hairy hands like black caterpillars and that horror between his legs. Poor boy. The only man in my life, luckily, the only man. I never danced again with any other man and . . . and I liked the tango. It's a funny world. I liked the tango . . .

*Pause.*

MIDDLE-AGED WOMAN. I didn't know you were here.

OLD WOMAN. Don't worry. You'll get used to it.

*Pause.*

MIDDLE-AGED WOMAN. Doesn't time fly.

OLD WOMAN. That's what they say.

MIDDLE-AGED WOMAN. You look great.

OLD WOMAN. That's not true.

MIDDLE-AGED WOMAN. Really.

*Pause. The* MIDDLE-AGED WOMAN *stares at the* OLD WOMAN, *grabs her by the hand and goes up to her. They*

*have a long French kiss. Suddenly, some soft, sentimental*
*music is heard. The sound quality is slightly defective.*

OLD WOMAN. Shall we dance?

MIDDLE-AGED WOMAN. Let's have a go.

*They get up. They clutch each other. They dance.*

OLD WOMAN. It's unbearable.

MIDDLE-AGED WOMAN. It's horrible.

OLD WOMAN. Oh, that's enough.

*They stop dancing.*

MIDDLE-AGED WOMAN. How awful.

OLD WOMAN. Stop it!!!

*The music stops.*

MIDDLE-AGED WOMAN. Is it always like that?

OLD WOMAN. Stupid old nurses.

MIDDLE-AGED WOMAN. Always like that?

OLD WOMAN. I've told them hundreds of times, but it's no
use.

MIDDLE-AGED WOMAN. How terrible.

OLD WOMAN. If that music equipment were mine . . .

MIDDLE-AGED WOMAN. If it were ours . . .

OLD WOMAN. No way. No way. Old people's music, old
people's music, the bloody nurses like old people's music,
they love it, they're crazy about it, and they won't
understand that I hate it and I'm not the only one. No way,
no way, I'm going to complain again!

MIDDLE-AGED WOMAN. That's it, let's complain.

OLD WOMAN. Yes, the two of us together, it'll be better with
the two of us together.

MIDDLE-AGED WOMAN. Don't worry, I'll help you.

OLD WOMAN. We'll have to be very firm.

MIDDLE-AGED WOMAN. Well, let's be firm.

OLD WOMAN. And take drastic measures.

MIDDLE-AGED WOMAN. Such as?

OLD WOMAN. A hunger-strike. A hunger-strike.

MIDDLE-AGED WOMAN. That's it. Until they play the music we want.

*Pause.*

OLD WOMAN. Maybe they'll let us die.

MIDDLE-AGED WOMAN. Maybe they will.

OLD WOMAN. I've only got a little time left.

MIDDLE-AGED WOMAN. No.

OLD WOMAN. Yes.

*Pause.*

MIDDLE-AGED WOMAN. We've got each other.

OLD WOMAN. Don't worry. You'll get used to it.

*Silence.*

MIDDLE-AGED WOMAN. It's lucky you're here.

OLD WOMAN. Why?

MIDDLE-AGED WOMAN. It's lucky we met up again.

OLD WOMAN. What do you mean?

MIDDLE-AGED WOMAN. I thought I'd lost you.

OLD WOMAN. What do you mean?

MIDDLE-AGED WOMAN. You taught me so many things.

OLD WOMAN. *What?*

MIDDLE-AGED WOMAN. About life. In such a short time.

OLD WOMAN. Sorry.

MIDDLE-AGED WOMAN. What.

OLD WOMAN. I really don't remember you.

*The* MIDDLE-AGED WOMAN *cries.*

## Scene Four

*A street. A container.* OLD WOMAN *and* OLD MAN.

OLD MAN. You're a slag dressed up as an old woman.

OLD WOMAN. What are you looking for.

OLD MAN. Food.

OLD WOMAN. It's more than ten years since we've seen each other.

OLD MAN. I'm hungry.

OLD WOMAN. Aren't you going to say anything to me?

OLD MAN. Slag.

OLD WOMAN. Aren't you going to say anything to me?

OLD MAN. Slag slag slag. Go away I'm hungry.

*Pause. The* OLD MAN *rummages about in the rubbish.*

OLD WOMAN. I've only got twenty minutes left. Because the home shuts at nine. Somebody said you were here. Today I've finally come to a decision. Ten years is a long time but you haven't changed. Half past eight, half past eight. I've been walking for six hours. Because I left after lunch. And I've been walking round and round. I don't know these streets. Even though they're in the city centre. They told me you were here. I know you sleep in the street. Your bedspread's a newspaper. Ten years I've known and today I've finally come to a decision. I don't know why. Or perhaps I do, I don't know.

OLD MAN. A sardine!!

OLD WOMAN. I don't feel sorry for you.

OLD MAN. Three sardines!!

*The* OLD MAN *takes out of the container a bag he has just ripped open. He sits down on the ground and takes out an open can of sardines.*

OLD WOMAN. I don't feel sorry for you.

OLD MAN. Go away you slag they're mine.

OLD WOMAN. I don't want to eat.

OLD MAN. Bastard bastard I know who you are I know who you are.

OLD WOMAN. You know who I am.

OLD MAN. Yes: a slag dressed up as an old woman: a disguised policeman. No! no! no! don't cut my hair I want to be here I don't want to have a wash I'll fart don't clean my shit up I like dry shit so my arse doesn't get cold the sardines are mine.

OLD WOMAN. Why don't you come to the home.

OLD MAN. I don't want my arse to get cold shit shit I want shit.

OLD WOMAN. Why don't you come to the home.

OLD MAN. My sister lives in the home.

OLD WOMAN. Your sister.

OLD MAN. Slag dressed up as an old woman.

*Pause. The* OLD MAN *greedily eats half a sardine.*

OLD WOMAN. I've got to go.

OLD MAN. Little sardine little sardine. Nice little sardine.

OLD WOMAN. Come on.

OLD MAN. Ugh disgusting I'm thirsty it's salty it's salty.

*He throws the sardine into the* OLD WOMAN's *face.*

OLD WOMAN. Oh. What are you doing.

OLD MAN. Little sardines covered in salt for old slags. I'm thirsty, I'm thirsty.

*The* OLD MAN *rummages in the container again.*

OLD WOMAN. And if it were the last time we saw each other? You're strong, you're mad, madmen are strong, too strong to die before their time. I'm ill and I'm older than you. Only a little but I am, only three years, but they're years just the same. Huh, before . . . what were three years for us before? Nothing. And we've always got on, and we've always understood each other, especially before. When they switched off the light in our room we used to whisper to each other and laugh, we understood each other. We weren't scared, we used to tell each other everything.

OLD MAN. Chicken!!

OLD WOMAN. Don't try to make me feel sorry for you.

OLD MAN. A half-eaten chicken!!

*He takes out another bag which has already been ripped open. From it he takes out chicken bones. He sits down on the ground. Dirt all around him.*

OLD WOMAN. Don't try and make me feel sorry for you.

OLD MAN. Roast chicken good pickin'. I won't give you any you old lemon slag.

OLD WOMAN. I don't want to eat, I'm not hungry.

*He eats. She looks at him, crouches down and sits by him. He looks at her, surprised.*

OLD MAN. You're not a policeman.

OLD WOMAN. No.

OLD MAN. You're an old woman.

OLD WOMAN. Yes.

OLD MAN. An old woman who was once young.

OLD WOMAN. Yes.

OLD MAN. Are you good?

OLD WOMAN. Yes.

OLD MAN. That means I can tell you a tiny little secret.

OLD WOMAN. Yes.

*He shows her one of his fingers with a ring on it.*

OLD MAN. Do you like it?

OLD WOMAN. Yes.

OLD MAN. I had a wife.

OLD WOMAN. I know.

OLD MAN. You don't know anything.

OLD WOMAN. Come to the home.

OLD MAN. A wife all of my own.

OLD WOMAN. Your wife.

OLD MAN. She died.

OLD WOMAN. A long time ago.

OLD MAN. She left me.

OLD WOMAN. Too long ago.

OLD MAN. She left me before she died.

OLD WOMAN. That's not true.

OLD MAN. We used to live together.

OLD WOMAN. What are you eating.

OLD MAN. We didn't see much of each other.

OLD WOMAN. Don't speak so much.

OLD MAN. My wife had a girlfriend. Hee hee.

OLD WOMAN. Come to the home.

OLD MAN. What lovely chicken.

OLD WOMAN. I'm good.

OLD MAN. I was the one who did the cooking.

OLD WOMAN. I'm dying.

OLD MAN. My sister.

OLD WOMAN. Not seeing you for ten years.

OLD MAN. And while I did the cooking . . .

OLD WOMAN. Sorry.

OLD MAN. My wife had a girlfriend: my sister.

*Silence.*

OLD WOMAN. I'm hungry.

*The* OLD MAN *holds out a half-eaten chicken bone for her. They eat. They gaze into the distance.*

*Pause. The* OLD WOMAN *gets up with difficulty.*

OLD WOMAN. A quarter to nine. The home shuts at nine. You don't want to come. I'm going.

OLD MAN. You slag dressed up as an old woman. You're dying.

*He bursts out laughing.*


**Scene Five**

*A street. Steps of a bar which is closed.* OLD MAN *and* LITTLE BOY.

LITTLE BOY. Hey you, what've you got in your pockets?

OLD MAN. Go to sleep little boy go to sleep.

LITTLE BOY. If you've got any money, give it to me.

OLD MAN. What time is it? Isn't it very late? Isn't it very late? Isn't it three o'clock? Isn't it four o'clock?

LITTLE BOY. Shut up.

OLD MAN. Oh. I'm not saying a thing not a thing.

LITTLE BOY. What is it you've got in your pockets?

OLD MAN. You're a little boy it's dark it's very late. The bar: closed.

LITTLE BOY. Give it to me.

OLD MAN. Oh you son of a slagbitch son of a slag your mother's a slag.

LITTLE BOY. My mother isn't a slag, you idiot.

OLD MAN. Oh you want to mug me. Sons of slagbitches go in for mugging and beating people up mugging and beating people up.

LITTLE BOY. Huh. What are you looking at, gaga face? Is there something funny about me?

OLD MAN. Not funny no. You're a little boy. Little boys don't live in the dark. I do. If you do you're not a little boy. You're a devil an animal.

LITTLE BOY. You really are an animal.

OLD MAN. Oh no oh no oh no. I'm a man I'm a man I'm a man.

LITTLE BOY. Do you want a cigarette?

*The* LITTLE BOY *takes out a cigarette and smokes.*

LITTLE BOY. They're great. The best. They cost me five forty, because they're the best.

OLD MAN. A cigarette.

LITTLE BOY. Here, I think you're dirty and gross but I'll give it to you if you don't say nothing to the cops when they come.

OLD MAN. I won't say a thing I won't say a thing.

LITTLE BOY. Here. I mean you haven't even seen me, yeah?

OLD MAN. No no. No no.

*The* LITTLE BOY *hands him a cigarette and a gold lighter.*

OLD MAN. Ha ha. Your father's.

LITTLE BOY. Oh yeah man! My father doesn't even smoke, you moron; I nicked it from a bloke who was really wicked and he thought I was wicked and that's why he'll never think I nicked it from him, do you want me to tell you about it?

*The* OLD MAN *inhales the smoke with delight.*

OLD MAN. Oh yes yes. Oh yes yes. Yeeeeees.

LITTLE BOY. Ha. Well the bloke I nicked this from he's a
bloke I met in the tube right and he sold this hash to me,
right, he was only asking twelve fifty, shit, it was fucking
excellent, shit, fucking hell, I've finished it, 'cause I've got
this cruddy mate who's a louse yeah and he smoked half of
it, shit he's mental he is, and the bloke in the tube took us to
his flat, right, shit what a flat, shit, and we had a shower
there 'cause it was a week since me and my cruddy mate
had had a wash, and when we were in the shower we saw
the bloke was going around his room starkers and there was
a bird there who was starkers and she goes 'who are those
two little boys?' and he told her we'd come to buy some
hash and the bird got up starkers right and came into the
bathroom, shit, her cunt was all black, shit, and me and my
mate started laughing: it turned out she was the singer from
a fucking wicked group called Spunksmell me and my mate
had gone to see four days ago on our mates' motorbikes,
shit what a coincidence, and she said we were very young
and I asked her if she was the bird from Spunksmell and she
said she was and asked us how old we were, right, and I
was starkers and told her the group was fucking wicked and
I was thirteen, and then the bloke came in and his cock was
this big and he was smoking a joint and he goes 'get
dressed and piss off' and he sold us the hash, and he was
only asking twelve fifty and we became mates, and since we
still had forty-three twenty left from the hundred and sixty-
five my mate had nicked from his old man, we bought it,
and then I nicked the lighter and we went out pissing
ourselves, shit what a laugh, and we smoked all the hash in
a night, shit, and we got really stoned and we spent the
night at this really crappy squat, right, shit what a trip man,
I was flying high like a little angel with beer and spliffs, and
in the morning I was still hallucinating like I was in heaven,
I wasn't making no noise or shouting or nothing, how
peaceful and how cruddy when I saw my mate sleeping like
an idiot.

OLD MAN. Like a little angel.

LITTLE BOY. But we left that squat and went to another one some punks had given us the address of, and the door opened and we go 'can we sleep here?' and they go 'okay okay but only for one night'; the singers from Social Shit were there, the bird from Dirty Sheets and the drummer from Fucking My Mother, it was wicked, and we thought fucking shit, we've still got eleven sixty-seven left and these blokes must have a trip we could buy, shit that's cool, and they gave us half a trip for a tenner, that's really cheap, they said, and me and my cruddy mate go shit that's cool! and we bought it right and had it all there, bloody hell man what a fucking shit cool what a cool trip, everything in all these colours yeah and we were flying so high and we were in heaven and I was in heaven like an angel and I wasn't thinking nothing and I wanted to laugh.

OLD MAN. Like an angel.

LITTLE BOY. But the next day we had one sixty-seven right and since we left the squat at ten and everybody else was out of it snoring we nicked a tenner from the bird from Dirty Sheets and we got the bus and all the mental old women and queer old men like you moved away 'cause they were shit scared and I thought if my mum saw me now she'd be shit scared as well. And with the tenner we had left we scoffed a four seasons in a park full of fucking snobby little cunts, shit they make me puke, going about dressed up as queers with their hair all nice and combed and if I had the bread those prats have shit I'd fill up with grass and fixes shit, it'd be fucking wicked, but after the pizza we only had six fifty-three right and we spent three eighty on a pack of fags, a fuck of a lot, but not as much as the pack I bought this afternoon, that cost five forty 'cause they're imported, they're cool aren't they, twenty-seven pee a cigarette, eh, man?, you're smoking twenty-seven pee, eh?; so we were knackered wandering through the park, right you see we don't have no OKUPATION to do all bloody day, we don't want to do nothing, sometimes I can't be bollocked to do nothing, I can't even be bollocked to roll up a joint; and we were stretched out on a swing till some mates brought us beer free, wicked man!, I thought, wicked!, I'll go up to the clouds tonight as well; but no way, 'cause it was a litre and we had to share it with my cruddy mate and the other four, who were the ones who had been my brother's mates; so I could only get four or five slugs, but one of the mates had a little joint of grass and with that and the glue we were sniffing we ended up making a night of it, but they had to go 'cause they haven't run away from home and I made them swear by my brother that when my parents called round to their house they wouldn't say nothing and they went off and I was real cool on a swing and I dreamt of my brother.

OLD MAN. A little angel.

*Pause.*

LITTLE BOY. How do *you* know?

OLD MAN. I'm so sleepy. You speak and speak and speak and I can't understand you.

LITTLE BOY. How do *you* know?

OLD MAN. Little angels little angels. I'm so sleepy. Pain in the neck you're just a pain in the neck and you don't speak like me.

LITTLE BOY. That's not true.

OLD MAN. Sleep sleep that's enough talking that's enough enough.

LITTLE BOY. That's not true. My brother isn't a little angel. My mum tells me he is, every day, she told me that for three months; it just slipped out now, because I say he's not, god doesn't exist, heaven's a con.

OLD MAN. Shut up shut up son of a slag go to sleep and shut up.

LITTLE BOY. My brother isn't a little angel, they told me lies at school, and angels don't ride motorbikes, have you ever seen an angel with their head split open? God doesn't exist, it's a lie.

OLD MAN. Go to sleep little boy go to sleep.

LITTLE BOY. It was over there. There's still a black and red mark from his crushed brain.

OLD MAN. Sleep sleep dream.

*Silence.*

LITTLE BOY. Come on, give me your fucking money, you prat!

OLD MAN. Little angels little angels.

*The* LITTLE BOY *starts kicking the* OLD MAN *in the stomach and goes through his pockets.*

LITTLE BOY. Come on, you prat, bloody hell, come on! Fucking shit, you queer, you bastard! Shit the wanker doesn't have nothing shit!! . . . The ring!

*The* LITTLE BOY *wrenches off the* OLD MAN*'s ring, spits in his face and runs off.*

OLD MAN. Oh. Oh. Oh. Son of a slagbitch son of a slag son of a slag of a little angel!!

## Scene Six

*Bathroom in a flat located in the city centre. Bathtub.* LITTLE BOY *and* MAN.

*The* LITTLE BOY *is in the bath. The* MAN *is standing up, looking at him.*

MAN. Big, eh?

LITTLE BOY. Not like yours.

MAN. Almost.

LITTLE BOY. I'd like it like that.

MAN. Lots of hairs, already, eh?

LITTLE BOY. Not as curly as yours.

MAN. You'll get it all soon.

LITTLE BOY. We'll see.

MAN. You'll see.

LITTLE BOY. Why are you looking at me like that?

MAN. And you?

LITTLE BOY. Do you want to have a bath?

MAN. No.

LITTLE BOY. And mum?

MAN. She's sleeping.

LITTLE BOY. Don't you want to have a bath?

MAN. No.

LITTLE BOY. All right, eh.

MAN. Who?

LITTLE BOY. What do you think? The water.

MAN. Oh.

LITTLE BOY. Who did you mean?

MAN. What do you think?

LITTLE BOY. Mum.

MAN. Is she all right, then?

LITTLE BOY. She's not bad.

MAN. She's not bad.

LITTLE BOY. There are better ones.

MAN. Of course! Of course!

LITTLE BOY. But there are worse ones as well.

MAN. Yes. Yes, yes, obviously.

LITTLE BOY. But a lot, eh?, a lot of worse ones as well.

MAN. You think so?

LITTLE BOY. You've got eyes in your head. Can't you see?
Can't you see them when you're in the street?

MAN. Sometimes.

LITTLE BOY. Liar.

MAN. Can you?

LITTLE BOY. I always do.

MAN. Oh, come off it, shut up.

LITTLE BOY. Don't you want to have a bath?

MAN. No.

LITTLE BOY. My fingers are already wrinkly.

MAN. Get out then.

LITTLE BOY. I don't want to.

MAN. You'll shrivel up even more.

LITTLE BOY. Oh, come off it, shut up!

MAN. Shall I sponge down your back?

LITTLE BOY. No need.

MAN. Do you want anything?

LITTLE BOY. No.

MAN. Did you know that . . . ?

LITTLE BOY. That.

MAN. Tomorrow . . .

LITTLE BOY. Tomorrow?

MAN. There'll be a surprise.

LITTLE BOY. What?

MAN. No. I can't tell you.

LITTLE BOY. Why?

MAN. It wouldn't be a surprise.

LITTLE BOY. Come on. Tell me.

MAN. No, no.

LITTLE BOY. And mum doesn't know about it either?

MAN. No.

LITTLE BOY. What is it?

MAN. You'll love it.

LITTLE BOY. Is it for me?

MAN. For everybody.

LITTLE BOY. For mum as well?

MAN. It's for everybody.

LITTLE BOY. Okay. And who'll like it most: you, me or mum?

MAN. You'll like it more than mum.

LITTLE BOY. And what about you?

MAN. I love it, I'm crazy about it.

LITTLE BOY. Shit shit shit! A new car!

MAN. Yes, yes, but don't tell mum.

LITTLE BOY. Shit shit, cool.

MAN. I'll get it in the morning.

LITTLE BOY. Hey, when you get back we'll have a drive, okay?

MAN. Are you happy?

LITTLE BOY. Yes.

MAN. So am I.

LITTLE BOY. Hey, mum'll like it as well, won't she?

MAN. Yes. Sure.

LITTLE BOY. What car is it?

MAN. You'll be really amazed.

LITTLE BOY. I bet I will.

MAN. Yes. Shhht. Don't say anything to anybody.

LITTLE BOY. Wow.

MAN. I've ordered one in red.

LITTLE BOY. Cool, that's my favourite colour.

MAN. That's why I asked for it in red.

LITTLE BOY. I'm going to wake mum up and tell her now.

MAN. No, no.

LITTLE BOY. Oh come on.

MAN. No. It'll be better if we call her down to the street tomorrow and she sees both of us in it. You just see her face.

LITTLE BOY. Yes. I already can. Ha.

MAN. Yes. It'll be funny.

LITTLE BOY. Yes.

MAN. What a laugh.

LITTLE BOY. Don't you want to have a bath?

MAN. No.

LITTLE BOY. I'll put some more hot water in.

MAN. What you should do is get out.

LITTLE BOY. A little bit more. Now's the best bit.

MAN. It can't be good for you to be so long in the water.

LITTLE BOY. Why?

MAN. Because it can't.

LITTLE BOY. Well, if you're going to tell me off, you'd better go, okay?

MAN. Who's telling you off?

LITTLE BOY. You are.

MAN. What have I said?

LITTLE BOY. You're already starting to go on.

MAN. Who? Me?

LITTLE BOY. Who do you think? The mirror?

MAN. When have I gone on?

LITTLE BOY. Get out, it can't be good, you'll catch a cold, huh.

MAN. I didn't say anything about a cold.

LITTLE BOY. It doesn't matter. You were going to.

MAN. Sometimes I don't understand you.

LITTLE BOY. Well sometimes you're just too much to put up with.

MAN. I'm going to sleep.

LITTLE BOY. Sure you don't want to have a bath?

MAN. No.

LITTLE BOY. With me?

MAN. Will we both fit?

LITTLE BOY. Of course! Don't you remember?

MAN. Make room for me.

*The* MAN *starts getting undressed.*

LITTLE BOY. And has the new car got an alarm?

MAN. What do you think?

LITTLE BOY. How should I know.

MAN. Of course.

LITTLE BOY. What else has it got?

MAN. Well . . . air conditioning . . . electric sunroof . . . chrome fittings . . . remote control centralised locking system . . . electronically adjustable wing mirrors as well . . . catalytic converter . . . boot and petrol cap you can open automatically from the inside . . . oh, and a stereo system with a cassette player and hi-fi CD player.

LITTLE BOY. A hi-fi CD player!

MAN. Yes.

LITTLE BOY. Wow!

*The* MAN *gets into the bathtub.*

MAN. Oh. It's boiling.

LITTLE BOY. What do you mean? It's cold.

MAN. For you. Because you've been here for so long.

LITTLE BOY. Don't jump in.

MAN. No.

LITTLE BOY. A lot bigger, eh?

MAN. What?

LITTLE BOY. Yours.

MAN. My what?

LITTLE BOY. Christ, can't you see it? Yours is much bigger than mine.

MAN. That's what you think.

LITTLE BOY. And what a hairy hand.

MAN. You'll get it all soon.

LITTLE BOY. We'll see.

MAN. You'll see.

LITTLE BOY. Look how the water's going up.

MAN. God all right, eh.

LITTLE BOY. Mum?

MAN. The water.

LITTLE BOY. Dad.

MAN. What?

LITTLE BOY. Look.

MAN. What?

LITTLE BOY. Touch.

MAN. Why?

LITTLE BOY. I'm ahead of you now.

MAN. You're ahead of me?

LITTLE BOY. Look how big it is now.

MAN. You've got a hard-on.

*Silence.*

LITTLE BOY. Mum's snoring.


**Scene Seven**

*Central station. Plastic seats.* MAN *and* GIRL.

GIRL. How did she know?

MAN. The smell of your cunt.

GIRL. Fuck off.

MAN. I admit it was my fault. Last time I didn't have a wash.

GIRL. And what did you say?

MAN. Nothing.

GIRL. Nothing.

MAN. That it was her imagination.

GIRL. Did she fall for that?

MAN. No.

GIRL. And what are you going to do?

MAN. I don't understand you.

GIRL. I asked what you're going to do.

MAN. Nothing.

GIRL. Don't you want to tell her about it?

MAN. Have you gone mad?

GIRL. I don't understand you.

MAN. You'll miss the train.

GIRL. No. I'm staying.

MAN. Great. Then, would you be so good as to tell me what we're going to do here?

GIRL. Talk about my cunt and your carelessness, your rudeness.

MAN. You know what? It'd be better if you and me called it a day.

GIRL. Yes. Stopped.

MAN. You can still make it.

GIRL. What?

MAN. Catch it.

GIRL. What?

MAN. The train.

GIRL. Oh.

MAN. Of course, it wouldn't be a bad idea if you washed more often. It'd have spared us a few problems.

GIRL. What are you going on about now.

MAN. Your cunt, of course. (Problems? . . . did I say problems . . . ?) It smells too strong, that's it. I mean all cunts smell, obviously, they smell sweet, and have a bit which really stinks, but it's only a bit, usually it's not at all unpleasant. But yours . . . now that it's over with us, I can tell you . . . yours really stinks to high heaven . . . it's strange . . . it's not the usual smell of dried or rotting fish that dirty cunts have during menstruation, no, no, yours, the smell of your cunt, is something else, it's more sour than

sweet, like ammonia, more like a mixture of ammonia and
rotting meat . . . I've always thought it was unusual, in
you . . . I mean seeing you like this, with clothes on, I'd
never have said so; until I found out for myself . . . I was
so surprised the first time (when was that, three months
ago?) . . . normally, the first time people have a wash, to be
clean for the date . . . I'm sorry, I honestly don't know if
this thing of yours is about being dirty, perhaps it's only
physiological, I mean a sort of internal illness, some
glandular malformation or infection (because glands are
what you've got inside, haven't you?) . . . like somebody
who's got bad breath, which generally means his stomach's
dirty or he's about to puke up, if he hasn't already . . . so
the first time, when you took your knickers off, I couldn't
believe it, I swear to you; sorry I'm telling you this now,
after we've done it so many times, they're things you can
only say when you've broken up and there are no
obligations or ties or bonds, when you feel as free as I do
now, that's it; well, the first time I almost felt sick, what a
stink, I remember, I looked at your crotch holding my
breath thinking I'd see some thick vapour, a fog come out of
it, the smell was so strong; but in spite of yourself you get
used to these things; sometimes . . . sometimes . . .
sometimes it didn't even go away after I washed my dick
with soap three times, and I had to carry it around (the
smell of your cunt) for the rest of the day (because mostly,
if not every time, we did it at midday, do you remember?);
so there was no way I could forget you. In fact, I don't
know how she didn't notice before; she obviously can't
have such a fine sense of smell as me . . . of course, in any
case, on the days I did it with you I tried not to take off my
pants in front of her or near her . . . I went to the bathroom
with my pyjama bottoms, soaped myself down for the last
time and put my pants straight into the washing machine,
after I'd smelt them and inevitably prevented myself from
retching . . . That's funny, when I was young and I only had
the smell of my balls in my pants, I liked smelling them.
Now, it's different . . . huh, there are some things I just can't
understand. Aren't you going to say anything? Why aren't
you saying anything?

GIRL. I dreamt all this a couple of days ago.

MAN. You can still catch your train.

GIRL. But it was different.

MAN. It's getting late for me.

GIRL. The dream was different, but not so different. We
agreed to break up, we could see it coming. You told me
your wife had found out. It was strange, we were in a
station as well. But you were the one who had to catch a
train. I remember you insulted me. More or less like you've
just done. But what I remember better was what I said to
you. I shouted at you, it was very noisy, I was surrounded
by people, passengers with suitcases, newspaper sellers,
ticket inspectors and especially . . . sweepers dressed in
yellow (there were a lot of them, thousands and thousands
of phosphorescent sweepers gaping and listening to what
I said, in front of us, sitting on the ground, with their
brushes by their feet). I was furious but clear-headed. I told
you that bad luck isn't the result of chance. You men have
a dangerous tendency to think so. Women don't. I don't.
I'm a woman. I said you were guilty. I shouted at you. I
said you were guilty in front of everybody. You, guilty. Of
everything. Absolutely everything. All your bad luck: your
wife's hysteria, the onset of impotence, your younger son's
instability. And especially: the death of your elder son. Yes.
You, guilty. You alone. And everybody started clapping.
Everybody cheered. Then you went off. By yourself. You
caught your train. By yourself. And it came off the rails.
And we saw how the train came off the rails with you
inside, only you. By yourself. And everybody cried out for
joy. And I cried out for joy. And I was glad. And we were
all glad. When I woke up, I wanted to believe it was a
nightmare. Now I know it was only a mere premonition.
I'm going. I don't want to miss the train . . . Aren't you
going to say anything? Why aren't you saying anything?

MAN. Your breath stinks. Your breath . . . stinks . . . as well.

GIRL. My cunt. My breath. You know what you stink of? Bad
luck. Scratch a little and out it comes.

MAN. You've missed your train.

GIRL. No I haven't. Your watch is fast.

MAN. If I'd had a wash last time . . .

GIRL. Nothing would have happened?

MAN. No.

GIRL. Probably not.

MAN. Everything the same as usual.

GIRL. Could you let me have your newspaper?

MAN. Why?

GIRL. To read it during the journey.

MAN. Will you be able to?

GIRL. Are you okay?

MAN. Have a good trip.

GIRL. Do you regret not washing your dick?

MAN. Mmm . . . I don't . . . think so.

GIRL. So, why are you crying?

MAN. Goodbye.

GIRL. You don't have any reason to. In fact nobody noticed. Nobody knows. Nobody heard me. Anyway, nobody cares about your bad luck. Not even the station sweepers. Don't worry. This smelly cunt of mine and my bad breath are saying goodbye without screaming or hysterics or shouting or nervous attacks or anyone listening to us.

MAN. Dreams are dreams.

GIRL. And this is not a theatre.

MAN. Dreams are lies.

GIRL. And trains don't come off the rails.

MAN. Goodbye.

*Silence.*

GIRL. I hate you.

**Scene Eight**

*Kitchen in a flat located in the city centre. Marble surfaces.*
GIRL *and* MIDDLE-AGED MAN.

GIRL. What are you making.

MIDDLE-AGED MAN. A salad.

GIRL. And will that be it then?

MIDDLE-AGED MAN. No.

GIRL. What else are you going to make?

MIDDLE-AGED MAN. Do you want to help me?

GIRL. Do you want me to help you?

MIDDLE-AGED MAN. No.

GIRL. Good. I prefer watching you.

MIDDLE-AGED MAN. Like you used to.

GIRL. I don't know why you like doing it so much.

MIDDLE-AGED MAN. What?

GIRL. Cooking.

MIDDLE-AGED MAN. You've always refused.

GIRL. What?

MIDDLE-AGED MAN. To learn how to.

GIRL. It was enough to have just one person who could do it
    reasonably.

MIDDLE-AGED MAN. Hand me that knife.

GIRL. I said I'd watch you, that's all.

MIDDLE-AGED MAN. You're right.

GIRL. I don't like those trousers. They look . . .

MIDDLE-AGED MAN. Fish.

GIRL. What?

MIDDLE-AGED MAN. Fish. After the salad, a nice piece of fish. It's fresh.

GIRL. Terrible. They look terrible on you. They're meant for young people.

MIDDLE-AGED MAN. I am young.

GIRL. Yesterday I met a friend and she told me a lie.

MIDDLE-AGED MAN. This lettuce is full of worms.

GIRL. Throw it away.

MIDDLE-AGED MAN. Which friend?

GIRL. I don't like worms.

MIDDLE-AGED MAN. I know the salt is near you.

GIRL. It's in my hand.

MIDDLE-AGED MAN. Look at me. Look at me. I'm not asking you for anything. You see? I'm coming for it myself. Can you let go of it? Thanks. Good, now carry on watching.

GIRL. A school friend. It was years since I'd seen her.

MIDDLE-AGED MAN. I think I know who she is.

GIRL. What are you doing with the salt?

MIDDLE-AGED MAN. They're so shiny.

GIRL. How disgusting.

MIDDLE-AGED MAN. When you grab them they curl up. Little balls.

GIRL. She often sees you in the street.

MIDDLE-AGED MAN. When you put them in a pile of salt, they explode.

GIRL. She told me you're the most interesting mature man she's ever met.

MIDDLE-AGED MAN. Splat!

GIRL. It's repulsive.

MIDDLE-AGED MAN. Oh. I know who she is.

GIRL. She lives nearby.

MIDDLE-AGED MAN. And what was the lie she told you?

GIRL. She told me you're the most interesting mature man she's ever met.

MIDDLE-AGED MAN. And what was the lie she told you?

GIRL. Will you stop playing with those worms!! You'll make me throw up.

MIDDLE-AGED MAN. You're not watching the way you used to. You've grown up. You're too old. Before you only watched. Now you watch and speak. You criticize.

GIRL. You haven't even asked me how the trip went.

MIDDLE-AGED MAN. How did the trip go?

GIRL. That apron isn't yours.

MIDDLE-AGED MAN. How did the trip go?

GIRL. Very well, as usual, I'm very pleased with my job, very pleased and I like travelling and being away from this lousy city and this trip went very well.

MIDDLE-AGED MAN. There are no more worms.

GIRL. Look carefully, make sure there are none left.

MIDDLE-AGED MAN. You're right, it's your mother's apron.

GIRL. You gave it to her as a present.

MIDDLE-AGED MAN. What a memory.

GIRL. What a stupid present.

MIDDLE-AGED MAN. Practical.

GIRL. Stupid. You gave it to yourself.

MIDDLE-AGED MAN. I like it more than mine.

GIRL. I gave it to you.

MIDDLE-AGED MAN. Look at these sole fillets!

GIRL. The most boring fish. It's been a month since I've come
    to see you and you choose the most boring fish and a
    pathetic salad full of worms and an insipid piece of fish; I
    call you from six hundred miles away, six hundred miles
    and I say: 'I'll be here tomorrow and I'll come and see you
    both, I'll come for lunch, because the day after tomorrow
    I'll be leaving again' and you rack your brains to serve up
    the most appropriate dishes, I can just see you, I can just
    imagine you: selecting for the occasion what the occasion
    calls for: boring daughter, normal visit, together by force,
    insipid meeting, boring meal. Salad and sole fillets.

MIDDLE-AGED MAN. You're leaving out what goes with
    them.

GIRL. With what.

MIDDLE-AGED MAN. The sole fillets.

GIRL. What.

MIDDLE-AGED MAN. Boiled potatoes. Small. Round.

GIRL. What have I done to you.

MIDDLE-AGED MAN. They're so good.

GIRL. Will you take long? You know what's wrong?, well, you
    see, the thing is . . . the thing is . . . the thing is I'm in a bit
    of a rush. I really am. Anyway, what about mummy?
    Shouldn't she already be here? Or is she going to shut up
    the shop even later since she knows I'm here?, just to see
    me for as little time as possible? What do you think?

MIDDLE-AGED MAN. It's a good meal if you don't want to
    put on weight.

GIRL. About mummy. What do you think.

MIDDLE-AGED MAN. What about you?

GIRL. I think she should be here.

MIDDLE-AGED MAN. Maybe she should. No. No. She'd
    make the kitchen dirty.

GIRL. We'd finish sooner.

MIDDLE-AGED MAN. She'd mess everything up.

GIRL. She doesn't get obsessive.

MIDDLE-AGED MAN. Everything.

GIRL. At least *she* doesn't.

MIDDLE-AGED MAN. It would be awful.

GIRL. It would be human.

MIDDLE-AGED MAN. She doesn't like cooking: she does it all wrong.

GIRL. Why do you like it?

MIDDLE-AGED MAN. It's a gift.

GIRL. A load of crap.

MIDDLE-AGED MAN. An inheritance.

GIRL. A lost one. A lost one. I can't stand you. A lost inheritance. I don't have it, I didn't receive it, I didn't want to learn.

MIDDLE-AGED MAN. It's not something you can learn, really.

GIRL. So I know I haven't failed you, as you think.

MIDDLE-AGED MAN. They're so small, the potatoes.

GIRL. I haven't failed you.

MIDDLE-AGED MAN. They're so difficult to peel.

GIRL. Your inheritance stops with you.

MIDDLE-AGED MAN. I think your mother's coming.

GIRL. It stops with you.

MIDDLE-AGED MAN. Can't you hear her on the staircase?

GIRL. And you won't have anything left.

MIDDLE-AGED MAN. Can't you hear the noise of the keys in the door-lock?

GIRL. Anything at all.

MIDDLE-AGED MAN. Can't you tell her perfume?

GIRL. You're alone.

MIDDLE-AGED MAN. Go and say hello.

GIRL. It's not my fault.

*Suddenly, the* MIDDLE-AGED MAN *throws all the kitchen utensils to the floor. Great noise.*

*Silence.*

MIDDLE-AGED MAN. Why don't you do the lunch.

GIRL. Why do you love yourself so much, daddy.

**Scene Nine**

*Small attic studio in the centre of the city. A bed.* MIDDLE-AGED MAN *and* BOY.

*The* MIDDLE-AGED MAN, *with an enormous parcel.*

MIDDLE-AGED MAN. A present.

BOY. What is it?

MIDDLE-AGED MAN. Guess.

BOY. From the shape, it's easy: a picture.

MIDDLE-AGED MAN. No. Don't unwrap it. Not yet.

BOY. Why?

MIDDLE-AGED MAN. You'll see.

BOY. Leave it over here.

MIDDLE-AGED MAN. Give me a whisky.

BOY. I don't have any.

MIDDLE-AGED MAN. You don't have any.

BOY. You finished the bottle.

MIDDLE-AGED MAN. I can't remember.

BOY. I was pouring you out glassfuls.

MIDDLE-AGED MAN. I can't remember.

BOY. Only to be expected.

MIDDLE-AGED MAN. What's up, then?

BOY. I'm nervous.

MIDDLE-AGED MAN. In the way of drink. What's up in the way of drink.

BOY. Water.

MIDDLE-AGED MAN. Not much.

BOY. I wasn't expecting you.

MIDDLE-AGED MAN. Why are you nervous?

BOY. Today . . . at my mother's. My sister was there as well.

MIDDLE-AGED MAN. I saw her the other day.

BOY. Exactly.

MIDDLE-AGED MAN. In the street, as usual.

BOY. We should live further away. Together, further away. This area's a dump. Everybody's always bumping into everybody else. There's no privacy.

MIDDLE-AGED MAN. Yes if you want to.

BOY. What do you mean.

MIDDLE-AGED MAN. Do you know how old I am?

BOY. I don't want to know.

MIDDLE-AGED MAN. Why?

BOY. I don't know. It would make me sick.

MIDDLE-AGED MAN. Fifty.

BOY. It makes me sick.

MIDDLE-AGED MAN. Who would think it?

BOY. Nobody, really.

MIDDLE-AGED MAN. Fifty, and that doesn't stop your sister . . .

BOY. She does it on purpose. And in front of mother. She said it in front of mother. Like before. And when she says it, she looks at me.

MIDDLE-AGED MAN. You think she looks at you.

BOY. She looks at me. She says it because of me. So that I know she knows everything.

MIDDLE-AGED MAN. Obsessions. Let's change the subject.

BOY. I'm scared.

MIDDLE-AGED MAN. Sick. Scared. Too young.

BOY. No.

MIDDLE-AGED MAN. Give me some water.

BOY. Shall I open the packet?

MIDDLE-AGED MAN. I'm thirsty. Not yet.

BOY. Help yourself.

MIDDLE-AGED MAN. You help me.

BOY. Make yourself comfortable.

MIDDLE-AGED MAN. I already am.

BOY. What were we talking about?

MIDDLE-AGED MAN. I can't remember.

BOY. Privacy.

MIDDLE-AGED MAN. Oh, yes: I'm fifty years old.

BOY. I'll shut the window.

MIDDLE-AGED MAN. And not even my daughter knows anything.

BOY. These bloody flats.

MIDDLE-AGED MAN. Do you want to suck me off?

BOY. Yes.

MIDDLE-AGED MAN. My zip's open.

BOY. If you don't close it they'll see everything.

MIDDLE-AGED MAN. Your lips.

BOY. Bloody neighbours.

MIDDLE-AGED MAN. Come on. Quickly.

BOY. Didn't you want some water?

MIDDLE-AGED MAN. Afterwards. Take your clothes off.

BOY. You take your clothes off, as well.

MIDDLE-AGED MAN. Take my clothes off for me.

BOY. You'll drive me crazy.

MIDDLE-AGED MAN. Put your hand on me.

BOY. You're driving me crazy.

MIDDLE-AGED MAN. Do you like me.

BOY. Yes, a lot.

*The* MIDDLE-AGED MAN *violently pulls the* BOY*'s clothes off.*

MIDDLE-AGED MAN. Now. Now. Now.

BOY. What.

MIDDLE-AGED MAN. Grab the packet. Quickly.

BOY. Now? Now?

MIDDLE-AGED MAN. Yes. Quickly.

BOY. What do I do? What do you want? What do I have to do? What is it you want?

MIDDLE-AGED MAN. Put it here. In front of the bed. Here. Yes. Upright. No, on two chairs. Yes. That's it. Yes. That's it. Very good.

BOY. And what do I do now? What do I have to do?

MIDDLE-AGED MAN. Don't be scared.

BOY. I'm not scared.

MIDDLE-AGED MAN. You've gone limp.

BOY. I'm not scared of you.

MIDDLE-AGED MAN. Tear away the paper and come over here.

BOY. It's a mirror!

MIDDLE-AGED MAN. Come on. Come on. Quickly. Here. Your mouth. That's it. Do it properly. Easy now, easy. I want to see it properly. Till the end. Your skin. I'm alive. Easy now, easy. I love it. I love it. You're so good. No, no, no! Don't look. You don't look. Don't look. What are you doing!

BOY. I want to see myself as well. I want to look.

MIDDLE-AGED MAN. Afterwards. Afterwards. Go on. Till the end. That's it. Yes. That's it. Afterwards I'll do it to you. And you'll look at yourself. You'll look at us. That's it. That's it. Just the four of us, all by ourselves. Just the four of us. Just! No, there really are four of us! That's it. That's it. Oh. You three . . . the only ones who love me.


**Scene Ten**

*Dining room in a flat in the city centre. Table and chairs.* BOY *and* WOMAN.

BOY. That was a great dinner.

WOMAN. Today I spent so long looking at myself in the mirror; I hadn't for days, perhaps weeks, perhaps . . . ten years; so long, for the first time, I kept looking; I'd come back from the market and I was in such a bad mood: things go up and up so fast, I wish I could get up the stairs of this decrepit old building so fast, I mean it's just right for an old woman like me, and I was carrying so much . . .

BOY. Make me a coffee.

WOMAN. And just as I opened the door the telephone rang and you'll never guess who it was.

BOY. The landlord's agent to say the rent's going up.

WOMAN. Don't you think it's strange for the telephone to ring just as you're taking your key out of the lock in the main door? Don't you? Well I do, I don't know if it's ever happened to me before, it's like the two things were connected; anyway, as you know, it's not often somebody calls here, it's not normal, it's abnormal, you know that better than I do, much better; I've always thought that the main reason you left me, I mean became independent (that's how you put it, isn't it?) was that the telephone rang so little here, really, I've always thought that; just imagine my face then on the doorstep, I was tired and worried, with plastic bags from the supermarket cutting my wrists and my purse empty, when there's still some time to go before the end of the month. To get to the phone, not to miss the welcome call, I just dropped them on the floor and broke seven eggs; so, I ran to the study like a mad woman, and in thousandths of a second I thought how I'd love to hear a pleasant voice saying hello and telling me pleasant things and perking me up and encouraging me for the rest of the day, days, the rest of my days.

BOY. I'm going to have a pee.

*The* BOY *goes out. The* WOMAN *carries on speaking as if nothing had happened. As she speaks, she gets up and goes through the pockets of the* BOY*'s jacket, which is hanging on his chair. She finds his wallet and looks for money.*

WOMAN. But no. It was a friend of my elder sister who lives in one of those places for people like her, one of those places I'd never in my life think of setting foot in. She'd been going through some papers and found my telephone number and was calling me so I would go and visit her, her and her friends and . . . and go somewhere in a coach full of people . . . like us. How awful! She said 'like us'. Can you imagine. In the end I pretended to be as confused as I could by speaking to her about trivial things and about my excellent state of health and about how friendly and nice the people are around here and that I'm delighted to be living here and I hung up in an instant, and almost sleepwalking I went to the toilet and looked in the mirror. What had she imagined, that old woman?! How had she dared to call *me*?! But it wasn't anything, I immediately calmed down: I still haven't got a single wrinkle. I'll be fine for another ten years without looking in the mirror again.

*She removes a banknote from the* BOY*'s wallet and puts it in her cleavage. The* BOY *had already come back without her realising it.*

BOY. What about the coffee?

WOMAN. Oh! You frightened me! Always behaving like that, you'll never change. You're a sadist, you're a sadist; why did you turn out like this?, why? I still can't figure it out.

BOY. I think I've got to go.

WOMAN. Who did you take after? Who?

BOY. I said I'm going.

WOMAN. Definitely not after your father, he was all sweetness and charm.

BOY. Sit down.

WOMAN. Still less after your sister, she's sensitive, delicate, incapable of harming a fly.

BOY. Calm down.

WOMAN. It's just that you can't go around frightening women like you do; because if you frighten me, I'm sure you frighten other women as well.

BOY. Which women.

WOMAN. Oh, the ones I imagine you take to the matchbox you call your home to do whatever you do there.

BOY. Why don't you come to see me one day?

WOMAN. I've got to take my pill.

BOY. Will you sit down?

WOMAN. You don't even invite me. I must get in your way.

BOY. I'll have my coffee somewhere else.

WOMAN. You'll have it here, with me.

BOY. How much do you want.

WOMAN. I've already told you next time you can come with a girlfriend, if you want. Me, I'm not bothered by company, quite the reverse. And us women we get on with each other. It'd be less boring. Why are you so boring? Oh, my pill. Why are you so boring?

BOY. No! Afterwards! You take it afterwards!

WOMAN. After what?

BOY. I don't know.

WOMAN. What?

BOY. I don't know, my mind's gone blank.

WOMAN. I'm going to make the coffee.

BOY. No.

WOMAN. Oh, so you don't want any now?

BOY. No.

WOMAN. Is there anybody at all who can understand you.

BOY. I don't think so.

WOMAN. You should see a doctor.

BOY. Have you gone mad?

WOMAN. There are some very good ones now. They keep you company.

BOY. I've gone blank. I don't understand a thing. I asked you a question and you didn't answer me. I don't know why we like wasting so much time. You call me, you call me, you call me almost every day and insist, I should come, I should come and see you; I already know you're the best cook, I don't doubt it, I've never doubted it; if you knew the publicity I give you everywhere you wouldn't believe that

what I say are really my words. And I give in and come and
see you; but I don't know why I stay so long, perhaps
through masochism, you know what that means? Yes, of
course you do, of course if you know what sadist means,
you'll also know what masochist means; no, no, don't be
frightened, I've gone blank because I don't know why
something is telling me I can't leave before you answer me,
I'm waiting for your answer in the same way you were
waiting with concealed pleasure and desperation for my
question; and I've got to go through a whole unbearable
dinner—excellent, I won't deny it—but slow and boring,
stuffed full of your empty talk . . . we can spare ourselves
all that, from now on, really; I don't like going blank like
this, mother, it makes me ill; I tell you to make me a coffee
and you don't, and time stretches out and it's all useless,
because in fact you're waiting and I'm waiting and waiting
is tiring and it hurts and everything stops and it harms us
and it ruins us. So this time don't shy away from the
question or pretend you're deaf, because I want to go,
mother, and don't worry: I'll come back, I'll come back
another day, another week, perhaps another year because
I'm your son. How much do you want.

WOMAN. A hundred.

*The* BOY *takes the notes out of his wallet.*

BOY. Ten. Twenty. Thirty. Forty. Fifty. Sixty. Seventy.
Eighty . . . and ninety.

*He violently puts the notes into the* WOMAN*'s cleavage.*

BOY. I'll give you the other ten another day.

WOMAN. Thank you, son.

BOY. An excellent dinner.

WOMAN. You're having a coffee somewhere else, are you?

BOY. Yes.

WOMAN. It's just that I've got to have my pill and you know
how sleepy I get.

BOY. Is there anybody at all who can understand me.

WOMAN. I can, son, I can.

*Silence.*

WOMAN. Goodbye, dear.

BOY. Goodbye.

WOMAN. I'll call you tomorrow.

BOY. If I'm having a screw I won't pick it up!

WOMAN. Are you starting to joke around now that you're going?

*The* BOY *leaves. The* WOMAN *goes to the table. She sits down. She takes the banknotes from her cleavage and carefully flattens them out. The doorbell rings . . .*

## Epilogue

*. . . The doorbell rings. The* WOMAN *gets up and walks stealthily to the door. She looks through the peephole. She half-laughs and opens up.*

YOUNG MAN. Good evening.

WOMAN. Come in, young man, come in. Excuse the mess.

YOUNG MAN. Could you do me a favour . . .

WOMAN. Of course, of course; won't you sit down?

YOUNG MAN. There's no need. It's just for a moment.

WOMAN. Well, then . . .

YOUNG MAN. Would you be kind enough to fill this little glass with olive oil for me? It's just that we've run out. I'll give it back tomorrow, I promise.

WOMAN. With pleasure, with pleasure, and there's no need to give me anything back.

YOUNG MAN. Thank you so much.

WOMAN. But . . . but . . . oh . . . what have you done to your face?

YOUNG MAN. It's nothing . . .

WOMAN. Have you been hurt?

YOUNG MAN. No. It's nothing.

WOMAN. Oh, sit down, sit down please . . . You did it on the stairs, didn't you?, you fell down on the stairs, didn't you? What bad luck, what bad luck. Wait a minute, come on, come on, sit down, don't worry.

*The* WOMAN *goes over to a piece of furniture and takes out cotton wool and hydrogen peroxide.*

WOMAN. Sit over here.

*The* YOUNG MAN *sits down.*

WOMAN. Don't be afraid. I'll treat you like a mother. Even better.

*Slowly, and very carefully, the* WOMAN *dabs the* YOUNG MAN's *face with a piece of cotton wool soaked in hydrogen peroxide. In silence. He looks at the* WOMAN *and allows himself to be treated. She delicately wipes away the trickles of liquid with a dry piece of cotton wool. He relaxes and smiles. She gently caresses his hair. He takes her hand. She kisses him on the forehead. He kisses her on the hand. They look into each other's eyes. The air is a mist of warm sensuality. Two strangers have just 'met'. The banknotes which were on the table have fallen to the ground.*

*End.*

# THE SCORCHED GARDEN

*by*

## JUAN MAYORGA

*translated by Nick Drake*

Juan Mayorga was born in Madrid in 1965. In 1988 he graduated in Philosophy and Mathematics. He continued his studies in Philosophy in Münster, Berlin and Paris. He has published papers on Philosophy and Drama Theory in various specialised magazines and has also worked for many years as a Mathematics and Physics teacher in a secondary school. He now teaches playwriting, philosophy and sociology at the Real Escuela Superior de Arte Dramático in Madrid. Three of his texts have been produced: *Más Ceniza* (1994), *El Hombre de Oro* (1996), and *El Sueño de Ginebra* (*1996*) His published plays include: *Siete Hombres Buenos* 1988, *El Traductor de Blumenberg* 1993, and *Concierto fatal de la viuda Kolakowski,* 1994. His most recent play, *Cartas de amor a Stalin* won the 1998 Premio Borne Prize and was produced at the Maria Guerrero Theatre of the Centro Dramático Nacional in the Autumn of 1999.

*The Scorched Garden* (*El Jardín Quemado*) was first performed in English as a rehearsed reading in the *Voices from Spain* season in the Theatre Upstairs on 9 April, 1997 with the following cast.

| | |
|---|---|
| PEPE | Allister Bain |
| GARAY | Alan David |
| DON OSWALDO | Roger Frost |
| PEREQUITO LILA | James Greene |
| MAXIMO CAL | Roy Hanlon |
| BENET | Gary McDonald |

*Director*   Caroline Hall
*Translator*   Nick Drake

*Spain, at the end of the seventies.*

**Prologue**

*Midnight. The port. Young* BENET *is observing the reflection of the moon in the water.*

STATUE. You're new to the Island.

*Since he thought he was alone,* BENET *is surprised by the voice of the* STATUE. *The* STATUE *is of a man about to throw himself into the sea.*

STATUE. I know everyone on the island. They all come by, sooner or later, to have a laugh at the old monster.

*With the slow and painful movements of an old man, the* STATUE *gets down off his pedestal.*

STATUE. No need to be afraid of my scar.

BENET. What scar?

STATUE. Look.

*He points to his face near his lips.* BENET *still can't see a scar. The* STATUE *goes to the water's edge and points at the reflection of his face.*

STATUE. See?

BENET. Just about.

STATUE. Don't try to make me feel better. The man who did that to me will get what he deserves.

*He looks into the water.*

STATUE. If it wasn't for the water, time would never seem to pass.

*He touches his wrinkles.*

But time passes.

*He looks up towards the top of the hill.*

It'll soon be Doctor Garay's birthday. Would you kindly give him my best wishes?

BENET. Do you know Garay?

STATUE. He once said to me: 'You won't survive even for one hour outside San Miguel'. Well I've shown him; I don't need him.

*He shows his cap, full of coins, at the foot of the pedestal.*

I'm never going back to San Miguel.

*He looks at his scar reflected in the water again.*

I thought in time it would fade; I thought my wrinkles would hide it. But the only truth is in the waters of this port. They don't lie: the scar grows deeper every day.

BENET. It's not ugly. It makes you look like you're smiling.

STATUE. My smile frightens people.

*The STATUE walks back to his pedestal.*

BENET. How long did you live in San Miguel?

STATUE. How long? Strange you ask me that today of all days. I dreamed they poured all the ash from the garden into an hour-glass.

*Wearily, he gets back onto his pedestal.*

Don't go into the garden with Garay.

BENET. Were you there during the war?

*But the old man has turned back into a statue looking out to sea.*

BENET. What's your name? Can we talk more?

*The STATUE doesn't react. Silence.*

If I buy you a hot meal, will you tell me about those times in San Miguel?

*The STATUE doesn't react. Silence.*

Come down, you can't spend the whole night up there.
You'll have to move soon, it's turning cold.

*The* STATUE *doesn't react. Silence.*

Nobody's watching; you don't have to be a statue if no-
one's watching.

*When he realises this is hopeless,* BENET *moves away,
somewhat frightened, keeping his eyes on the* STATUE.
*Then he approaches again for the last time:*

I'll be back tomorrow.


**Scene One**

*Midday.* GARAY*'s office.* GARAY, *an elderly man, receives*
BENET, *and invites him to sit down. A large window gives
onto a burned garden.*

GARAY. To what do I owe the pleasure? Since you arrived,
    we've hardly had a moment to talk. Have you had enough
    rummaging around in the archives?

BENET. Let's say I've allowed myself a few minutes off to
    wish you a happy birthday.

GARAY. Now how did you know . . .

BENET. I noticed the preparations for a party, I asked, and –

GARAY. Ah ha.

BENET. Have I spoiled the surprise?

GARAY. It was my boys' idea. But birthdays always put me in
    a foul mood. How am I supposed to celebrate old age?
    Retirement draws closer like some horrible shadow. I don't
    know what I'll do with myself after that: dither about all
    day, nothing to do but dawdle along the coast path. Still, I
    know such things can be seen from a different point of view
    entirely: your generation is graduating now, full of fresh
    ideas, wanting to start everything over again, make it all
    new – including San Miguel – always supposing a young

person actually *wants* to come and work here. I must say I'm surprised that you, with all your impressive qualifications, chose us for your practical.

BENET. Why?

GARAY. I suppose I attributed it to the island's attractions; I thought perhaps you had come for a holiday after all that studying. However, those dusty archives haven't left you time to set foot on the beach. And have you visited the city yet?

BENET. Recently I've been taking a late night stroll down to the port.

GARAY. Oh the port, there's nothing down there.

*He takes out two glasses and pours some wine.*

Try this. With all due modesty, you won't find better wine anywhere else on the island.

BENET. I came across an interesting character: a statue-man.

GARAY. A statue-man? Really.

BENET. Yes, according to him he lived here years ago.

GARAY. How interesting. What was his name?

BENET. Pink Budgie.

*GARAY is surprised.*

BENET. Must be a nickname.

GARAY. Indeed.

BENET. That's all I know about him. When I tried to ask him more personal questions, he went as silent as a stone.

GARAY. An old patient, perhaps?

BENET. There's no file on him in the archives. Could he have been a nurse? One of the cleaners?

GARAY (*with a look of utter incredulity on his face*). Pink Budgie? Perhaps it was a joke? The island's full of jokers.

BENET. Anyway, he seems well looked-after. His cap is always full of coins.

GARAY. They pay him not to move. People are in such a hurry these days they're fascinated by someone who simply stands still. So you've found the ugliest spot on the island; but you know the city is really quite pleasant. Wouldn't you prefer to stay there? I'm worried this place isn't comfortable enough for you. The cries of the boys at night –

BENET. There's no place in the world I'd sleep better than here. The truth is I want to get to know San Miguel. Which is to say, I want to get to know you. Would you believe me if I said your fine example inspired my own vocation? Your ethical example, I mean.

*GARAY makes a gesture to show he doesn't want to listen to such praise.*

BENET. Everyone speaks of you as if you were a saint.

GARAY. Everyone flatters me on my birthday.

BENET. I've seen it with my own eyes. You live for them.

GARAY. I'm just a modest healer.

*He changes the subject.*

Do you need anything? Anything at all?

BENET. On the contrary. I'm in your debt. You've given me so much help with my work . . . Of course, I would have liked to deal personally with the patients, as was my original intention –

*He doesn't let GARAY interrupt.*

Yes, I know you have your reasons for not granting me access.

GARAY. I'm so pleased you've finally understood my point of view. The boys live in a delicate but precious state of equilibrium, and I won't risk that for anyone. So that's the only reason I welcomed you a little cautiously perhaps. But you've been so respectful of our ways . . .

BENET. Well, in the end this is just a routine job at the end of
my course. It's not worth disturbing the patients for. It's
more a matter of making contact with the centre and, in
practice, planning some strategies for the future. There are
fresh breezes blowing through psychiatry too.

GARAY. The Dictatorship's over, and suddenly the whole
country wants to change from top to bottom. You know
yourself my sympathies lie with the new government. But
I'm worried that all this insecurity brings a dangerous
turbulence with it too.

BENET. There's nothing to be afraid of; everything will turn
out for the best – and for San Miguel, too. I'd love to
discuss with you some proposals I'm thinking about
developing in my report.

*He takes out a notebook.*

I'm going to argue for some architectural alterations.

*He sketches a plan of San Miguel.*

The grass in the patio should be replanted, and the wall –

*He points through the window to a wall –*

What lies behind that wall around the patio?

GARAY. A view of the port.

BENET. I'll suggest it's knocked down.

GARAY. *Open* the garden?

BENET. I think it's a priority. Together with a new
gymnasium. The most suitable spot would be where Block
Six stands.

GARAY. We'll need to talk through this more carefully.

BENET. Psychometric equilibrium is an essential objective,
especially for the 45-65 year-olds. A fixed timetable,
concrete activities and clear responsibilities, that's what
those men need. I'm sure you'd agree that work is the
primary factor in socialisation. It should be complemented
by integration in a local context: groups of volunteers who

would accompany the men into the city, introduce them to their families . . . Similar programmes have had an eighty percent success rate in German asylums . . .

GARAY (*interrupts*). I see you take your practical placement seriously.

BENET. It's the least I can do for San Miguel. I like it here.

*He pauses.*

I'd like to run San Miguel.

GARAY (*uncomfortable*). In that case, San Miguel will be fortunate indeed. Your qualifications are magnificent. So good that when the place here falls vacant, I'm sure you'll change your mind. You'd have your pick of the best hospitals in Madrid. I'm sure you'll choose somewhere else in the end . . .

*He is interrupted by a noise of voices and movements. GARAY and BENET look through the window. BENET looks at his watch.*

BENET. The running of this centre never ceases to amaze me. They eat when they're hungry, they sleep when they want, they idle the day away in the patio –

GARAY. *Garden.*

*Looking into the patio as if it were a giant aquarium, GARAY and BENET observe the patients as they enter the garden.*

BENET. How are they?

GARAY. Have you heard people speak of angels?

BENET. Some of them are very old.

GARAY. Old angels.

BENET. There's a man with one arm.

GARAY. Poor Nestor.

BENET. A war wound?

GARAY. An accident.

BENET. At any rate, at his age he must have fought in the war. Does he ever talk about it?

GARAY. I've never heard him.

*He comes away from the window.*

Shall we take a stroll together? I'd like to show you an interesting spot on the beach. A rock with corals –

BENET (*interrupting*). I understand the repression was very bad on the island.

GARAY. No worse than on the mainland.

BENET. But isn't a civil war on an island different?

GARAY. Don't believe what they tell you. In a time of civil war, fear exaggerates everything: the shadow of a penknife becomes the shadow of a sword. Luckily, our civil war finished years ago . . . Now let's take that stroll. I think I'll show you my vineyard up on the hill.

BENET (*without taking his eyes from the window*). In other centres I've seen them take all kinds of precautions: they take away their shoelaces, remove any sharp objects . . . Here none of that is necessary. These people seem infinitely content.

GARAY. I'm thrilled that's how you see San Miguel.

BENET. No tranquillisers, no stimulants: you don't believe in prescribing drugs?

GARAY. We don't use them. There's no need.

BENET. Why don't the nurses come out into the patio with them?

GARAY. What for? It would only disturb them.

BENET. Disturb them? They're nurses. And why don't you hire more staff? I'm amazed you can control so many with so few.

GARAY. There's only a few of them, but they're all professionals, and they're identified with San Miguel. We'll take that walk up to the vines now. You can't say no, it's my birthday. Work is forbidden today.

*He invites him to follow. But* BENET, *one more time, turns back to the window.*

BENET. There's nothing in the patio.

GARAY. And you'd rather see it full? Full of what?

BENET. They need – manual work to occupy their hands, or a basketball hoop. And they particularly need some spatial reference points, such as –

GARAY. Yes?

BENET. They're just shadows drifting in emptiness.

GARAY. 'Shadows in emptiness'?

BENET. Why not teach them a trade? Why not get them used to being with people? Are they all incurable? We're taught our mission is to return people like him to society.

*He points to a patient through the window.*

GARAY. You don't approve of the way I run San Miguel.

BENET. Your ethical example always moved me. You stood firm at the front of the hospital during the war, you never abandoned your patients –

GARAY. But you don't approve of the way I run San Miguel. Unfortunately for you, you'll have to wait until I retire. Then you can take your turn.

*He motions him to leave the room.*

GARAY. As a doctor, allow me to prescribe a couple of days' rest at the beach. It's affecting you, spending all this time shut away in that dusty old archive. And now, if you'll pardon me, I need to make a couple of calls. Will you come to my birthday party?

BENET. Your party will have to wait.

*He hands him a telegram.* GARAY *reads it.*

BENET. Yesterday I called Madrid. I informed them in detail of the way this centre is being managed.

GARAY. Is this how you repay our hospitality? I receive you as a friend and –

BENET (*interrupting*). I have seen enough evidence of irregularities –

GARAY (*interrupting*). So for my birthday present you betray me.

BENET. Why don't you use proper sanitation, or any kind of therapy, any kind of medicine? Why are family visits so restricted as to make them practically impossible? Why do I find everywhere the same apparent *will* towards decay?

GARAY. You are making a serious mistake; believe me you will come to regret this.

BENET. Oh come off it. 'This will cost you dearly. I have friends. They'll kick you off the island.' Don't threaten me. Hasn't anyone here noticed the Dictator is dead? Or do you still believe you have friends in high places? So call them and then we'll see who comes running.

*He offers him the telephone.*

How many friends will you have when the truth is passed from person to person on the island?

GARAY. Truth? Have you got no closer than the *truth*?

BENET. I'm very close. I just need a couple of answers to a couple of questions. I don't believe you'll answer them. But here in San Miguel some one will.

GARAY *offers him the phone.*

GARAY. Who do you want to start with? Doctors, nurses, the kitchen staff?

BENET. I'm not interested in them. As you just said, they all identify with San Miguel. I'd prefer to ask the others – no-one ever asks them anything.

*He points to the patients on the other side of the glass.*

GARAY. Do you think a medical tribunal will admit their evidence?

BENET. We'll hear if they've anything to tell us.

GARAY. I won't let you near them. I have medical reasons –

BENET. Didn't you read that telegram? I'm in charge here now.

*He takes out some files, and searches for something.*

We'll begin with the cripple, the one-arm man.

*He finds the file, and reads.*

Nestor Sorel. Please call him over.

GARAY. You'll have to do that yourself.

*Pause.* BENET *and* GARAY *are face to face.* BENET *goes over to the door to the garden. He opens it. The patients stare at him. Pause.* BENET *returns to* GARAY.

BENET. Don't you want to come with me?

GARAY. You're not afraid to go into the garden by yourself are you?

BENET. They know the truth and I want you to be there to hear it.

*Pause.*

GARAY. Don't worry, I won't leave you alone. I couldn't forgive myself if any harm came to *anyone*.

BENET (*looking at the garden*). All I see are shadows trapped behind glass. They don't look dangerous.

GARAY. Dangerous? On the contrary. They're so vulnerable that any self-seeking fool could do them great harm. Any professional careerist seeking his own glory.

*GARAY puts on a white coat. He gives another to* BENET, *who hesitates before he refuses it.*

BENET. Democracy is going to unmask a lot of people. Here in this patio too.

GARAY. *Garden.*

BENET (*looking into it*). How can you call this place a
    garden?

**Scene Two**

GARAY *enters the burned garden.* BENET *does not pass
through the doorway.*

GARAY. Are you afraid to step into emptiness?

    BENET, *hesitating because he's so full of emotion, steps
    into the garden.*

GARAY. There you are. That wasn't so bad, was it?

    BENET *touches the ash.*

BENET. Who set fire to it?

GARAY. The war.

BENET. The ash is cold. Why hasn't it been replanted?

GARAY. The war razed it for ever.

    *Silence.* BENET *follows behind* GARAY *uncertainly. On
    the ground he sees the shadows of birds which never land in
    the garden.*

BENET. A garden without birds.

    *In the garden the patients shuffle about alone, or in groups.
    Reverentially or perhaps fearfully they allow* GARAY *to
    pass. Even if they long to reach out to him, they don't dare
    to go near him.* BENET *notices their wariness.*

BENET. Your relationship with them isn't right.

GARAY. They know they can always count on me.

    BENET *stops one of the old men. He looks at him in
    silence. Then he lets him continue on his way. He stops
    another old patient. He observes him closely.*

BENET (*to* GARAY). Why is Block Six empty?

GARAY *is surprised by the question.*

BENET. There are no records of any visits to Block Six for the last fifty years. Since each visit to each Block is recorded in the archives, the inference is that no-one lives there. Unless no-one in Block Six has any family or friends.

GARAY. They're old. Over time everyone has forgotten them.

BENET *lets the old man carry on walking. He observes the others.*

BENET. Precisely; I've carefully studied the files of the oldest patients; González, Quintás, Reverte, Cohen . . .

GARAY. Good people.

BENET. . . . Baez, Cal, Sorel, Barrio, Casares . . .

GARAY. Also good people.

BENET. Which staff look after them?

GARAY. I deal with the oldest ones personally.

BENET. That makes things simpler then. You will recall that some of the oldest men arrived at San Miguel in the spring of '37. Wasn't that when the Fascists occupied the island?

GARAY. What's that got to do with –

BENET. Turbulent times. Who would have been a statue-man? Keep quiet while everyone else around you goes mad?

*Silence.*

BENET. The register states there were twelve admissions that spring.

GARAY. Perhaps.

BENET. But one date has been omitted on those twelve files.

*He shows him the files.* GARAY *looks at them uninterestedly.*

GARAY. Back then we didn't pay much attention to such bureaucratic details.

BENET. It's an important date.

GARAY. I never bothered with paperwork. I don't remember who was in charge of the register back then –

BENET (*interrupting*). The final date is missing in all of them.

GARAY. I don't know what you're talking about.

BENET. 15th May, 1939. Now do you know what I'm talking about?

GARAY *shakes his head. A pause.*

BENET. Dr Garay, I known why this place is so difficult to understand. It's because what is today a psychiatric asylum was once a prison. The guard was positioned over there –

*He points to the office window.*

– from where he could watch the prisoners killing time in the patio. Do you remember what happened to those twelve men? Did they know they were going to die? Did they walk slowly around the patio, just waiting for their last moment to come?

GARAY. Did you discover all this snooping about in the archives?

BENET. Everything in the archives is a lie, including the names. The truth is, Doctor Garay, that twelve sane men were handed over to you in April '37. And two springs later just after the war was over, you stood them in front of a firing squad.

*Pause. BENET and GARAY look at each other. Some of the patients pass between them.*

GARAY. My hands are clean. Who sent you to smear me? This so-called 'national reconciliation'?

BENET. The country will not pardon you. One of those men was Blas Ferrater.

GARAY. What?

BENET. Blas Ferrater.

GARAY. Blas Ferrater, here in San Miguel?

BENET *looks at his notebook.*

BENET. He arrived on the island in April '36. He was leading a group of intellectuals supporting the Republicans.

GARAY. You mean the 'Ship of Poets'?

BENET. On that voyage, Ferrater composed 'Among the Orange Trees', his last poem of which only the first verse has survived. 'So that the angel awakes – '

GARAY. 'So that angel awakes' – I'd have wished for nothing better than to meet Blas Ferrater: the finest poet of his generation, a man capable of risking his life for an idea. Unfortunately, and as everyone knows, the 'Ship of Poets' sank a few miles from the port, and there were no survivors. They say a German submarine . . .

BENET (*interrupting*). Pink Budgie saw Ferrater in San Miguel.

GARAY. Pink Budgie?

*He remembers*

Ah, the statue-man?

BENET. He swears he saw him here, Ferrater and eleven other Republicans.

*Pause.*

Dr Garay, not only will you be thrown out of San Miguel; not only will you be barred from medical practice. Find a good lawyer: I'm going to drag you in front of a judge.

GARAY. And do you think a judge will condemn me on . . . on the word of a poor fool who lives rough on the streets, his face smeared with flour? Do you seriously believe a jury will accept his testimony?

BENET. Ferrater arrived on the island; he was captured by the Fascists and locked up in San Miguel under another name, until you stood him in front of the firing squad.

*Silence. He crouches down. He touches the ash.*

The truth lies buried under this ash. They never left here. Blas Ferrater and eleven other men.

*He looks at the ground.*

Doctor Garay, call your men. Tell them to dig here.

*He points to a spot on the ground.*

GARAY. Am I talking to a policeman now? I would like to know if I'm talking to a doctor or a policeman.

BENET *looks at the oldest men.*

BENET. One of them will remember Blas Ferrater. One of them must have seen those twelve men stood against the wall.

GARAY. So you still insist on talking to them? What if they don't want to talk to you?

BENET. Do you seriously think your madmen won't collaborate with me?

GARAY. You are very wrong to call them that.

BENET. You think they won't testify against you? Don't you see how they're desperate to cry out the truth? Until now their lives have been nothing but the lies you recorded in the archives.

GARAY. Even if they screamed the truth, you wouldn't be able to hear it. Nor will you be able to make them understand you. You're just a petty bureaucrat of the spirit. What do you know of the soul? You're just a novice. All you'll do is frighten them.

BENET. They want to talk to me.

GARAY. No: you speak a different language. They speak with the tongues of angels.

BENET. I know I will get to the heart of all these lies.

GARAY. And what will you do when you get there?

BENET. Justice will be done.

GARAY. Justice? You don't have the first idea what justice is. You aren't strong enough. You're not strong enough to walk in the garden.

*BENET doesn't understand these words. He takes a handful of ash; he watches it fall to the floor between his fingers.*

BENET. Why was the garden burned down? What did they find that they didn't like?

*But GARAY isn't listening, he has disappeared amongst his patients. BENET finds himself alone. He doesn't know where to go.*

## Scene Three

*A group of men in white coats are digging at the spot to which BENET pointed. But for how long has he been standing still, indecisive? Then he recognises a patient walking across the garden. Hurriedly he searches through his files.*

BENET. Calatrava!

*CALATRAVA stops dead. BENET looks at the old man, who looks at him from eyes cast down, warily. BENET reads his file.*

BENET. Tomas Calatrava, right?

*CALATRAVA doesn't reply or move. BENET doesn't know how to start a conversation with him.*

BENET. So – you came to San Miguel aged 19, is that right?

*CALATRAVA doesn't respond, move, or look directly at BENET.*

BENET. Come on, relax. Don't look at me like that, I'm not going to hurt you.

*He invites him to sit next to him, beneath the scorched orange tree.*

I would like to be your friend. But first I need to get to know you, you know – what you like, what you don't like. So shall we have a little chat?

CALATRAVA *moves his head, but the gesture is neither of consent or refusal.*

Is there anything you would like to do which you aren't doing? Anything you're missing here in San Miguel?

CALATRAVA *does not respond.*

Do you know what I miss, Tomas?

*He whispers something crafty to him.*

I bet you miss them too. I could get you a night pass. If you behave yourself, of course. Are you going to behave yourself?

CALATRAVA *doesn't choose to respond.*

You must have heard of that famous writer who lived here years ago. A poet, in Block Six – remember him? I'm writing a book about him, it's a biography, so I need to find out more about what things were like here then. I'm going to show you a photograph of this man, and if you can tell me anything about him – you get a reward! A night pass, I promise. Anything at all you can remember, you tell me, OK?

*He passes him an old photograph.* CALATRAVA *looks at it in silent surprise.*

His name was . . . Well anyway, they'll have called him something else in here. You must recognise him, the whole world knew who he was. You can't have forgotten him.

DON OSWALDO. You're wasting your time.

DON OSWALDO *is another of the old men; he has been prowling about with gloves, a whip and a stick.*

DON OSWALDO. You've got the wrong man. Don't waste your time with this one.

CALATRAVA (*recites*). 'So that the angel awakes.'

*Silence.*

He was here just five minutes ago.

BENET *is perplexed.*

CALATRAVA. The one who writes the poems. Didn't you see him? He was just here, beneath the orange tree, five minutes ago.

BENET *is confused. He looks for* GARAY.

BENET (*calling out*). Are you laughing at me, Doctor Garay? Is this some sort of joke?

*The patients look at* BENET. *He turns back to* CALATRAVA *to speak to him, but* DON OSWALDO *interrupts.*

DON OSWALDO. Haven't you noticed this man is mad? He can't tell you what you want to know. But I can. You don't have to tell me why you're here; I already know. Just tell me first: which is your favourite; greyhounds, circus-dogs, hunters . . . ? Well, you're in luck, I've got some magnificent specimens for sale. I have an animal for every occasion: to guard a farmhouse, to protect the children; each one is carefully trained for the role it will fulfil in society.

*He throws a stick off-stage .*

Fetch, Gaitan!

*His eyes follow the trajectory of the stick as it falls to the ground.* CALATRAVA *has made use of the distraction to disappear.*

You're too slow, Gaitan.

*He talks confidentially to* BENET, *who now notices that* CALATRAVA *has vanished.*

He misses his old master. But I won't accept secondhand goods, it's not easy to manage an animal with bad habits. There are too many con-men in this profession, and it's all too easy to teach a dog bad tricks.

BENET *wants to look for* CALATRAVA, *but* DON OSWALDO *makes him stroke the non-existent dog.* DON OSWALDO *pats the dog on the back and sends him off.*

If you want an animal to show off, then don't forget Philip the Second. An exceptional pedigree.

*He strokes the coat of Philip II.*

Look at him, the brute, isn't he a fine specimen? The small head, the shining eyes, the sharp ears . . . He knows he's being admired. And what do you think of his legs? What speed would you say they'd reach?

*He strokes Philip II's legs and watches the animal walk away. Satisfied,* DON OSWALDO *strokes another dog which also does not exist.*

Now I present to you Emmanuel Can, the very best for herding.

*He whistles and walks the dog in a circle.*

Observe his coat, see how its colour changes depending on the light. But no, it's not going to work; do you see his hackles rising? Better to leave him be. It means you don't like him. Don't be offended, the man must like the animal as much as the animal the man. Don't worry, I'm sure we'll find you something; each man has his dog.

*He looks at various non-existent dogs; finally, he points to one.*

Ah yes, here we are. The patience of Job!

*He takes him by the collar.*

Don't worry about the burned paw, his speciality is self-sacrifice, he's the best at sniffing out explosives.

*He thinks the dog is about to lick* BENET.

It's alright, he's just being playful.

(*To the dog.*) What are you doing? Why are you wrinkling up your nose?

(*To* BENET.) He's always sniffing, he works hard with his nose, he can find a dead body under a ton of rubble. But this one don't seem to like you either. See how he stays dead-still, guarding his territory? You must have a great many enemies, my friend.

*He goes up to another non-existent dog.*

In that case, Schmitt is your dog. A tough son-of-a-bitch. You won't find a better fighter anywhere.

*He points out the shadow of a bird on the ground.*

See how he goes for the doves?

*He takes off the muzzle, gives the dog a sweet, opens his mouth, examines his teeth.*

Trained to hunt men. He can track a three-day old scent; five if the earth is damp.

*Suddenly he draws back his hand, as if Schmitt has bitten him.*

Bastard!

*He tries to stop the pain.*

He's practically taken off a couple of fingers.

*He whips the dog.*

He gets more insolent every day. Do you know how many of these things there can be in just one litter? Look around you. Other than Winnie, all the bitches are pregnant. They keep on breeding, and every day I get weaker.

*He points to Schmitt's bruised body.*

But now my whip has no effect.

*With an effort, he cracks his whip authoritatively.*

They're circling me, just waiting for the chance to strike. I've no friends among them; the moment I close my eyes they'll attack.

*He points to a scar.*

Would you believe that's the work of Dolar, a mere puppy. But you have nothing to fear. Chose one, pay the price and he'll respect you like a master. I am only his trainer.

BENET. I'm not here to buy a dog.

DON OSWALDO (*very surprised*). Oh? So why are you wasting my time?

BENET. Wouldn't you like to have more space for your training?

DON OSWALDO. I've got more room than I need: time's what I really need. Chatting away all day long isn't how I earn my money. People pay me because I do my work well, and because what they're really buying is peace. The Mayor's wife, she's one of my best clients, she's always telling me that now when she walks through the streets with the dog, the blacks back right off, and that's a very agreeable feeling.

BENET. I'm carrying out an investigation.

DON OSWALDO (*surprised*). Don't tell me: it's about Hansel and Gretel. I swear I'll punish them. I swear my teaching's not at fault. Even if no-one trains them, they still bite the blacks. Those anarchists say I train them to do it, but the fact is that if there's one black and a thousand whites, the dobermans always go for the black. What can I do about that? It's just Nature. No other breed is born knowing who to attack and who not to attack. Dobermans are, and they go straight for the balls.

BENET. I'm not here about the dobermans.

DON OSWALDO *looks at* BENET *with great mistrust.*

DON OSWALDO. I won't answer any questions about feeding or training techniques. That's all top secret.

BENET. Have you ever seen a dead dog on the hard shoulder of a motorway?

DON OSWALDO. A motorway?

BENET. A dead dog at the side of the road. You know that's how you'd feel if we took away your animals.

DON OSWALDO. Take away my animals? You couldn't do that to me. The dobermans –

BENET (*interrupting*). Do you think I'm interested in the stupid games of your dobermans? What worries me is that these dogs are a menace to society. Why did you hide the fact that they're riddled with disease?

DON OSWALDO. My dogs are healthy!

BENET. I'm afraid you're going to have to find a new job. This is too important to leave in the hands of an irresponsible person. Your pupils constitute a serious threat to public health. The situation has deteriorated so badly that perhaps the kennel isn't the answer anymore. When were they last innoculated against rabies?

DON OSWALDO. Rabies? Look at their tongues –

BENET. Society no longer has faith in you. You let one of the animals escape.

DON OSWALDO. I have never lost a dog.

BENET. It bit a child.

DON OSWALDO. A child?

BENET. A white child.

DON OSWALDO. Impossible. My dogs know that –

BENET (*interrupting*). A long time ago we received an anonymous letter informing us of everything. Only now are we able to verify the accusations.

DON OSWALDO. It's a lie. Which miserable bastard –

BENET. Citizen Ferrater helped us with this information.

DON OSWALDO *looks frightened. Pause.*

BENET. Blas Ferrater is the name he used. Perhaps it's a pseudonym, to protect himself. What's indisputable is that he lived here: the letter gave detailed descriptions of this place.

*Pause.* BENET *observes* DON OSWALDO's *reactions.*

BENET. I'd like to believe that this Ferrater had some personal vendetta against you. In which case, his testimony will be invalid. But what would he hope to gain by perjuring himself? Think back. What do you remember about him?

DON OSWALDO *is in pain; he looks everywhere as if for help. His eyes light on* GARAY.

DON OSWALDO. Do something, Garay. They're going to take my dogs away.

BENET *sees* GARAY; *he had not noticed him reappear.*

BENET (*to* DON OSWALDO, *who looks imploringly at* GARAY). Mr Garay can no longer help you. He too has lost his job.

DON OSWALDO *looks at* GARAY, *who nods to confirm that what* BENET *has said is true.*

DON OSWALDO. This is madness –

(*To* BENET.) Are you a complete fool?

BENET (*interrupting*). Don't judge me too quickly. I also have my duty to perform.

GARAY (*to* DON OSWALDO). You must co-operate with Mr Benet, professional to professional. He's been sent to find out the truth regarding an accusation against me.

DON OSWALDO (*to* BENET). You're wrong, it's not his fault. He's the one who feeds the dogs.

BENET. What? Is Garay the dogs' master?

DON OSWALDO. He feeds them.

BENET. Does he work for you?

DON OSWALDO. On the contrary, he changed my life by giving me this job. I couldn't tell a dog with its head in the air from one slinking along with its nose to the ground; Garay taught me the different breeds, and the language of whistles. He has friends amongst them. He sits down beneath the orange tree, and they sleep at his feet. I'd be nothing without my whip. But all he needs to do is look at them, and they're peaceful as lambs.

BENET. The person who feeds the dogs –

DON OSWALDO. Apparently he's only the person who feeds them. But if he wasn't here, what use would my whip be?

BENET. When Garay leaves, there'll be no need for whips.

DON OSWALDO. You don't know what you're saying. You should have known him in those years, when the port was over-run with dogs.

BENET. When?

DON OSWALDO. There was a wolf loose among the dogs. Hidden among the shadows, waiting for a ship full of children to arrive. But before he could attack them, Garay went down to the port and killed the wolf with one embrace. The others surrounded the beast. And so Garay managed to reunite them and bring them up the hill. They followed him obediently like a pack.

BENET. When did this happen?

DON OSWALDO. A long time ago. But it could happen again at any moment. When food is short, their eyes shine bright . . .

BENET. They'll never be hungry again.

*He points to the window of the office.*

I'll put a gunman there. He'll deal with them in a couple of minutes.

DON OSWALDO. You can't kill all the dogs, it's impossible.

*He points to a scene that only he can see.*

Look at Marilyn, she's nearly ready to give birth again. If she keeps going like this . . .

BENET (*interrupts angrily*). That's enough!

*His anger shocks DON OSWALDO.*

Remember you're still charged with a serious offence. Now; we're trying to recall Blas Ferrater. Would it help you to see a photograph?

BENET *makes him look at the old photo. It pains DON OSWALDO to look at it. He looks back at GARAY.*

GARAY. Don't look at me like a beaten dog. What can I do, if someone's denounced you? Unless you can prove it's a question of slander . . .

BENET. Doctor Garay, kindly leave me alone with my patient.

GARAY. Would you be willing to confront Ferrater in person?

BENET *is perplexed.*

GARAY (*to* DON OSWALDO). Let's settle this once and for all. Bring Ferrater before us, and let's confront this head on.

BENET. What sort of game are you playing at, Garay?

GARAY. I have to warn you, if you don't agree to this confrontation, Mr Benet will have to believe Ferrater's testimony.

*Pause.* BENET *doesn't understand.* DON OSWALDO *goes up to a non-existent bitch.*

DON OSWALDO. Winnie is on heat. I don't like to keep her tied up, but I have to, for her own good. She mustn't get out to the blacks' mongrels. It's part of my responsibility to see that the pedigree dogs don't mate with the mongrels. And that's not easy on an island like this, where there are so many of them, and all uncastrated.

*Silence. He's furious.*

How dare Ferrater claim my animals have rabies!

GARAY. Well he has, word for word, it seems.

DON OSWALDO. What the fuck does he know. He's kept well away from them. He's frightened. He always thought I stank like a dog.

BENET. What are you talking about? When was the last time you saw Ferrater? Five minutes ago? Forty years ago?

GARAY. What else, other than five minutes or forty years?

DON OSWALDO'*s gaze looks for something without finding it. He points to something.*

DON OSWALDO. Ask those loony chess-players. I'm sure they'll know where he is. They always got on well with that pedant. Ferrater is a deep man, but he's not always right. Let's hope this time he's wrong. If rabies gets out, what will become of the Republic?

*He points to the non-existent Marilyn.*

Look at the useless creatures Marilyn has given birth to. Are they born with rabies? Are they rabid from the moment of birth? Is that why there are no longer any women in this country?

PEPE *and* NESTOR *burst onto the stage in the direction pointed out by* DON OSWALDO. *One-handed* NESTOR *carries a box;* PEPE *a chess-clock. The men in white coats have dug a deep pit. Some of the inmates stare at them in terror; others simply do not see them.*

**Scene Four**

PEPE. How come the board isn't set up yet? It's time for the game.

NESTOR *sets the clock up where it can be clearly seen, and draws the lines of a chess board in the ash. Next to* PEPE *he takes a seat on one side of the board. He opens the box and strokes the pieces. The men in white coats dig the pit even deeper. When* BENET *manages to overcome the uneasiness which seizes him, he consults his files. He goes to sit on the other side of the board, but* PEPE's *alarmed voice stops him.*

PEPE. You can't sit there!

BENET. Can't I?

PEPE. That place is reserved for maestro Bakhtin.

BENET. Oh. Sorry.

PEPE. He should be here by now. You haven't seen him in the stadium?

BENET *shakes his head.*

PEPE. I hope nothing's happened to him. I saw him in the
hotel dining room this morning, and he looked terrible.
I felt like asking him and his dear mother to join me at my
table for breakfast. Does that surprise you? No, courtesy
and valour are not mutually exclusive. Opponents need not
behave like enemies. I was the first person to recognise his
talent in Moscow, where he was one of 89 schoolboys
playing a simultaneous display. Since then we've played
each other 17 times. I've seen him grow up, and he's seen
me grow old. Are you surprised I like the boy? In the end, a
player has more in common with his opponents than with
his own countrymen. That boy and I live on the margins: we
go from hotel to hotel, sleeping with different women every
night . . . We are never far from the 64 black and white
squares, and yet I'm certain both of us feel the same weari-
ness on our endless journey around the chess-boards of the
world.

*He's disgusted to see* BENET *take a white knight out of the
box.* BENET *speaks to* NESTOR.

BENET. Such a beautiful creature. I bet it could jump right
over this wall.

*He points to the wall.* NESTOR *stays silent.*

PEPE. You doubtless have a wife and a home, so you must be
wondering why I carry this cross upon my shoulders.
Conversely, my young opponent who is going to take his
place on the opposite side of the board has never asked why
I have sacrificed everything for the game. We both represent
our countries.

*He points to a branch of the orange tree.*

The flag.

*He looks emotionally at the non-existent flag.*

BENET. You'll be able to rest very soon now. Sooner or later
every opponent must lose.

PEPE *looks at* BENET *in astonishment as he sits on the far
side of the board.*

PEPE. I repeat: I am waiting for maestro Bakhtin. You do not
seem to have noticed the transcendent nature of this game.
Up until now we have drawn every game. But today's
combat is exceptional, no other game has raised such
expectations around the board. I was shocked by Bakhtin's
pallor this morning, but it's only natural: he bears an
enormous responsibility.

*He points to the other inmates.*

Dignitaries and representatives of both countries are here
for the game. Do you realise how many millions of souls
are depending on us?

BENET. Let's play before Bakhtin gets here. A quick game.

PEPE. Impossible. I wouldn't know which flag you were
defending.

BENET *is distracted by* NESTOR, *who has begun to
arrange the 32 pieces on the board.*

BENET. Sorry?

PEPE. Which federation?

BENET. I'm playing for free.

PEPE. Another stateless person. Every day there's more! It's
all very sad.

BENET *finishes setting up his pieces.*

PEPE. This is highly irregular. Show me your credentials.
What's your position on the ICF ladder?

BENET. There's no need to be afraid of me.

PEPE. You won't win.

BENET. We'll see.

PEPE. You won't win. I've drawn against all my opponents
throughout the world.

BENET. You're afraid of me.

PEPE. I've hardened myself in combat against the most
terrifying opponents. Every day they are better trained.

They're like robots. When they were babies they were taken away from their mothers and had engrained in their memories all the variants, checkmate strategies with thirty anticipatory moves. Some days I thought everything was lost, when I was surrounded by black pieces. Nevertheless, my king always escaped. One way or another I find the way out, the magisterial solution that forces a draw.

BENET. If that's the case, neither of us need be afraid.

*BENET takes a white pawn and a black pawn and hides them behind his back. He motions to PEPE to choose a hand.*

PEPE. I only play white.

*Pause. BENET puts the pawns back on the board, and motions curtly to PEPE to begin. But he does not move.*

PEPE. We can't start without the adjudicator.

BENET. Don't you trust me?

PEPE. We can't play without him. Only he knows all the rules and the exceptions.

*He points to GARAY. BENET looks at the doctor.*

BENET. We'll consult him if we disagree about anything.

*More forcefully, he gestures to PEPE to play. But PEPE won't bring his hand near the board.*

BENET. Would you rather the ICF disqualify you?

*Pause. PEPE looks at the board as if finally he'll start to play.*

PEPE. I always feel so emotional at the beginning of each new game. What are we, you and I, before those millions of watching eyes. What does our little board mean here at the centre of the world? Because this board is definitely at the centre of the world.

*NESTOR touches a white pawn.*

PEPE. Is it because I'm growing old that the pieces affect me more and more every time I touch them?

*NESTOR moves a pawn, and starts the clock. BENET moves and presses the button. Immediately NESTOR moves again and presses the button. PEPE seems deeply moved.*

PEPE. Isn't this what the Ancients called Beauty? The rules are unchangeable, the movement of the pieces is fixed. And isn't this also what the Ancients called Liberty?

*Moving his piece and pressing the button, BENET interrupts PEPE. NESTOR takes a black pawn, and presses the clock. He lets the piece fall into the box. PEPE smiles in a macabre way.*

PEPE. Isn't it like a knife in the heart every time a piece is taken and falls with a crash back into the box? After so many victims, who'd ever believe it was just a game? We live in grief. In sacrifice.

*BENET moves and presses the button. NESTOR reaches out to a white piece, but BENET takes his wrist and looks into his eyes. Only then does NESTOR come out of his deep trance.*

BENET. For years I studied all your games looking for an error. In the end I decided you were unbeatable. Until someone told me your weak point. Because I know you have a weak point.

PEPE. How dare you? Don't you know who you're addressing? I am a Grand Master. Let me inform you there are only twelve Grand Masters officially recognised by the ICF.

BENET (*to NESTOR who is trying in vain to seize with his one hand a white piece*). I'm certain to win. Ferrater taught me how to beat you.

*PEPE and NESTOR are astonished.*

Ferrater taught you?

*NESTOR gets up from the board and goes to find GARAY. PEPE looks at NESTOR helplessly.*

PEPE. I don't remember ever having played Ferrater. Furthermore, I refuse to believe that he –

BENET. I'd just like to point out I'm threatening your Queen.

*PEPE looks at the board in terror. He implores NESTOR to intervene. But NESTOR doesn't respond.*

BENET. Do you resign?

PEPE. I ask for an adjournment. I can't play in these conditions. A spectator on the third level is spoiling my concentration with his continual whispering. And the smell of the carpet is giving me a migraine.

BENET. I knew you were a failure. Ferrater told me so.

PEPE (*to* GARAY). Why don't you intervene?

*GARAY does not move. PEPE appeals resentfully.*

Stop the game before it's too late.

*GARAY studies the game.*

GARAY. Your position certainly looks difficult.

BENET. Anyway, Mr Garay can't help you. I've just dismissed him.

PEPE. What?

BENET. Don't look so surprised. Unless you're blind you'll have noticed that Mr Garay is guilty of countless irregularities.

PEPE. I don't understand. You must be wrong.

GARAY. The Competition Committee is never wrong. It just needs some evidence to justify the resolutions it is taking against me. If you have that evidence, you must give it to Mr Benet.

PEPE (*to* BENET). You won't find it. Garay has always been vigilant in keeping the game clean. Thanks to him, the games have never degenerated into a row. Someone needs to know the rules in these difficult times. So by what law can you judge him? On the contrary, out there where the law is silent, his word creates the law.

*Pause. BENET stares at NESTOR.*

BENET. Until today, only Garay's word has been valid. Now everyone can speak.

GARAY. Anyone who has anything to say.

BENET (*to* NESTOR). Everyone is free to say whatever they think.

GARAY. Now there are too many words.

BENET (*to* GARAY). I'm on their side, Doctor Garay. And you – which side are you on?

(*To the patients.*) When the war came to the island, did anyone know which side Garay was on? Which were his pieces? Did anyone know if he played black or white?

(*To* GARAY). He held on to Ferrater, and waited to see which way the situation would go in the country. He had to wait for one side or the other to win, so he'd know who was a friend and who an enemy. And when the war was over, he chose the winning side. He stood twelve men before a firing squad. To prove his loyalty did he even ask to be the executioner? Did he ask to give Ferrater the *coup de grace*? Was that his reward?

*Pause.* GARAY *puts a patient in front of* BENET.

GARAY. What if this were Blas Ferrater?

*He puts another one in front of* BENET.

Or this one?

*He points to all the patients.*

Or if any of them were Blas Ferrater, the great poet?

*Silence.* BENET *looks at them.*

BENET. So is that your version of events? You made them pass as mad in order to save them? You locked them up for the sake of humanity? Only they weren't meant to go mad themselves? Don't try to trick me, Garay. None of these men is Blas Ferrater.

GARAY. If you didn't talk so much, you might still hear the echoing crack of the rifles. Can't you hear them?

*Silence.* GARAY *points to the air, as if he can hear the shots.*

For a long time the war was forgotten in San Miguel. We began to believe the soldiers would never open that door, never set foot in the garden.

*He touches two lines on the wall.*

Do you see those two lines of holes, like stripes of a flag? One corresponds to their heads, the other to their hearts. Twelve hearts. They were buried where they fell.

*Silence.* BENET, *shaken, looks at the ground where* GARAY *is pointing.* GARAY *gestures to the men in white coats to dig at that point.*

GARAY (*to* BENET). You're a skilful player, but in the end you lose confidence. You threatened to finish it off quickly, but you're scared to check-mate him.

*He makes* PEPE *look at the board. He says to him:*

My friend, if the black pieces are worth anything, they will knock over your King with one blow.

*Shocked,* PEPE *looks back at the board. He still doesn't dare to move, his hand shakes above the pieces.* GARAY *points to the clock.* PEPE *looks desperately at the ticking hands.*

GARAY. Every night you dream the clock has stopped, that history has stopped, and that nothing has happened since you sat down to play that first game. You dream that history and death no longer exist. Have you heard the ticking of a watch on the wrist of a dead man? The watch continues to tick while the body rots. The worms consume the strap of the watch but not its ticking. Have you heard the ticking of a watch on a skeleton?

*Suddenly,* PEPE *makes a move and presses the button. Pause. Trembling, he looks up at the other patients.*

PEPE. Why are you staring at me? Did I make a mistake? Don't try to influence me. No matter what you do, the public always side with the opponent. They applaud all the most vulgar moves and boo my best games. I've played a great game. I offer a draw.

*He offers his hand to* BENET. *But* GARAY *takes a white piece with a black piece, and presses the clock.*

GARAY. Mate in three.

*PEPE looks at the board in fear.*

PEPE. Impossible. You're wrong. The English champion, the Polish champion . . . none have taken my King. I drew at Lunachersky in 1951, at Montreal, with two Rooks, at Brend in 1953, in Kinchassa, with Bishop and Queen –

GARAY. And at Metz in '61, in Bogota with three Pawns. The best game in memory. But all that turns out to be a lie. Ferrater was right; did you think you could get away with cheating forever?

*PEPE looks at GARAY in agony like a naughty child discovered by his father. He wants to protest, but he can't speak.*

GARAY. Ferrater often warned me. You're nothing unless you cheat.

*Slowly, weeping with rage, PEPE throws himself on one of the patients, hits him, and repeats:*

PEPE. I've always played by the rules!!

*Some of the other patients separate them. They try to calm him down.*

BENET *looks at the patient hit by PEPE and at the pit dug by the men in white coats.* NESTOR, *meanwhile, has leaned out over the abyss of the board.*

NESTOR. Where does the horror come from? From the Rooks? From the Bishops on their diagonals of blood? From the mad roar of the Knights? No: it comes from this little Pawn at the front of the column smiling at the King; he's the source of the horror. He knows he's Death's worker.

*He speaks to the patients. His one hand moves in the air like a solitary chess-player.*

One, Pawn to King 6; two, Knight to Bishop 4; three, Pawn to King 7.

*Commotion among the patients.*

And if we reply with King to Knight 3?

*Hope rises among the patients.*

Then black Bishop to King 8, King to Knight 2, Knight to King 7, taking the Rook and the game.

*Deep sigh from the patients.*

Not Pawn to Rook 4, not Knight to Knight 5, not Rook to Bishop 6. See how the enemy dominates the heart of the board while his pawns advance? Black is preparing for Knight to Queen 7. Our King is going mad and spreads panic and disorder among his people.

*Disorder and panic among the patients. The men in white coats not knowing if this is the right moment to intervene, look at* GARAY. *He gestures for them to stay back.*

NESTOR. The situation is desperate. Only the greatest sacrifice can save us now. There is one last alternative – sacrifice the Queen.

*He moves the White Queen.*

NESTOR. A draw.

GARAY (*to* BENET *who keeps looking at the patient attacked by* PEPE). Is everything clear now? Is there anything else to say?

PEPE (*to* BENET, *re-establishing calm*). And now, please forgive me. The moment has come to defend the Republic.

*He points off into the distance.*

Here comes maestro Bakhtin, holding his mother's hand.

NESTOR *sits by his side and sets up the pieces to begin a new game. Elsewhere in the garden,* DON OSWALDO *makes his Great Danes jump.*

**Scene Five**

*The men in white coats take a break beside the pit. They have found what they were looking for.* BENET *looks alternately at the bottom of the pit and at the man* PEPE *attacked. From time to time this man goes over to the wall as if he could see right through it.*

GARAY. So you still don't understand. How much longer are you going to wander about in the garden?

BENET *looks at him vacantly.*

GARAY. Why don't you close your eyes? It might help. Imagine San Miguel occupied by the victorious military in their clean uniforms and shining medals.

GARAY *looks at the window of his office.*

Close your eyes and look over there. Can you see me, much younger than I am now, pouring my best wine for the soldiers?

*He pretends to raise a glass in a toast.*

To victory! Do you see the soldiers' eyes misting over? See how they're starting to forget what brings them to San Miguel? See how Garay's wine transforms them into peaceful lambs? And then the young captain, the only one who stays silent, covers his glass as I offer him more wine. This gesture is important. Remember, it is May, 1939. Peace has come. The captain goes over to the window, looks into the garden and says to me: 'Your wine is excellent, Garay. What a pity the stink of those Reds coming from the garden prevents one from savouring the bouquet. There must be at least twelve Reds out there.'

BENET. And thus Garay delivers up his twelve Reds.

GARAY. One must help fall that which is going to fall. In war there must always be a winning side. Because if no-one wins the war will never end.

GARAY *stands next to the* MAN PEPE *attacked.*

GARAY. Those soldiers had won a war. They wanted twelve men and they had them. They shot twelve men, and then they left. And they forgot us, and the world left San Miguel in peace.

BENET *would like to answer, but he can't speak. GARAY brings the MAN closer to BENET.*

GARAY. Talk to him. He saw everything. Or don't you believe the words of madmen now?

BENET *doesn't want to listen to any more. He needs to leave the garden. But GARAY stands the MAN before him.*

BENET. Did they shoot twelve innocent men? Is that what you hope I'll believe? This isn't Blas Ferrater.

*He doesn't look at the MAN. He looks at the old photograph. He doesn't even look like him.*

GARAY. Would you prefer to believe Ferrater is down there in that pit of bones? Which of those twelve skeletons is the dead poet?

BENET *won't look at the pit. He wills himself to look at the MAN. GARAY stands back.*

BENET. And who do you think you are?

*The MAN looks at him, does not understand.*

BENET. I've met a dog trainer and an unbeatable chess-player. What's your role?

*The MAN looks at him as if trying to remember him.*

MAN. You must be the man who's going around asking everyone about me. Have we met? Have we talked during the voyage?

BENET. So you're on a voyage. Like an astronaut going round and round above the spinning planet? Or Marco Polo perhaps?

*The MAN extends his hand.*

MAN. Blas Ferrater.

*Pause.* BENET *doesn't shake hands. He looks at him surpressing who knows what sort of joy or despair. He searches for the* MAN's *file. He shows it to the* MAN.

BENET. You are Maximo Cal.

CAL. Your information is incorrect. My name is Ferrater. And you must be –

*He tries to remember.*

– the American photographer. Your Spanish is excellent.

BENET *stares at him in amazement.*

What's the news from the Ebro, or from Madrid? Do you know the latest position? I'm sure the Front is holding up. Isn't it a beautiful day to arrive? Let's hope the sun's shining when we disembark.

*He stares through the wall.*

We just need to dock, then we can march ahead to the front, we can urge the soldiers onwards with our songs and build a defence of poetry for the Revolution. And when the war is over, from out of the ruins will rise the Land of Poetry.

*He brings* BENET's *attention to the voices of the other inmates.*

Isn't this symphony of foreign voices beautiful? Don't you just feel we're going to found a new country? Poets of all nations summoned together to proclaim one idea: the island must not fall. It will be a death-trap for reactionaries. We're all fighting men here, you included; in fact, you're one of the most important. Through the lens of your camera the democracies of the world will see the Republic is in danger. We need the support of the Free World, and of all men of good will. They won't allow Spain to fall into the hands of Fascism. So now do you realise how important you are to us? Don't forget; you're fighting for the Republic. With your camera you can stop this war; you can stop all wars. And that's why I want you to promise me not to help the victims. Promise me that if you see a wounded child you won't stop to help. Concentrate instead on capturing his agony, put all his pain into your camera. Photograph the pain of the world.

*He shows him a scrap of paper covered with crossed-out words.*

CAL. I too am preparing my weapons: a poem. I don't know how to load a rifle, but I will march armed with poetry. If I can find exactly the right words they will turn into action, they will prevent this Evil. I've re-written this poem thousands of times since we set sail, but I still haven't found exactly the right words. I just can't concentrate. I won't be able to until we disembark.

*He checks that the other inmates are standing away from him, and whispers confidentially:*

Can I tell you a secret?

BENET. Of course.

CAL. When we set off from Valencia, everyone seemed to be loyal to the cause. But even here on the ship Fascism is advancing. At night I can hear men prowling about near my cabin. I feel the noose tightening around me. I'm just a simple poet, but I represent something important to many people. The people turned me into a symbol. If anything happens to me, you must safe-guard my words and return them to the world.

*He shows* BENET *an unbound manuscript. He looks up at the sky.*

It's clouding over.

BENET *opens the manuscript. He recites with emotion:*

BENET. 'So that the angel awakes
    a thousand mothers sacrifice their sons
    to the red dream of the dawn . . . '

CAL. It's called 'Among the Orange Trees'.

*Silence.* BENET *looks at* CAL.

BENET. Ferrater, I bring you good news. You are a free man.

CAL *looks at him without understanding. He stands as if the wind has just swept across the deck of the ship.*

CAL. Can't we sail faster?

BENET. There's no need to be afraid. The war is over for ever.

*CAL doesn't take any notice of him. He stands as if the ship is entering a storm.*

CAL (*to* GARAY). Won't we arrive too late?

GARAY. How do you sleep at sea, Benet? Does the sound of the wind and the cry of the seagulls affect you? Do you feel seasick? Be careful; in the last storm a sailor fell overboard.

BENET (*to* CAL). No-one will be persecuted for their ideas any more. No-one needs to be afraid.

GARAY (*to* BENET). Have you noticed how time passes differently at sea? Doesn't it seem as if a whole century has passed by since we set sail?

BENET (*to* CAL). Your poems are sung in the streets, children recite them at school. You don't need to hide any longer.

GARAY (*to* BENET). You're lucky to be on the Ship of Poets. Did you know this ship used to carry millionaires on pleasure cruises?

(*To the patients*). Didn't the Republic do well to requisition it for the people?

*The patients agree enthusiastically with GARAY. So does CAL.*

BENET (*to* CAL). Don't listen to this nonsense!

(*To the patients*). Don't listen to Garay!

CAL *and the others are astonished.*

CAL. Have you gone completely mad? Are you inciting the crew to mutiny against the Captain?

BENET. Now you must believe in *me*.

(*To the patients*). Don't be afraid of Garay. He can't hurt you anymore.

*Astonishment spreads among them.*

CAL (*to* GARAY). Shall we throw him overboard, Captain?

GARAY. No. You must learn to respect Mr Benet. From today
you must obey *his* orders.

*Commotion and confusion among the patients.* GARAY
*calls for silence.*

GARAY. Mr Benet is investigating an accusation against me.
An anonymous accusation. But the details are so precise
that it can only have come from a member of the crew or
from a passenger. It accuses me of –

*He turns to look at* BENET.

What *does* it accuse me of Mr Benet?

CAL (*to* BENET). Only a Fifth Columist could have denounced
him. Garay has navigated the ship up to now. He managed
to trick the blockade, and showed great courage when an
armoured Fascist ship tried to board us. If he had not been
at the helm, the traitors would have changed the ship's flag.
The Poetry is ours, but only the determination and intelli-
gence of the Captain will guide the ship to the island. If
anyone is able to guide us through the storm, it is this man.

BENET (*to* GARAY). You're lucky you live in a democracy.
You'll have a fair trial and imprisonment without torture.

GARAY. Do you think I'm frightened of prison? I don't
suppose you'd believe me if I told you my only concern is
their welfare? What's going to become of my boys?

BENET. Your boys? Your prisoners, you mean.

GARAY. Prisoners? Are they in chains? Do you see any signs
of punishment?

BENET. You took everything away from them, even their own
names. The firing squad wasn't enough for you. You gave
them a fate worse than death.

GARAY. They're not afraid of death. They're just children
playing.

BENET. You cast them into emptiness.

GARAY. So you still can't see anything but emptiness? You still can't see what I have made here? In this emptiness I have built a home.

BENET. You'll pay for your crime, Garay, you owe it to your victims. To all your victims.

*He points to the pit.*

GARAY. My victims? Do you think it was me who pointed out those innocents? 'There must be at least twelve Reds out there', said the captain. I went into the garden and told the boys what the soldiers wanted. And it was the boys themselves who found the answer.

*BENET shakes his head, he can't accept what GARAY is telling him. GARAY invites him to look at the patients.*

Will you put *them* before a judge?

*CAL is euphoric, walking around the pit as if it didn't even exist, and pointing through the wall.*

CAL. The lights of the port! See the crowd which has come out to welcome us! Listen to those joyful shouts! The whole town is on its feet waiting to greet us!

GARAY. You won't find a judge who could judge me. What am I accused of? Of planting flowers in the ash of a burned garden? I have given them an eternal spring.

*CAL is still staring through the wall.*

CAL. The orange trees are in flower! This is going to be the last spring of the war.

BENET. You stupid poet, can't you see you're sailing into disaster?

CAL. Poets must not be cowards. We're going to arrive in time to save the island from falling into the clutches of Fascism. We're going to support the Front! We're going to encourage the men with our Song of Liberty!

BENET. The Fascists have surrounded the port, can't you hear the shooting?

CAL. We'll sing louder, stronger than the bombs!

BENET. No-one will disembark with you. The ship will depart without you, abandoning you.

CAL (*to* GARAY). Captain, don't retreat. Even if only I land. No matter what happens, no matter what the cost, my words must be heard. The poet's voice will save the people, for it is the spirit of the Republic. Helmsmen, hold steady! Stoke the engines below! Deckhands prepare the landing boats!

BENET. Can't you hear the silence in the port? Can't you see it's a tomb? No-one has come to hear you speak.

CAL (*points to* BENET). What are you waiting for Captain – stand him in front of a firing squad.

GARAY. A firing squad? What's the charge?

CAL. Spreading subversive propaganda that the enemy has broken through the front. If it gets out to the crew, they'll force you to retreat. If this man isn't a fascist infiltrator then he must be a defeatist, which also helps the enemy. Are we going to allow a fifth columnist to break the spirit of the Ship of Poets?

*The patients surround* BENET.

BENET (*points to the imaginary port*). The only thing awaiting you there is Death. The flag has been changed. Fools, can't you see the island is overrun by the enemy? Everything is lost.

(*To* GARAY *with a violent gesture*). Tell them the orange trees are dead. Enough make-believe. Tell them the truth! The Truth!

*Furiously he forces* CAL *to look down into the pit. His violence upsets the patients and even surprises himself. Pause.*

BENET (*to* GARAY). Tell them you have no intention of returning them, healed, to the world.

GARAY. They know I can't do that.

BENET. Tell them you think they will never be cured.

GARAY. 'Cured'? What does 'cured' mean?

BENET. I will cure them.

GARAY. No medicine on earth will cure a patient who decides to stay sick. But their souls are the best, the healthiest, on the island.

BENET. I'm going to separate the sick from the well.

*He tries to distinguish between them, but can't.*

I'm going to release the healthy men.

GARAY. And who do you suppose is waiting for them? What's out there for them? They won't even recognise the country on the other side of that wall. These men *lost*. They can't go back to a country which for them is an impossibility. Outside this garden they will not survive.

BENET. I'll get them out of here . . .

GARAY. Why? What's the use of more statue-men?

BENET. Statue-men?

*He doesn't understand.*

Don't try to trick me like you do them, Garay, you won't change my mind.

GARAY *shows* BENET *a file from the archive.*

GARAY. Do you recognise him without his scar? Antonio Roca, alias Pink Budgie. The night he left San Miguel, I took his file from the archives. Read it: he was admitted on the same day as his eleven comrades in Block Six. He's handsome, isn't he? You should know that Blas Ferrater was in love with him; he wouldn't share him with anyone.

BENET *looks at Ferrater, who stays at the edge of the pit as if mesmerised by what he sees at the bottom.*

DON OSWALDO. He says he's drawn a big smile on his face, with his pen, out of love. But he's done it to destroy his beauty – with a bite-mark.

PEPE. Yes, he is jealous, so he's slashed Budgie's cheek with the sharp edge of the Bishop.

*NESTOR makes a cut in the air.*

GARAY. Budgie thought he could survive outside San Miguel. But the wolf howls and two black horses circle the foot of his pedestal. There is so much pain on the other side of this wall . . . only a statue could bear such pain. Don't take these men out of the garden. The only thing awaiting them out there is the dark night. In the garden we are surrounded by ash, but out there is a bush that burns endlessly. Is that what you would condemn them to? Their place is here. Beyond time. Beyond pain. Don't drag them back into time and pain. Don't drag them back to war. Forget San Miguel. Leave the dead in their graves.

*Pause. GARAY points upwards, and addresses the patients.*

I am up on the hill, on the other side of the wall, waiting for you. See how the crowning branches of the orange trees thrust out above the wall. It is a garden. That's where you'll all find peace.

*BENET stands before the patients, who seem now to be a unified group.*

BENET (*to* GARAY). I will return these men to the world.

GARAY. Return them to hell. Take them all, take even one if you dare. They'll still come back. They'll climb the walls to get back to my side.

BENET. They won't be back. Come this way now!

(*To the men in white coats*). Open all the doors!

GARAY. Why are you letting the demons in?

*BENET wants to take CAL off. But he stands fixed beside the pit, looking down into it as if into the abyss.*

BENET. We'll destroy this place. Knock down the walls!

*But his voice is drowned out by CAL's who shouts down into the pit.*

CAL. Why are you staring at me? Haven't you understood yet? How much longer do you need before you'll see things from History's point of view?

*He points down as if at twelve people.*

It isn't my hand that chose you, but History. History decides who lives and who dies. What are the lives of twelve men when humanity itself is at stake?

*He goes to the wall, and turns his back to the pit. The other patients go with him. As if they are standing in the prow of a ship, he calls out to those waiting at the port. His words are heard over the sound of crashing waves.*

CAL. We fight for a universal cause! Comrades, workers and peasants, our struggle is your struggle! We are here, poets, travellers, brought together to dig the deep grave of fascism.

*He points to the dead orange tree.*

The flag of the Republic shines brighter than ever. Don't the colours glow more brightly in the storm? Workers, peasants and poets, all united, to the barricades! No Pasaran! The destiny of mankind is at stake!

*They all listen to* CAL. *In* BENET's *hands, the manuscript of 'Among the Orange Trees' is scattered by the wind.*

**Epilogue**

*Day or night, in the Port.* BENET *with his luggage. He speaks to the* STATUE.

BENET. Tell me he isn't Ferrater.

Why did Garay let you go?

Why did the others stay behind?

How many statue-men are there?

My boat's leaving soon; won't you talk to me? If I attack you with a hammer until there's nothing left but your feet, would you talk to me then?

Tell me who set fire to the garden.

Tell me when they went mad.

Was it your smile sent them mad?

Will you keep smiling forever?

*The statue-man does not move.*

# BAZAAR

*by*

## DAVID PLANELL

*translated by John Clifford*

David Planell was born in Madrid in 1967. He studied Cinema
and Television at the Universidad Complutense de Madrid and
has been a script writer for television since 1990. In 1995 he
took part in the Royal Court International Summer School
where his play *Prime Time* was given a workshop directed by
Roxana Silbert. *Bazaar* is his first play to be produced. It is
the winner of the Comedias Hogar de Teatro prize and
premiered in Puerto Santa Maria (Cádiz) in August 1997
followed by a tour throughout Spain. *Bazaar* had its British
premiere as part of the New European Writers' Season at the
Royal Court Theatre Upstairs in November, 1997. He also co-
translated Rebecca Prichard's *Essex Girls* as part of Nueva
Dramaturgia Británica in December, 1987.

*Bazaar* (*Bazar*) was first performed in English as a rehearsed reading in the *Voices from Spain* season in the Theatre Upstairs on 10 April 1997 with the following cast:

| | |
|---|---|
| HUSSEIN | Henry Goodman |
| RASHID | Chand Martinez |
| ANTON | Andy Serkis |

*Director*   Roxana Silbert
*Translator*   John Clifford

The British premiere was staged at the Royal Court Theatre Upstairs as part of the New European Writers' Season, first performance on 25 November 1997 with the following cast:

| | |
|---|---|
| HUSSEIN | Nicholas Woodeson |
| RASHID | Nitzan Sharron |
| ANTON | Adrian Edmondson |

*Director*   Roxana Silbert
*Translator*   John Clifford
*Designer*   Simon Vincenzi
*Lighting*   Chahine Yavroyan
*Sound*   Fergus O'Hare

**Characters**

HASSAN

RASHID, *his nephew*

ANTON, *a guy from the neighbourhood*

*Setting:* the backroom of a Moroccan shop in the city centre.

*Act I:* 16 August, 7pm.

*Act II:* next day, 8.30 pm.

## ACT ONE

*Heaps of boxes in disorder in the room at the back of the shop. Boxes of different sizes containing different kinds of merchandise: radio cassettes, small electrical appliances, cheap novelties, watches, brightly stamped teeshirts hanging on heaped up hangers, and loads of other things that we'll never get to see because boxes fill all the available space.*

*Not much furniture. A small table. There's a door leading to the shop, and a window looking out on the street. No other exits.*

*ANTON has his arm in plaster. The plaster is all scabby and covered with pictures and signatures. RASHID is putting prices on boxes with a gun that puts on sticky labels.*

ANTON. So. Do you want the job?

RASHID. I've got a job.

ANTON. No I didn't mean that.

RASHID. It's struck eight. I've got to put prices on all this stuff.

ANTON. No. You don't understand. That's not a job. That's work. And work is work. And a job is a job. And you work because you've got to. Usually because you got to eat. Or pay your rent. You just have to. End of story. But a job… a job is something you do because you want to, and you do it well, because you like doing it. Do you get it? A job is rock and roll, but work… Work is fish fingers . . .

RASHID. I see.

ANTON. Fish fingers in the fullest sense of the word. And another thing. When you do a job, you get the profit. When you work, some other bugger does. Like Hassan. Whether he's your uncle or not. And don't get me wrong. Your uncle, as far as I'm concerned, is a great guy. His shit comes out his backside. But. Think about it. And it's not just something I'm saying. It's the truth. It's the real world. Such as it is. Hassan has a job. You work. And that's the difference between you. It's easy to see. Fancy a joint?

RASHID. Well...

ANTON. What?

RASHID. Yes.

ANTON. Roll one for us.

RASHID. You'll roll one better.

ANTON. How do you expect me to roll a joint? With this stump?

RASHID. Oh yeah. Your arm. I didn't think.

ANTON. I've had it on for almost three weeks. It's got more graffiti than a shithouse wall. I'm telling you, with your arm in plaster you're on a different fucking planet. My right arm, too. It's the fucking limit. You can't imagine what a fucking drag it is after fifteen years, having to learn to wank left handed. Still. With a bit of luck they'll take it off me next week. OK, where is it?

RASHID. Where's what?

ANTON. This joint.

RASHID. I don't know. Still. OK. But make it a quick one.

ANTON. What?

RASHID. Give me.

ANTON. Give you what?

RASHID. The shit.

ANTON. I don't have any.

RASHID. You don't have any?

ANTON. Didn't you tell me you had a joint?

RASHID. No I don't have one. I want one.

ANTON. For fuck's sake. I asked you if you had one.

RASHID. I thought you asked me if I wanted one.

ANTON. What a disaster.

*Long pause. It looks as though they're not going to get their smoke. All of a sudden,* ANTON *brings out a lump of hash.*

ANTON. There. But make it a small one.

RASHID. Oh. So you do have shit.

ANTON. Yes, fuck it, but hardly any. Make it a small one. Take it.

RASHID. I don't know.

ANTON. Now what's wrong?

RASHID. My uncle doesn't like it.

ANTON. So what if your uncle doesn't like it? He's not going to throw you out for smoking a joint.

RASHID. He doesn't like it. It's against the law.

ANTON. Smoking a joint is against the law. What a joke. But your uncle's a moor. A moor from Marrakech. What are you on about?

RASHID. He's not from Marrakech, he doesn't smoke joints, and he doesn't like people who do.

ANTON. Look just make up your mind. Roll a joint or don't roll a joint. But stop farting around.

RASHID. He'll be here in a minute.

ANTON. Look I'm begging you. Even if it is just a short one. Even if he's just outside the fucking window! Roll me a joint. I can't roll it with my arm in plaster. And I want a joint! I want a fucking joint!

RASHID. Have you hurt yourself?

ANTON. No. Not at all. This pissy plaster. I want it to disappear.

RASHID. Give me.

ANTON. Thanks. Here. Papers.

*Pause.* RASHID *starts burning the hash.*

RASHID. It smells good.

ANTON. It tastes even better. It's so strong it knocks your head off.

*Pause.*

So. What do you think. About this job. Interested?

RASHID. I can't do it now. Hassan'll be here soon. He's tense.

ANTON. What's his problem?

RASHID. It's just he wants to make the shop bigger. Rent the place next door.

ANTON. So business is good.

RASHID. He still needs money. And planning permission. Loads of money.

ANTON. The same old story. Money. Fucking money. Working your arse off to earn a fucking peseta. That's why I told you about this job.

ANTON. What job?

ANTON. Rashid, I told you yesterday.

RASHID. I didn't really understand.

ANTON. You pretend your camera's been stolen, you go to the police and you report it. And then you claim the insurance. And if you do it well, you make so much money you can wipe your arse with it.

RASHID. So . . . ?

ANTON. For fuck's sake. It's so hard to talk to you. You report the theft of your camera and you get half a million from the insurance company.

RASHID. So someone has to steal your camera.

ANTON. A camera or whatever. Something valuable.

RASHID. But first you need a camera. Or something.

ANTON. OK listen. You go on a trip . . .

RASHID. Here. It's ready.

*He gives him the rolled joint.*

ANTON. What a joint. What a fucking joint! Christ man you know how to roll them. You moors must have joint rolling genes. No, you light it.

RASHID. No. Probably better not.

ANTON. Yes, man. Fuck. Don't be stupid. Give it a couple of drags.

RASHID. No really. I've got to work.

ANTON. So have some. Putting prices on things is graft. And if you got to graft, do it with a joint. You do it better.

RASHID. No.

ANTON. Yes, Christ, I'm telling you. Light it.

RASHID. OK.

*He lights the joint.*

ANTON. So. let's see. You buy a ticket to go somewhere. Let's say Seville. When you buy the ticket you insure your luggage and you insure the camera. So it's all insured and you get on the bus. So you get to where you're going, Seville or wherever, you get a room in a hostel, you leave your luggage, and you go straight to the police station.

RASHID. You go to the police station? What a way to earn a living. That is weird.

ANTON. Listen. You've to report you've been robbed. You've got to do it right away. Report the robbery you're supposed to have suffered, right? Right. So you report the robbery, then you sign the form. Then you come back here, with the police form and the receipt for the camera, and you go to the insurance company and you claim your money back. Get it?

RASHID. Yes

ANTON. Are you sure?

RASHID. Yes.

ANTON. There you are then. It costs you eight thousand for the ticket, ten thousand for the insurance. two thousand for the hostel. About twenty thousand. And that's fine. That's your investment. You put in twenty thousand, you take out half a million. Hey, pass us the joint.

RASHID. Half a million?

ANTON. Yes, what do you think? That's the usual sum.

RASHID. OK. But it isn't true.

ANTON. What isn't true?

RASHID. It isn't true they robbed you in the bus station.

ANTON. Of course it isn't. I mean that's the whole point.

RASHID. So it's against the law.

ANTON. Well, yes. It's against the law. Obviously. I mean what are we talking here? Are we talking you falling out with your granny? No. Are we talking you sitting the entrance exam for police academy? No. So what do you think we're fucking saying?

RASHID. It's just dangerous. I don't want to get into trouble with the police.

ANTON. What do you mean, trouble. What trouble?

RASHID. Police don't believe me. If I went into a police station and told them I'd been robbed, I know what'd happen. They'd put me in jail.

*Short pause.*

ANTON. Yeah but . . . You don't go to the police.

RASHID. I don't?

ANTON. I don't seem to have explained this very well. I'm the one who goes to the police. I told you, I'm the expert. I know what I'm doing. I'm the one that reports the theft.

RASHID. So what do I do?

ANTON. You take care of the camera.

RASHID. I take care of the camera?

ANTON. Yes. For the insurance. The receipt for the camera. The insurance company will ask us for the receipt. The receipt for the camera that's been stolen. And they do that to prove that we did in fact own a camera.

RASHID. I see.

ANTON. All you have to do is ask your uncle to make you a receipt.

RASHID. I have to ask my uncle?

ANTON. Yes. See, it's Hassan who owns the shop, so it's Hassan who writes the receipt. See, that's logic. If we don't have a receipt, we can't claim the insurance. And if we can't claim the insurance, we don't make any money. Do you get it?

RASHID. But I'm not buying a camera.

ANTON. No, you don't buy the camera. All you do is get the receipt. And the receipt has my name on it and says that I bought the camera in this shop. Hassan just stamps it and signs it.

RASHID. Hassan won't want to do that.

ANTON. Why not?

RASHID. Because he's got to sell the camera. Otherwise it's against the law.

ANTON. For fuck's sake. Shit me a banana. This again. What difference does it make? We're not going to mug anybody. We're not going to kill anyone. All we're going to do is rip off an insurance company. And that's all. Alright it's against the law. But what's really against the law is what the insurance companies do, which is line their pockets with the pitiful few pennies that every poor bastard has scraped together working his arse off in some shit job for the whole of his shitty little life! THAT's what's against the fucking law . . . (Short pause.) Fuck, what a head banger.

*We hear the little bell at the door of the shop and the same time the phone rings.*

ANTON. Telephone.

RASHID. No, it's the door. Throw out the joint.

ANTON. It's the phone.

RASHID *looks through the door which connects to the shop.*

RASHID. It's my uncle. Throw out the joint.

ANTON. There's still two drags left.

RASHID. Get rid of it. get rid of it!

ANTON. Calm down mate. Calm down. It's nearly finished.

RASHID (*fanning with his hands to disperse the smoke*). It really stinks.

ANTON. Calm down.

RASHID. The whole place is full of smoke.

ANTON. Stop it will you? You're making me nervous.

RASHID *starts putting prices on packages.*

ANTON. Why isn't he coming? What's going on? Does he know we're here?

RASHID. He's talking on the phone. Will you waft. Waft.

ANTON. Fuck mate, you're so tense. What's the matter. Does he eat people for breakfast?

RASHID. Are you going to waft or not?

ANTON. Alright, I'll waft. I'll waft.

*Enter* HASSAN.

HASSAN. Hello.

RASHID. Hello.

ANTON. How's it going Hassan. How's things.

HASSAN. Incredible.

RASHID. What's happened?

HASSAN. They just phoned me. On the phone. Just now.
Phoned me. I was just coming in . . .

ANTON. What's up?

HASSAN. It's the video. They chose the video. The television
people. They liked it. They've selected it. It's incredible.

ANTON. Hassan, don't tell me you sent a video to the telly.

RASHID. A video?

HASSAN. The crash.

ANTON. What crash?

HASSAN. The bicycle. When the bike crashed. They've
selected it.

ANTON. What?

RASHID. The accident.

ANTON. What are you talking about?

RASHID. The bicycle accident.

ANTON. The bicycle accident?

HASSAN. Yes. Your bicycle accident. I recorded it, through
the window. A month ago. The day we were trying out the
new video recorder. Remember.

ANTON. No.

HASSAN. Yes. I was trying out the camera. Through the
window. Just recording. You got on your bike and went
down the hill.

ANTON. Wait a minute. Wait a minute! Are you telling me
that you filmed me smashing into the flower stall?

HASSAN. Yes. And I sent it to the telly. From when you get
on the bike till when you fall off it at the end. All of it. You
going down the hill, you smashing into the flower stall, you
flying through the air. And they chose it. They've just
phoned.

ANTON. You mean you sent a film of my accident to a TV programme? You're taking the piss.

HASSAN. No.

ANTON. You mean one of those programmes when people fall over and smash their heads open. Or when some bride falls face down into the wedding cake? You sent off my crash?

HASSAN. Yes. 'You've been Framed.' Saturday nights. With that funny guy. People falling over. People bumping into things. People's television. Home videos. And we've been selected. Fifty thousand pesetas. Just for being selected.

ANTON. Fifty thousand fucking pesetas!

HASSAN. Twenty-five for you. Twenty-five for me. No?

ANTON. You're going to give me twenty-five grand?

HASSAN. Of course. You fall off your bike, I send it to the telly. It's fifty fifty.

ANTON. Fuck that's great. That's fucking great.

HASSAN. But I don't have the money yet.

ANTON. No. Well obviously not, if they just called you. What else did they say?

HASSAN. I couldn't hear really. It was a mobile phone. I got cut off.

ANTON. Fuck, what luck. Twenty-five thousand for a broken arm. If only I'd known. I'd have broken the other one.

HASSAN. And that's not all. Just listen. We're also in for the final. The grand final. The five best videos. That's what he said. And it's true. I've seen the programme. There's five who qualify.

ANTON. You're joking.

HASSAN. We could win. You know how much the prize is?

ANTON. Fuck. I don't want to know. 500 thousand. A million . . .

HASSAN. Two millions.

ANTON. Two million pesetas. But do you know what you're saying?

HASSAN. I'm saying two millions. One for you. One for me.

ANTON. You fucker, you're a genius. Eat my cock.

HASSAN. If it wins. If it doesn't win . . .

ANTON. Then it doesn't, right. But we've still got the fifty thousand.

HASSAN. Yes fifty. We've been selected.

ANTON. Well, fifty grand, you don't look a gift horse in the mouth.
And when does it go out this programme?

HASSAN. 'You've been Framed'. Saturdays. Tonight.

ANTON. Fuck a donkey. I want to see it. Can you imagine? No, I can't. Two million. It's too good to be true. It can't win. But fuck. What if it does?

*The phone rings.*

HASSAN. I bet it's them.

HASSAN *goes out.* ANTON *and* RASHID *are alone.*

RASHID. Fucking hell.

ANTON. Yeah, fucking hell. On a donkey. It can't be true. It'll be some shit taking the piss. Hassan's off his trolley with it. Not that I'm surprised. Fuck me. Two million. Just like that.

*Short pause.*

You going to tell him about the receipt?

RASHID. I don't know.

ANTON. Well maybe now's not the best moment. Or on the other hand maybe it is. The guy's so happy. Who wouldn't be when they're going to give us two million for fuck all.

RASHID (*sceptical*). Two million?

ANTON. You know something? Hassan's a good man. Soft-hearted. Generous.

RASHID. Now listen to you. The boss is a good man all of a
    sudden.

ANTON. Well, yes. I mean, listen. I mean just think what life's
    like. I mean sometimes, right, SOMETIMES the bosses can
    be good people. I mean look at him, right now, there he is
    giving out millions like sweeties. Yeah? I said yes?

RASHID. Yes.

*Enter* HASSAN.

HASSAN *comes in with a bit of paper in his hand.*

ANTON. What's up boss?

HASSAN. Rashid, did you call the shop in Algeciras?

RASHID. Eh?

HASSAN. The Algeciras order. Did you phone to confirm it?

RASHID. No. I'll do it on Monday. It's after eight. It's too late
    now.

HASSAN. Why wait till Monday? You were meant to phone
    today. You've had all day.

RASHID. Yes, all day to put prices on.

HASSAN. Rashid, I am getting tired of this. You forget about
    the orders, you don't answer the phone. Yesterday you just
    walked out the shop.

RASHID. I've priced fifty hair-dryers.

HASSAN. Listen, this isn't Morocco. Rashid, in Europe they
    work. This boy hasn't been to Belgium. Or Switzerland.
    Here you have to work. Any idiot can sit on his arse for
    hours pricing things. But I need someone to LOOK AFTER
    THE SHOP.

*Slight pause.* RASHID *does not reply.*

Listen, I love your father like a brother. He is my brother.
But don't think that's why you're here.

RASHID. No, not because he's your brother. IN SPITE of him
    being your brother. If I wasn't your nephew I'd never put in
    fourteen hours a day.

HASSAN. You're just a boy and you don't understand. You don't mean to, but all you're doing is insulting those of us who REALLY work fourteen hours a day. (*Slight pause.*) Rashid, you're here because you want to be here. If you don't like the job then get out of here and get another one. Is that clear?

RASHID *looks at* ANTON.

ANTON. It's OK, Hassan, don't get angry with the boy. With this video we're going to make a fortune. What else do you want? And what's for sure is that with your million your shop's going to end up like a palace.

HASSAN. What do you mean?

ANTON. You were keeping quiet about it, weren't you?

HASSAN. Quiet about what?

ANTON. Quiet about that. I mean, you're going to extend the business. Aren't you?

HASSAN. What?

ANTON. What's the matter. You going deaf?

HASSAN. What do you know about it?

ANTON. Nothing, I don't know nothing. That's why I'm asking. All I know is that the sweet shop's going to close. Hey but you don't think I'm fucking you around?

HASSAN (*to* RASHID). I don't think anything. I see what I see.

ANTON. Hey what's wrong? What have I said?

HASSAN. The boy's got a lot to learn. Hasn't he, Rashid? He's got to learn to work, . . . and work . . . (*He grabs his sideburns.*)

RASHID. Ow. Ow!

ANTON. Hey but listen mate. It was just a remark.

HASSAN. Work more. Talk less.

RASHID. Ow. Fuck!

ANTON. Don't take it like that, you're going to pull his
   sideburns out.

HASSAN. He's my nephew. I can take it any way I like. He is
   my nephew and this is my shop. I pay the rent. Every
   month.

RASHID. You're hurting me! . . . Jalini! (*Let go of me!*)

ANTON. But listen, fuck, I wasn't saying anything.

HASSAN. My nephew. My shop.

ANTON. Yes, right. Absolutely right. Your nephew, your shop.
   It was just a remark. I got it wrong.

HASSAN. I shit on the prostitute.

ANTON. What's wrong with you?

   HASSAN *lets* RASHID *go. Pause.*

HASSAN. The video's no good.

ANTON. What do you mean it's no good?

HASSAN. It's no good.

RASHID. What?

ANTON. But I thought you said they'd selected it? I mean,
   don't they like it? Isn't it good?

HASSAN. Yes, it's good. It's too good.

ANTON. What do you mean, too good?

HASSAN. They say it's too good. (*He reads from the bit of
   paper in his hand.*) That it's very obvious. That you can see
   it's been set up.

ANTON. Set up? These shits are arseholes. How can it be set
   up when . . . when it wasn't set up? I broke my fucking
   wrist against the fucking flower stall.

HASSAN. They don't know that. They want us to do it worse,
   'like it was more of an accident.'

ANTON. But it was an accident!

HASSAN. Yes, but it's a very well made accident. They say
they really like it. We're still selected. It's a good crash. It's
a really funny idea: you're on your bike, you look at the
blonde, the car brakes . . . you turn the handlebars to avoid
it but hit the bench instead, go through the air and hit the
flower stall.

ANTON. So?

HASSAN. They like it, but it looks set up. It's all too clear.
'The camera's got to move. It needs to be dirty. To look
worse. More . . . fuzzy'. That's what they say. If we want to
get into the final.

ANTON. It's crazy. I must be fucking dreaming! I mean, right,
out of pure fucking luck you record a fucking funny smash
up and it looks like it's been set up. So what we're supposed
to do is set it up so it looks like an accident. Fucking crazy.
More fuzzy?

HASSAN. But listen. They're all set up. All the ones on
television.

ANTON. You trying to take the piss or something?

HASSAN. Are you telling me that you think all those crashes
and prat falls on these programmes all really happen?

ANTON. Fuck yes. Obviously.

HASSAN. No. No They're not real. They're all set up.
Everyone knows that.

RASHID. They're false?

ANTON. Really?

HASSAN. Yes. Really false.

ANTON. No, I mean . . . Fuck. And I thought that . . . I mean
they look real.

HASSAN. They have to LOOK real. They don't have to BE
real.

*Long pause.*

ANTON. So . . . we have to do it again . . .

HASSAN. Yes, we have to do it again. And we have to set it up. The bike, the car, the smash, the flowers. Just like it was.

ANTON. We have to do it all over again?

HASSAN. And make it all the same. From the beginning right to the end. All the same. You want to do it?

RASHID. It can't be done.

ANTON. Well if we don't have a choice . . .

RASHID. Are you really going to do it again?

ANTON. Hassan says they like it. I mean, do they like it, or don't they like it?

HASSAN. They don't like it. They love it.

ANTON. Because if it's got to be done, I'll do it.

HASSAN. We're going to make it. And we're going to win.

ANTON. I mean, fuck, if the prize were a steam iron, forget it. But it's not a steam iron. it's two million.

RASHID. It's stupid.

HASSAN. What is?

RASHID. The whole idea. It's never going to turn out the same.

HASSAN. Why not?

RASHID. Because you can't do it again. It's impossible. It's already been done. You can't do it again.

HASSAN. Why not? Everyone does it. They set it up, and shoot it.

ANTON. Yeah why not? You set up the camera. And press the button. That's all there is to it. Isn't it?

RASHID. It was an accident. It was luck. And luck is luck. You can't make it happen again.

HASSAN. Your problem is you're ignorant. Luck doesn't happen. You have to make it happen.

ANTON. So I'll do it again?

HASSAN. Of course. It's your accident.

ANTON. And I have to smash myself up again?

HASSAN. Yes. Just like you did before.

ANTON. But . . . what do I do about my arm? Do I have to
break it again?

HASSAN. That's a point. Your plaster. When are they taking it
off?

ANTON. Next week.

HASSAN. Does your wrist hurt?

ANTON. No it's fine. But bearing in mind we have to repeat
the smash . . .

HASSAN. But you can't be on the video with a plaster on. It
would look wrong.

ANTON. No I mean obviously no-one should see the plaster.
So what'll we do?

HASSAN. You got any pliers? Those big ones . . .

ANTON. Yes. No! I mean I know as far as you're concerned
there's a problem with the plaster. And that's what matters
to you. But what matters to me is whether I break my wrist
again.

HASSAN. Oh. That.

ANTON. Unless we put down cardboard boxes.

HASSAN. Cardboard boxes?

ANTON. Yes, well really there's no reason why anything
should happen. But just in case. We just put down a heap of
cardboard boxes and there we are.

HASSAN. You mean mattresses.

ANTON. No. Boxes. Shit. Cardboard boxes. Don't you ever
watch TV? 'The making of Diehard 3'. What they do is put
a whole fucking heap of cardboard boxes down outside the
window so Bruce Willis doesn't break his head open.

RASHID. Well, let's see if you do break the other arm.

ANTON. That's great, mate. You just wish me luck.

HASSAN. The best thing are two thick foam rubber mattresses. But it's your accident. It's up to you. Whatever you prefer: boxes or mattresses.

*Pause.*

ANTON. OK you're right. Mattresses. I'll stick with the mattresses. And a pair of kneepads and Allah preserve us. He'll have to, that's all I can say. I like my arm. I don't want to spend the rest of my life wanking left handed . . . OK. What else? We'll have to get all the people back to get the show on the road.

HASSAN. Yes. And everything else. the car, the bike.

ANTON. But come to think of it, how are we going find the same people? We can't put a postcard up in the newsagents: 'Looking for those passing through Lavapies when I smashed myself up. All enquiries to Bazaar Hassan.'

HASSAN. Wait a minute. The people don't have to be the same. No-one's going to notice the faces. Just the crash.

ANTON. But it'll still be me.

HASSAN. Of course you will be. I'm talking about the others. The blonde and the rest of them.

ANTON. The blonde doesn't come from round here. I know all the good looking chicks from round here. I'd remember if I'd seen her before.

HASSAN. So we look for another blonde.

ANTON. And I know the perfect blonde. She's got everything you need in a blonde. Blonde hair. Platinum. Platinum blonde hair. Shoulder length. Works in the supermarket. I've been trying to get off with her for weeks. 'Do you want to work in a film?' It's the perfect opening. She'll love it.

HASSAN. It's really important. It's what made the accident happen. Her arse walking down the street. And you following it with your eyes. Right? She's just got to do the one thing, but she's got to do it well. Can you speak to her?

ANTON. That's just what I've been saying, haven't I? She's not got much else, but she's got an arse. It's an arse she's got. An arse of authority. One of those that's big, but tight arses. Must be because she's sitting on it all day. Almost West Indian . . . Fuck I'm getting a hard on just thinking about it . . . I'll go down right now and I'll tell her before they close.

HASSAN. Wait a minute. We also need the two old men on the bench. Those ones taking the sun.

ANTON. Oh yes them, the old men. Obviously. But that's no problem, this neighbourhood is full of old men. The jannies in my block, who've retired. Look no further. They'll do fine.

HASSAN. I'll have to see them first.

ANTON. Oh yeah of course. Like they do in films. You have to cast them. That's what it's called: casting. Choosing the actors. I've worked on a film. I've worked with Almodóvar.

RASHID. As an extra?

HASSAN. But this isn't a film. This is just twenty seconds.

ANTON. Don't be so modest, Hassan. What happened before was a bit of luck. But now you're going to direct a film. I mean OK a short film, but still a film. I mean I'm assuming you're going to be the director.

HASSAN. Well, yes, I suppose. I suppose so.

ANTON. Yes, you, christ, who else? Who else but you? And besides, you'll be directing the same film a second time . . . I mean we're not doing so badly . . . what a son of a bitch, our Hassan . . . Who would have known it. I mean Rashid, come on. Try to look interested. Think of the possibilities. Use your imagination.

HASSAN. Good. Then . . . You speak to the blonde and to the old men.

ANTON. Right. Tomorrow morning in the square. What time?

HASSAN. Wait. We've forgotten Fali, the gypsy in the flower stall.

ANTON. Uy, that's a problem. We'll have to find someone else.

HASSAN. Why? Fali can do it.

ANTON. 'Cause that gypsy can't stand the sight of me. Because a month ago I crashed into her flower stall and fucked up all her merchandise. You can't expect me to go back to her and say, 'Hey, Fali, you're a good friend. Just stay where you are a minute or two because what I'm hoping to do is wreck your stall all over again.

HASSAN. OK. I'll talk to her.

ANTON. She'll tell you to get lost.

HASSAN. Don't worry. I'll speak to the gypsy.

ANTON. OK OK. It's up to you. But don't come running to afterwards and telling me that Fali's giving you hassle. It's none of my business.

HASSAN. Fine. No problem.

ANTON. So it's all fucking brilliant. We've got it all sorted: the gypsy, the old men, the blonde . . . oh no I was forgetting something. The guy in the car.

HASSAN. What guy?

ANTON. We need the guy who was driving the car that went in front when I was on the bike.

HASSAN. I'll drive the car.

ANTON. You? Then who's going to hold the camera? Someone's got to be here with the camera.

HASSAN. Rashid.

ANTON. Rashid? Hey wait a minute. We got to think about this camera.

HASSAN. It's easy. He'll do it fine.

ANTON. You sure? I mean we don't want anything to go wrong. I mean these modern cameras have buttons all over the place. The zoom, the anti-glare button, all that.

HASSAN. The anti-glare button?

ANTON. See? It's not that easy. If it's a fine day the sun'll be shining all morning against that window. If you don't press the anti-glare button, it all comes out completely dark.

RASHID. I know about the anti-glare. I can work a camera.

ANTON. I'm just saying because we don't want to turn the whole neighbourhood upside down to get this film made and then fuck the whole thing up with some technical cock up.

HASSAN. Don't worry. Keep calm.

ANTON. No I am calm. I'm very calm. I'm just saying a video camera isn't like a hair-drier: with an ON button to turn it on and an OFF button to turn it off, two speeds and there you are.

RASHID. I know.

ANTON. I tell you what. Let's meet here half an hour early and have a look at the camera.

RASHID. There's no need for that. I can use a camera.

ANTON. Hassan, these details are really important. We'll have to check the video tape, see if we have to plug the camera in or whether it'll run on battery, just check the filming speed . . . I mean imagine if we made a mistake and filmed it in slow motion . . . I mean I don't even want to think about it. Without anti-glare and in slow motion . . . and we've fucked the whole thing up completely. I mean I know he's your nephew and that, but even nephews get things wrong sometimes.

HASSAN. All right. All right. Everyone at nine in the square. Us here at eight thirty.

ANTON. OK. I'll bring the bike. All right. All right? Absolutely fucking right. This thing with the video is just

so fucking brilliant. I'm off to the supermarket. 8.30.
Tomorrow.

HASSAN. Yes. Wait. You got pliers?

ANTON. Yes, don't worry. I'll take this off, even it takes a tin
opener.

HASSAN. See you tomorrow.

*Exit* ANTON.

HASSAN. Yuch. That man smells. That man smells horrible.
Have you noticed.

RASHID. Yes. Disgusting.

HASSAN. Every time he comes up to you. What a stink. He
can't have had a shower since he got that plaster on.

RASHID. It's not that. It's his breath. He doesn't clean his
teeth.

HASSAN. You're right. It's his breath. Or maybe his feet.
Someone should tell him. Tell him to clean his teeth.

RASHID. No. You can't do that.

HASSAN. And why not?

RASHID. You can't go up to him and say: Your breath smells.

HASSAN. Why not? He doesn't know. People whose breath
smells never know. I don't like him breathing all over my
face. He needs to be told.

RASHID. He's not going to like it.

*Pause.*

HASSAN. Rashid. I'm sorry about what I did before. I was
getting nervous. And it's no business of his whether or not
I'm going to expand this shop. He just talks talks talks. All
the time talks. You can't trust him.

RASHID. Why are you doing this. It's a piece of nonsense.

HASSAN. Rashid, we could win. And we could make this
shop into something really big.

RASHID. Oh yes. Winning a competition on TV.

HASSAN. It's two million. What difference does it make if it's a TV show, a lottery ticket, or something you inherit from your granny? Two million pesetas. Think about it. We knock down this wall. We build a proper storeroom to keep our orders in. This one's just a heap of shit. I never know where anything is. You can't work here. And we'll put in a new shop window. We need a proper shop window.

*Pause.*

Listen, I'm fifty-five. I'm getting tired. I need someone I can trust to run the shop.

RASHID. You don't trust me.

HASSAN. So. Prove to me I can trust you. You could earn real money. Business is good. Our suppliers are good. Our prices are good. And if we make the shop better, we'll be overrun with customers.

*Short pause.*

RASHID. Why don't you call Mustafa?

HASSAN. Who?

RASHID. Mustafa. He can do the prat fall.

HASSAN. The guy who hangs around with you?

RASHID. He's strong. And he doesn't have a broken arm.

HASSAN. That guy's a dealer. I don't like him hanging around here.

RASHID. Listen. Not everyone's a dealer.

HASSAN. Rashid, did you really leave Morocco just to stand on a street corner and sell hashish?

RASHID. I don't sell hashish.

HASSAN. You've been here three months . . . Are you going to spend your whole life with Moors? It's the same every day: you get together, you roll a joint, you spend all day sitting on your magic carpet drinking mint tea . . . Morocco

in Madrid. Welcome to the ghetto. All you need is a photo
of King Hassan on the dining room wall. Rashid, this is
another country. People live here in a different way. Can
you understand that?

RASHID. I don't know any other way of living. I just know
my own.

HASSAN. Your way of living. You don't read the papers.
People are getting out of Morocco on pedalos.

RASHID. I don't need to read the papers. I've seen it with my
own eyes.

HASSAN. Well then, what's the fuck the use of a way of life
people are so desperate to get out of they're prepared to
swim? Forget that way of life. Forget that country.

RASHID. Bbat M'stafa Yarya â cul âm (*Mustafa's father goes
back every year.*)

HASSAN. Rashid, I've told you once, I've told you a thousand
times. Don't you go talking berber language back at me.

RASHID. Mustafa's father goes back every year. Everyone
does. Every summer, for their holidays. But you never do.

HASSAN. I've been living here ten years. I used to go back, in
86, 87 . . . But then I understood. Here they live like rats.

RASHID. They? THEY??

HASSAN. Just saving, saving. And why? So they can go back
on holiday once a year? So they can buy a Mercedes?
Living here like animals, sleeping five in a bed, and going
about there like big pricks in their Mercedes, which they
drive around the village so everyone can see them, 'Look,
Hassan's got a big Mercedes.'

*Short pause.*

Do you understand? And here they've got nothing. Nothing
at all. And there? What the fuck would I do with a German
car?

RASHID. At least they've got their family. But you. Who have
you got?

HASSAN. Don't get me wrong, Rashid. I'm not like them. I'm not like them at all.

*Pause.*

RASHID. Then who are you like?

*Blackout.*

**ACT TWO**

HASSAN, *with the camera in his hand.*

RASHID. The fifth take.

HASSAN. Are you sure?

RASHID. Yes, the fifth's the good one. The last one.

HASSAN. We only made five?

RASHID. Yes.

HASSAN. Are you sure? We've been out there all day.

RASHID. Look for yourself. There's only five. And the last one is the good one.

HASSAN. I'm just going to. I'll have a look. Did you pay the Gallego?

RASHID. Who?

HASSAN. The guy at the café. The sandwiches. The cokes. Did you pay him?

RASHID. That guy's dangerous.

HASSAN. What?

RASHID. That Gallego. I went to pay for the sandwiches. I saw some mint on the bar and I asked to buy some to make tea. He wouldn't sell me any.

HASSAN. Why not?

RASHID. Because not. Because the mint is not for sale. Because it's there to make rum punches.

HASSAN. But you paid him.

RASHID. Yes, I paid him. But he wouldn't sell me any mint. That guy's a pig.

HASSAN. OK he's a pig. I must watch this video. Back in a minute.

RASHID. I asked him: 'Why should you care?' When you buy coffee in the supermarket nobody asks you if you're going to drink it black, or white, or with sugar. You pick it up, you pay for it, and you piss off. It makes no difference if you want the mint to make tea, rum punches, or to wipe your arse with it. That's what I told him.

HASSAN. You told him that? For fuck's sake why tell that to the Gallego?

RASHID. Because I don't get it.

HASSAN. Rashid, don't give me lectures. He uses mint for rum punches. Period. There's nothing to get about it. Everyone sells what they want. It's a free market.

RASHID. If it's free for selling it's also free for buying.

HASSAN. Listen.

RASHID. What!

HASSAN. Six or seven years ago I lived in the suburbs. Thirty kilometres away. Every day I came in by train. One day two women got onto the train and sat opposite me. About as far from me as I am from you. I was reading the paper. The women were staring at me. Staring all the time. Then they began to whisper to each other. Bsbsbsbs . . . Moors here . . . bsbsbsbs . . . Moors there. Moors everywhere.

RASHID. Fuck. So you see what I mean?

HASSAN. Wait a minute. 'It's just not right', one of them was saying, 'The whole country's full of Moroccans.' The ticket inspector came in asking to see our tickets. And they kept talking louder and louder. 'They're taking all our jobs.' I just couldn't stand this. They were talking about me as if I wasn't there. And the other one's saying: 'My son's been out for work for two years. It's just not right. Dirty Africans. Why don't they stay in their own country?' Blah, blah,

blah . . . The ticket guy was just behind us. One of them had got out her ticket. Just before he arrived, I leant forward, picked up her ticket and I put it in my mouth.

RASHID. You what?

HASSAN. I ate it.

RASHID. You ate the woman's ticket?

HASSAN. The inspector came. 'Tickets please.' The woman was red all over, she couldn't even speak. The other one pointed to me, trembling: 'The Moor ate her ticket . . . ! It was the Moor . . . the Moor ate it!'

RASHID. Fuck.

HASSAN. You understand? We have to think. Listen, we can live in this country, but we've got to use our heads and avoid problems. And we have to work. And anyone who wants to make it can make it. And anyone who wants to make a video for television can make it too.

RASHID. Yeah.

HASSAN. Are they after you? Bad luck. But if you try to go after them, then you're an idiot.

*Pause.*

HASSAN. Right. I'm going home.

*We can hear the bell ringing as someone enters the shop. ANTON enters, with a loud shirt on. He also has new plaster on his right arm, which goes up to his shoulder, and his left leg is bandaged up to the knee. There's a big dark bruise all over his face. He leans on a crutch.*

ANTON. Hi.

HASSAN. Fuck.

ANTON. Agreed.

RASHID. How's your arm?

ANTON. I'm collecting fractures.

HASSAN. What did the doctor say?

ANTON. I've broken my wrist. Again. Dislocated my shoulder, sprained my ankle and this eye won't open for a month.

RASHID. Uf.

ANTON. They've told me I'll have to keep the plaster on for two months. Still, it's done now. It was an amazing smash, no? There must be enough on tape to make you shit yourself.

HASSAN. That's just what I'm going to see.

ANTON. Well I hope so. Because I am definitely retiring from show business. I mean it's bad enough not being able to wank. But now someone's going to have hold my prick when I piss...

RASHID. And you won't be able to clean your teeth.

ANTON. Yeah that too. On top of everything else. Still. Who cares. I'm not into all that racaraca.

*Pause.*

HASSAN. Well. See you later.

ANTON. Listen, just out of curiosity. How much does a camera like that cost?

HASSAN. Why? You want to buy one?

ANTON. No. I'm just curious.

HASSAN. Don't worry. We're going to clean up. When you've got the money, I'll sell it to you. (*He jokingly assumes a cod Arab accent.*) And for you, my friend, at a special price.

ANTON. With a receipt and everything?

HASSAN. What?

ANTON. So if you sell me the camera, you'll give me a receipt?

HASSAN. Yes. But then I can't give it to you at a discount. I'd have to declare it. It's better to pay cash without receipt. Don't you think?

ANTON. Of course. Yes. I don't know.

*Pause.*

HASSAN. I'm going to see the videos. I'll be back in a
   minute.

ANTON. See you then.

*Exit* HASSAN.

RASHID. It's turned out well. That last smash was good.

ANTON. It'd better be. We were out there for twelve hours.
   What did it look like from here?

RASHID. They were all good, but the fifth is perfect.

ANTON. Yes, you're right, the fifth. The last one.

RASHID. Yes the fifth is the best one. That's for sure. At least
   it looked the best from here.

*Short pause.*

By the way, what happened to the blonde?

ANTON. The blonde?

RASHID. The blonde. You said she'd come.

ANTON. Wait till I tell you. Fucking tart. You remember,
   yesterday, when I left here, I went straight to the
   supermarket?

RASHID. Yes.

ANTON. To tell the chick the story. Get her involved. And, at
   the same time, see if she wouldn't . . . know what I mean.
   Well, fine, I go to the shop, and I go right to the condoms. I
   pick up a packet and go to the queue at the blonde's till.
   When I get to her she picks up the condoms and says: 'Is
   that all?' And I say: 'What else do you want? Want me to
   take the pill?' And she fell about laughing.

RASHID. And then what happened?

ANTON. I wait for her at the exit, we go to the Gallego's bar
   and I tell her all about it. That we're going to make a film,

that we need a blonde with long hair, etcetera etcetera. And because she's blonde, she's perfect for the blonde. And do you know what she said? She looks at me all alert all of a sudden and says 'You going to make a porno film?'

RASHID. She said that . . . She asked you if . . .

ANTON. If we were going to make a porno film. Just like that. Porno film.

RASHID. And then?

ANTON. Up all night fucking like crazy. Just like that. She's an animal. You can't imagine. Thinking about the film must have made her horny.

RASHID. OK. So she wanted to.

ANTON. Fuck, if that wasn't wanting to I don't know what was. I don't even dare think about it.

RASHID. So she wanted to make the video.

ANTON. Eh? Oh yes. Or at least, she did in the beginning. But then....Well . . . it was seven in the morning and I had to go to my place to take off the plaster before coming here. She was getting dressed, and she asks me, 'And since when have you been a film director?' and I say 'Me? No, it's not me, I don't direct films. . . . I'm the star, the director is Hassan, you know, the guy from the Bazaar.'

*Short pause.*

She has a face on her like you can't imagine. I say 'Hassan is the director' and all of a sudden she stops dressing, looks very serious, and then the little cunt says 'I'm not going nowhere to do nothing with no moor' Just like that. Out of the blue. And I say: 'But listen, what do you mean, Moor, or nigger or whatever? So what if he comes from Morocco or Outer Mongolia. It makes no difference. You don't have to jerk him off.

RASHID. Right.

ANTON. All you've got to do is walk along wiggling your arse so I lose balance and break my head open . . . it's a video

for the telly. And she says, like some mental defective.
'I don't know how come he doesn't disgust you.'

RASHID. Fuck.

ANTON. I'm not going to hold a knife to her throat and tell
her: 'Make the film or I kill you.'

RASHID. Obviously not.

ANTON. Still, between you and me, using a wig was pushing
it a bit.

RASHID. Why? We needed a blonde. There weren't any
blondes.

ANTON. There weren't any blondes, there weren't any
brunettes. But whose idea was it to make a bloke into the
blonde?

RASHID. Not a bad idea.

ANTON. And the greengrocer. You have got to be desperate to
use a greengrocer. Oh, so we haven't got a blonde? No
problem, we'll give the greengrocer a skirt and a wig and
action! I'm telling you, Hassan is desperate.

RASHID. He wasn't bad. Looking through the camera. From
the behind, he looks like a woman.

ANTON. The greengrocer a woman? You know the only way
the greengrocer is like a woman?

RASHID. What's that?

ANTON. Because he likes dicks.

RASHID. What?

ANTON. I'm telling you, he's a fucking queer. Every time I go
in to get some apples, first thing he does is look at my balls.
But that's not the same as him looking like a woman . . .
Come off it, Rashid. You ever been with a woman?

*The phone rings in the shop. Exit RASHID. ANTON
wanders about among the boxes, looking around. He
glances at the papers on the desk. RASHID comes back.*

ANTON. Well?

RASHID. It was the people from the telly.

ANTON. You're joking. What did they want?

RASHID. I don't know. To talk to Hassan.

ANTON. They'll be expecting the video. The amount of fucking money those people have. You didn't talk to your uncle about the receipt, did you?

RASHID. No.

ANTON. For fuck's sake. You could help me a little. Look suppose I stop pissing about and just ask him?

RASHID. What?

ANTON. Just that. Ask him. Do you think Hassan'll make out the receipt for me if I ask him?

RASHID. I don't know. He's nervous.

ANTON. Fuck his nerves. Why doesn't he just smoke a joint?

*Enter* HASSAN. *He carries the videotape and a piece of paper with notes on it.*

HASSAN. What's happened?

ANTON. What's happened with what?

HASSAN. With the tape. What's happened? Which was the good one?

ANTON. The last one. The fifth. Wasn't it?

RASHID. Yes. What I said. The fifth. The last one. Why?

HASSAN. Wait a minute. Let's just see. Let's just see. In the first one I brake too early and you smash into the car.

ANTON. Yes, that's where I got this bruise. Brilliant smash, but no use. I fell alright, but before the bottom of the hill.

HASSAN. Fine. So the second.

ANTON. In the second you could see the mattresses.

RASHID. That's right. I could see them through the lens. Beneath the flower stall. That's when we stopped again to hide the mattresses properly.

ANTON. You hid them properly all right. And now look at the state I'm in.

HASSAN. Look don't make me tense. The third. What happened in the third?

ANTON. Listen, I'm not making you tense. You're tense already.

HASSAN. What happened in the third?

ANTON. How am I supposed to know? Everyone was doing their thing. I was busy breaking my arms.

RASHID. It was the boy pissing.

ANTON. Exactly. The brat. Pissing all over his mother. Fucking unbelievable. Only that gypsy could have thought of bringing along her brat with her to make the video. What a fucking joke. That woman is completely fucking crazy.

HASSAN. So the fourth?

ANTON. That one I won't forget. It was the wig. The greengrocer had it on crooked. You could see his bald patch from a mile off.

HASSAN. That's right. the greengrocer.

ANTON. Look I'm sorry Hassan, I know this is a bit beside the point but . . . doesn't it seem a bit much instead of a blonde to have a bloke in a skirt and a wig?

HASSAN. A bit much? Where was the blonde?

ANTON. The blonde? I told you, she couldn't come.

HASSAN. You said 'I'll take care of the blonde.'

ANTON. Yeah, but the thing was…she was ill.

HASSAN. How, ill?

ANTON. She had her period.

HASSAN. Her what?

ANTON. Her period, man. Period. Don't they have them in Morocco? Look, all I'm saying is that it seems crazy to me to have a bloke playing a chick. I mean alright the greengrocer can be as queer as you like but, for fuck's sake, it sticks out a mile.

HASSAN. The greengrocer, the green grocer. He could be a postman. Or a baker. Or a plumber. It matters a fuck.

ANTON. You mean 'It doesn't matter a fuck.' But I'm telling you it does matter. The greengrocer does matter.

HASSAN. What matters is that he looks like a woman from behind.

ANTON. Oh yes. And what if I said what he looks like is the greengrocer in drag?

HASSAN. So what. No-one's going to look at the greengrocer. You're the star.

ANTON. Right. So I'm the star. And why does the star fall off his bike and break his arm? Because he swerves. And why does he swerve? Because he sees an attractive blonde walking along the street. So you have to see how the blonde looks. And everyone round here knows the greengrocer. And all my mates are going to watch that video. You want them to think I'm queer?

*Short pause.*

HASSAN. Please just listen. What about the fifth?

ANTON. Yes the fifth. That was the one that worked. Everything turned out fine. I ride down the hill, you brake, I swerve, I fly over the old farts and land on the gypsy. It was great. Fucking brilliant fall.

HASSAN. And you're sure it's the fifth?

ANTON. Yes. it's the one after the greengrocer's wig. Listen, what the fuck's wrong?

*Short pause.*

HASSAN. The fifth . . . It's missing.

ANTON. What do you mean it's missing?

HASSAN. You can't see anything. It's all black. Shadows.
Everything's shadows.

ANTON. But that's impossible. I mean we tested the camera a
dozen times. There can't be any mistake. Rashid, you and
me, we tested it this morning. And it was working, right?
We plugged it in, tried out the zoom, turned on the anti-
glare . . . (*Pause.*) Shit.

HASSAN. What? What's wrong?

ANTON. The anti-glare.

HASSAN. What do you mean? Didn't you put it on?

ANTON. Yes I put it on, of course I put it on, but then it got
late.

HASSAN. So?

ANTON. I didn't think it would get so late. But doing it over
and over and over again . . .

HASSAN. Do me a favour. I don't know what you're saying.

ANTON. When we started the last shoot it was six o'clock,
right. At six the sun doesn't shine on the shop window. It's
too low. So you don't need anti-glare. If you put on the anti-
glare when you don't need it . . .

HASSAN. What happens?

ANTON. It all comes out black.

*Short pause.*

HASSAN. Black . . .

ANTON. Black, yes, black. You've seen it, haven't you. How
did it come out?

HASSAN. Black. It came out black.

ANTON. Exactly what I'm fucking telling you!

*Pause.*

I'm saying what a fucking disaster. It's all black. The only
one that's any good and it's not worth shit. The whole
fucking day wasted. I shit on the father, I shit on the son,
I shit on the fucking holy ghost! And there's me like a
fucking twat breaking me fucking arms. Like fucking Sooty.

HASSAN. I don't believe this.

RASHID. So all we've done is no good?

HASSAN. Fuck.

*Pause.*

ANTON. Look I'm sorry, mate. It's my fault.

HASSAN. What is?

ANTON. It's my fault. That fucking anti-glare. It shouldn't
have been on all the time. I'm really sorry.

HASSAN. Let go. Let go!

ANTON. What's wrong? Hassan, I'm saying I'm sorry.

HASSAN. Listen. Why don't you brush your teeth?

ANTON. What?

HASSAN. You smell bad. You should brush your teeth.

ANTON. You're telling me I smell bad?

*Pause.*

You know something? I saw the programme last night. It's
not fifty thousand, it's a hundred thousand.

HASSAN. What?

ANTON. The video selection. They pay a hundred thousand
for each selected video. The first batch. It's a hundred
thousand.

HASSAN. What are you talking about?

ANTON. You told me it was fifty thousand. Don't pretend you
don't understand. It's not fifty thousand. It's a hundred. And
there was me thinking 'There's Hassan giving me half. How
generous.' Generous my arse.

HASSAN. And the knee pads. Where do you think they came from? A dustbin?

ANTON. Maybe I'm not hearing you right. I can't believe you're telling me that you spent fifty grand on kneepads.

HASSAN. Kneepads, petrol for the car, flowers for the gypsy, the videotape, the sandwiches . . . It all costs money. Shall I make out a list?

ANTON. You paid for the gypsy's flowers . . .

HASSAN. You think this is just a game. Like monopoly. You throw the dice, go past go, and they give you fifty thousand. That's not how it works. To earn money you have to spend money. You want two mattresses? OK. You can have two mattresses. But you have to pay for them.

ANTON. Don't try and get me muddled. I didn't want mattresses. I wanted cardboard boxes.

HASSAN. Go and shit yourself.

*Pause.*

ANTON. OK, you're right. I admit it. I'll go and shit myself. I admit it. It was my fault we fucked up. I'll go and shit myself right now. But I want what's mine. The twenty-five thousand. Not a penny more, not a penny less. Don't you go thinking I've broken my arms for nothing, Hassan.

HASSAN. Yes.

ANTON. I can't spend all night apologising.

HASSAN. Don't worry. We haven't fucked up.

ANTON. Oh haven't we?

HASSAN. We'll do it again.

ANTON. We'll what?

HASSAN. Do it again. All of it. The smash. From the beginning right up to the end. Right now.

RASHID. What? The video?

ANTON. Are you mad?

HASSAN. Rashid . . .

RASHID. Do it all again? Now? Never.

HASSAN. Everyone's out there. We've got to do it now.

ANTON. But you're crazy. It's night time.

HASSAN. Listen. This isn't going to be easy. Either help, or get out that door and don't come back.

ANTON. He's serious. He seriously thinks we should do it again. Look at him. He just likes being the director. I mean, what else do you want me to do? Kill myself? Game for a fucking laugh. The only bit of me that isn't broken is my teeth!

HASSAN. No you can't do it. Look at the state you're in.

ANTON. Thanks. How kind. Thanks a lot. So who . . . ? (*Short pause.*) Oh right. Obviously.

RASHID. Me?

ANTON. Give me my money. I'm off!

HASSAN. Look, you can't ride the bike, but you can lend a hand.

ANTON. Lend a what?

*He hits the table with the plaster.*

HASSAN. What are you doing?

ANTON. I've got an itch and I can't scratch it.

HASSAN. Go out to the street and find everybody. Half an hour ago they were all in the Gallego's bar. Tell them to wait, because we're gong to do it again. I'm coming right away.

RASHID. He's a right bastard that Gallego.

HASSAN. I want to see them all down there in fifteen minutes. The greengrocer, Fali, the old men . . .

RASHID. You can't have the old men. They'll be knackered. They've spent eight hours in the sun doing crosswords . . .

HASSAN. Who cares. There's enough old men about. Better still, let's cut the old men. It'll be fine. You hit the bench and there we are. And no old men. What matters is the smash. Get on. Move.

ANTON. Listen people aren't fools. I mean do you really think we just give the signal, and there they are, all in their places just because this guy gets on his high horse . . . if it's not too much to ask, how do you expect me to convince them?

HASSAN. Pay them.

ANTON. Sorry?

HASSAN. Ten thousand each. Ten for Fali and ten for the greengrocer. All they have to do is be there. The rest is our business. And this is a business. We're working. Mattresses, kneepads, flowers, production costs. And the ten thousands, labour costs. That's how you're going to convince them. How else are we going to recover our investment?

ANTON. Hassan, that gypsy is raking it in without doing a stroke of work. You call it labour costs to have someone stand behind a flower stall singing flamenco songs? 'El Camarón de la isla!' . . . Do you call it labour costs to pay someone to walk down the street waggling his arse like a tart? I'll tell you what labour costs are. THESE are labour costs. A broken arm. Three broken fingers. And a face like an aubergine. That's my fucking investment. Do you mind telling me what return I'm supposed to get?

HASSAN. We said twenty-five. Didn't we? So twenty-five. And if we win, then five hundred thousand.

ANTON. Five hundred thousand. If you win. Tell me if I'm wrong, but it used to be a million.

HASSAN. Yes. Before using the anti-glare when there wasn't any glare.

*Pause.*

ANTON. Agreed.

HASSAN. You'll do it?

ANTON. I'll do it.

HASSAN. You'll get the cast?

ANTON. I'll get the cast.

HASSAN. Right. In the next fifteen minutes. In the square.

*Short pause.* ANTON *is doubtful. He looks at* RASHID.

Run!

*Exit* ANTON. HASSAN *searches among the boxes.*

HASSAN. He's a bullshitter. Let's see. I'm sure we've got a
thousand watt bulb. We've got to have one somewhere. I
mean you know this, don't you? Don't trust him Rashid. He
talks and talks and talks and doesn't know what he's talking
about . . . Where the fuck is this bulb? Listen, if you want
kneepads, you'll have to go and get them. They're at home.
The mattresses are there too. But go now. You've got to be
quick.

RASHID. I'm not going to do this.

*Short pause.*

HASSAN. What. You're not going to do what?

RASHID. Hassan. You lied to him.

HASSAN. To whom.

RASHID. I was there. At first you offered him twenty-five
thousand. And if you're chosen it's not fifty thousand. It's a
hundred. He's right. You've robbed him of twenty-five
thousand.

HASSAN. Not that again. What's the matter with you? I've
already told him. Its deductible expenses. Fuck it Rashid.
What's your problem?

RASHID. When you offered him twenty-five there were no
expenses.

HASSAN. There's always expenses. Flowers, mattresses,
kneepads, petrol for the car . . . Expenses, Rashid. We had
to buy things to redo the video.

RASHID. To redo? Wait a minute. I was there. First the telly people called to say they'd chosen the video. And THEN you offered twenty-five. Then they called back to say it had to be done again. You'd offered him twenty-five before they called back again. BEFORE knowing there were going to be expenses. BEFORE knowing you would have to redo it.

*Pause.*

HASSAN. That guy's a big mouth. 'Don't worry, I'll take care of the blonde.' And then it so happens the blonde has her period. Did you really believe the blonde was having her period?

RASHID. Open your eyes. For fuck's sake. Just this once. Open your eyes. The blonde was going to come until she realised it was you who was going to make the video.

HASSAN (*incredulous*). In that case why did he tell me she had a period?

RASHID. I can't tell you. Think about it. Maybe he didn't want to spoil your day.

HASSAN. Rashid, you're so naïve. 'Don't worry, I'll take care of the anti-glare' The anti-glare, for fuck's sake. How does this work? You help me, I pay you. Right, I earn more. But the idea's mine, and I get together the means to make it happen. Do you really think it's unfair? This isn't Africa. Here you get paid for your work if your work is well done. But if all you do is big mouth and fuck up everyone else, then you're out in the cold. That's how things work. It's not my system, I didn't invent it. You think I'm being unfair . . . too bad. We disagree. That's great. Because the good thing about this country is that neither you nor I are going to be sent to jail for that. Where's the bloody bulb?

RASHID. Fuck.

HASSAN. There's no time to talk about it, Rashid. We've got to get this done. And get it done now.

RASHID. I won't.

HASSAN. Why not? All you have to do is bump into a bench and land on some mattresses. You scared?

RASHID. You scare me.

HASSAN. So you're just going to leave me to do it on my own?

RASHID. Call M'stafa.

HASSAN. You're afraid of breaking your arm. Fine, don't do it. I understand. But at least drive the car. That's all I'm asking. Drive the car to the square. It's just a hundred yards.

RASHID. M'stafa can drive.

HASSAN. Mustafa, Mustafa . . . what is it about Mustafa? Are you his father?

RASHID. He needs the work.

HASSAN. I've told you I don't like moors.

RASHID. I'm a moor!

HASSAN. Rashid, you're my nephew.

RASHID. You've got to stop. This isn't normal.

HASSAN. How much do you want? We can reach an agreement, can't we? Tell me how much you want. Just to drive the car.

*Short pause.*

Please. Rashid.

*Pause.*

I don't know who you take after. But you're not my brother's son. You little bastard.

*The phone rings.* HASSAN *goes to the door.*

*Exit* HASSAN.

RASHID *looks. Behind a huge heap of clothes he uncovers a box for a light bulb.*

*Enter* HASSAN *with a bag. He seems strangely serious.*

HASSAN. Oh. the bulb. That's one less thing to worry about.

*HASSAN begins to take clothes from the bag and starts putting on: a djellaba, some Arab slippers, an Arab head-dress . . .*

RASHID. What are you doing? What's going on?

HASSAN. Fuck. This is all crumpled.

RASHID. What are you doing?

HASSAN. You didn't want to do it. So I'll do it myself. By the way, where's the bike?

RASHID. What are you talking about? You can't go on the bike. You'll kill yourself.

*HASSAN has finished putting on the clothes over his own. He looks at himself in a mirror.*

HASSAN. Fuck. Some fucking Arab here. Eh, what do you think? The Arab's going to give himself a smash on his bicycle. They're going to love this disguise, I'm telling you. Why didn't I think of this before? Fuck, I look so like a moor . . . Eh don't I look like a moor?

RASHID. Hassan, what are you doing? This isn't a costume. These are your clothes.

HASSAN. I haven't worn them for years.

RASHID. Look, you can't see a thing out there. It'll be dangerous.

HASSAN. That's why I've been looking for the bloody bulb!

*The door bell rings. ANTON enters, with his shirt torn to shreds.*

ANTON. Fuck the prostitute who gave birth to that dirty gypsy bitch and all her brats...

HASSAN. Are they ready?

ANTON. Are they ready? You never paid Fali, did you?

HASSAN. Have you got the bike?

ANTON. Eh. You said you'd paid the gypsy for the flowers. Did you pay her or didn't you?

HASSAN. Not yet.

ANTON. Eat my grandmother's shit!

RASHID. But what's happened? Didn't you go to the bar?

ANTON. The gypsy's broken her wrist, and her friends were just about to cut my face. They've wrecked my new shirt. And the Gallego says you never paid for the sandwiches.

HASSAN. What?

ANTON. He says you and Mustafa stole the mint from his counter.

HASSAN. You stole from the Gallego?

RASHID. That guy's a pig.

ANTON. Can anyone tell me what the fuck is going on?

HASSAN. Nothing's going on. You're all going to get your money. You'll all get what is your due.

ANTON. Yes, fucking brilliant. I know. I just want to know when.

HASSAN. Tonight. As soon as the job's over.

ANTON. I'm sorry, don't get me wrong, don't take offence, but no-one's paid you yet. Or is it all going to come out of your own pocket?

HASSAN. Yes. Just as you say. Out of my pocket.

ANTON. Look mate. Look at the state I'm in. Are you trying to take the piss? What the fuck is this about you paying for everything out of your own pocket?

HASSAN. The television phoned. They've overspent their budget.

ANTON. What's that supposed to mean?

HASSAN. They don't have any money. They've overspent the budget and we're out. They're not going to pay a penny for the video.

*Short pause.*

RASHID. What?

ANTON. They're not going to pay.

HASSAN. They don't have any money left.

ANTON. Then what are we doing here?

HASSAN. It doesn't matter. We'll do it.

ANTON. Hang on hang on. Just explain this.

HASSAN (*to* ANTON). Quiet now. Christ's sake. You'll get your money, Fali will get her money, the greengrocer will get her money. His money. So we're just going to go ahead and get this bloody video made. Can you drive?

ANTON. Yes. With my prick.

HASSAN. Look I told you you'll get what's your due.

ANTON. But what's up with you? If they're not paying you for this . . . What's in it for you? I just . . . I just don't understand.

HASSAN. Look. Forget about the five hundred. They're not paying, so there's no half million. But the twenty-five thousand are yours. Right now, tonight. And if you help me with the camera, you get fifty. All you've got to do is look through the camera and follow me when I go down on the bike.

ANTON. Follow you? Shoot you? But I thought we'd agreed he was going to do it? . . . Listen mate you're off your head. (*To* RASHID.) They should lock him up. They really should. I'm not joking. That's why he's all dressed up.

RASHID. Hassan, what's up with you? I mean all this is... really strange.

HASSAN. Come on, yes or no. I'm in a hurry. Fifty thousand. Just for following me with the camera. That's all. You don't have to lift a finger.

*Pause.*

ANTON. You're really having a laugh, aren't you? If someone told me this as a story I wouldn't fucking believe them. I mean it's just brilliant: four fucking idiots going round in circles in front of Sir while Sir considers which will be the funniest way for fucking idiot number one to break his leg falling into a flower stall. And all this just so six million idiots can have a good laugh on a Saturday evening eating their chips in total fucking comfort in front of their fucking TV sets. Fucking brilliant.

HASSAN. I've told you. I'm the one doing the accident. Now please.

ANTON. Do you want me to help you?

HASSAN. I'm asking you to help me. Please.

ANTON. OK I think all this is ridiculous. Still. I want a receipt for a video camera.

RASHID. What?

ANTON. Fifty thousand and the receipt for a video camera. The one that costs the most.

RASHID. La! (*No.*)

ANTON. I give you a hand, whatever you want me to do, and in return you give me fifty thousand and the receipt. It's personal.

RASHID. Don't give him the receipt.

ANTON. Look darkie. Why don't you go and take a walk?

RASHID. Don't give him the receipt.

ANTON. You're scrambling my brains and I won't fucking stand for it!

HASSAN. Rashid, sri dreb dora (*Go out and take a walk.*)

RASHID. Lach, gadi taatih el factura? Lach? (*But why are you going to give him a receipt?*) You don't know what he wants it for.

HASSAN *opens the door.*

HASSAN. Kh'Rey! Kh'Rey! Ya llah. Ya llah! (*Out. Get out. Go on, out. BUT NOW.*)

*Pause. Exit* RASHID.

ANTON. The boy's off his head.

HASSAN. Where's the bicycle?

ANTON. Just at the door of the bar. Smashed to a fuck but still serviceable.

HASSAN. Right. So all we have to do is speak to the gypsy.

ANTON. Hassan, I don't want to get involved in anything that's not my business. And you're the boss. But you don't really think the gypsy's going to stand in front of a flower stall with a broken elbow and give you a beautiful smile.

HASSAN. I'll take care of the gypsy.

ANTON. Look that woman's hysterical. I've seen her. And her man is really pissed off.

HASSAN. I'm going to give them fifty thousand. I know them. They'll do it.

*Short pause.*

ANTON. Fifty thousand. Fine. You're the boss. I mean, some kind person should probably tell you you're walking straight into a huge pile of elephant shit. But don't worry, that person isn't me.

HASSAN. I need them. I need her for the flower stall and him to drive the car.

ANTON. The gypsy's going to drive the car? Fuck's sake. Some other kind person should probably tell you that when you shout 'Action' that guy's going to put his foot down and not stop till he gets to Barcelona. Still. Don't worry: that kind person isn't me either.

HASSAN. Good. In that case, you stay here with the camera. You can still hold it with your arm like that?

ANTON. Don't you worry. I'll be panning.

HASSAN. You just got to follow me.

ANTON. I'll follow you. No problem.

HASSAN. Just follow me till I fall over. Then look for the greengrocer.

ANTON. Right. Fuck's sake. Whatever you say. The receipt.

HASSAN. Yes, of course. The receipt and the fifty thousand. I know.

ANTON. No you don't know. I want the receipt NOW.

HASSAN. Now?

ANTON. Yes. Now. The money later. The receipt now. On the shop's note paper. With the date, a signature, a stamp, identity card number and all that receipt shit.

*HASSAN goes out. Pause.*

*He comes back with a book of receipts, a biro, and a rubber stamp.*

HASSAN. What's the date?

*ANTON goes to a calendar.*

ANTON. August 16th. San Miguel. Fucking wonderful.

*HASSAN writes and then seals with the rubber stamp. He gives ANTON the receipt..*

ANTON (*looks at it*). Sony, eh?

HASSAN. Yes. Sony.

ANTON. Three hundred and fifty thousand.

HASSAN. I've two models in stock. That's the most expensive.

ANTON. OK. Back in a minute.

*He exits. HASSAN is thoughtful. He looks at himself in the mirror. We can hear the bell from the shop entrance. RASHID enters.*

HASSAN. Look, I haven't time. Just one thing: you never paid for the sandwiches. And you took the mint. Wonderful. Just what they expect from you: another couple of moors. Heaps of shit.

Listen, Mustafa can get high on hashish or whatever he wants to do with his life. But now I've got to go down and

pay the Gallego for his sandwiches and explain that my
nephew has just come across from Morocco and is a stupid
creature who doesn't know how to behave. And then I have
to apologise. Apologise for MY NEPHEW.

RASHID. Mimti, mimti, mimti . . . (*For God's sake!*)

HASSAN. Rashid, I've done everything I can to explain this to
you, but you don't want to learn. If you use your head,
doors open for you. But you can't open doors bashing your
head against them. You've got to think.

RASHID. How long is it since you last went home?

HASSAN. Look, please. Not this AGAIN.

RASHID. Look Hassan. But this time YOU listen to ME. That
story of the train ticket is just a lie.

HASSAN. What do you mean?

RASHID. I told it to Mustafa. He already knows it. He said
everyone in Tangier knows that story. You haven't been
back for so long you don't know this. But boys tell it to the
tourists. The famous story of the brave Moor who ate his
train ticket.

HASSAN. This is a true story.

RASHID. Oh yeah I'm sure it's true. But you heard it
somewhere, didn't you?

HASSAN. Is it a good story or a good story?

RASHID. It's a very good story.

HASSAN. The only problem is you need balls.

*Short pause.*

RASHID. Hassan, what's happening to your plans to expand?
If you go on chucking money away you won't have
anything left.

HASSAN. OK, the telly won't pay. But they're going to
transmit it, Rashid, and that's all I want. Don't you
understand that?

RASHID. They're going to transmit it.

HASSAN. Yes. Because it's good. Because it's funny. Because the moor's going to smash himself up on his bike. And they're getting it for nothing. It's a present.

RASHID. But look what you've done today. One take and then another and another . . . Zid wa zid wa zid wa zid. (*One and then another and another . . .* ) Look at yourself. You look like a clown. Do you think you're in the circus?

HASSAN. Leave!

RASHID. Fuck's sake. I knew you'd do anything for money. But the only thing you want to do is smash yourself up on a bike so you can get on the telly.

HASSAN. So what? Everyone wants to get on the telly.

RASHID. But Hassan this is crazy. This is World War Three!

HASSAN. I'll do it as often as I have to, understand. As many times as I have to.

RASHID. Hassan, since when have you started to trust him?

HASSAN. I don't trust him. I just need him for a business deal. That's all.

RASHID. But you've given him a receipt for a video camera and he hasn't bought it.

HASSAN. What if I have? It's my receipt. Isn't it?

RASHID. But you don't know what he wants it for. It's got everything, your name, the date, the shop's stamp... Now he can do what he likes with that receipt. Don't you understand?

*Short pause.*

HASSAN. How do you know?

RASHID. Because he told me. Listen, Hassan: he just wants the insurance money. He's going to pretend he's been robbed in order to get money from the insurance company.

*Pause.*

HASSAN. Wait a minute. Wait a minute! How do you know all this?

RASHID. I've told you. He wanted us to do it together.

HASSAN. No I'm not talking about that. I'm talking about the receipt. The information on it, the dates...the shop's STAMP. Now you know very well I never stamp my receipts. So how do you know I put a stamp on this one?

*Short pause.*

When I wrote out the receipt, you were out in the street.

*Short pause.* RASHID *takes out the receipt.*

RASHID. Take it. It's yours.

HASSAN. Where did you get it from? If you stole it....

RASHID. I just gave him a shove. He didn't realise.

HASSAN. Why?

RASHID. Hassan, if there's any hassles with the police you'll be involved. I did it for you.

HASSAN. Rashid. O my God. Rashid.

*Short pause.*

RASHID. When did you last go home?

HASSAN. What do you mean?

RASHID. It's ten years, isn't it? It's been at least ten years.

HASSAN. I can't believe it. You're not going to give me this lecture all over again.

RASHID. Now I understand. You never go back on holiday. You don't want a German car. You want to go back on television.

HASSAN. Listen, boy, I can't waste any more time.

RASHID. Look at yourself. You look like a clown . . . You don't know what you're doing, or where you are . . . You don't even know who you are . . .

HASSAN. Rashid . . .

RASHID. They'll see it. You know that. You know they'll see you because over there they watch Spanish television. We're not that far away after all. Are we? Isn't that how you're thinking of going back? Going back to your own country? In a television channel? Playing the clown on television? Hassan, how old are you?

HASSAN. Kh'Rey, kh'Rey, Rashid. Men H'na. Men H'na. (*Leave. Get out of here.*)

RASHID. You've got it wrong, Hassan. You need help.

HASSAN. Fine. OK then. SO-WHY-DON'T-YOU-HELP-ME?

*Long pause.*

RASHID. OK. I agree. I'm going to help you.

HASSAN. You're going to help me?

RASHID. Yes.

HASSAN. I'm sorry Rashid. I just have to do this.

RASHID. Yes. We'll do it. Together. You and I. Eh?

HASSAN. Yes. Thank you.

RASHID. Wait for me here, I'm going to the Gallego's bar to look for Fali and the greengrocer. With any luck, they'll still be there.

HASSAN. Be careful with the Gallego, Rashid. He'll be really angry.

RASHID. Don't worry, I'll pay for the sandwiches, and say I'm sorry.

HASSAN. Be careful. Please.

RASHID. I will. I promise. I'm going to say I'm sorry nicely. Don't worry.

HASSAN. And what'll we do about . . . what's his name?

RASHID. Forget him. That guy's a menace. A real menace.

HASSAN. Fine. If you help me . . . But we need someone else. Someone to drive the car . . . If I'm on the bicycle, someone's got to drive that car.

RASHID. Yes. Yes you're right. Shit.

HASSAN. Do you think Mustafa . . . ?

RASHID. What?

HASSAN. He drives, doesn't he? You told me he did.

RASHID. Are you being serious? Do you really want him to do it?

HASSAN. No, the question is, are you sure he can do it?

RASHID. Of course. He drives really well. He'll make a good job of it.

HASSAN. It's ten thousand. Give it to him.

RASHID. Yes, I'll tell him. I'll go and find him. Don't you worry. NOW we'll get it right. There's no hurry, we've got the whole night. Hassan . . .

HASSAN. What?

RASHID. Thanks.

HASSAN. It has to happen, eh Rashid? We moors always stick together.

RASHID *gets ready to go. Suddenly we hear a shop window being broken at the shop entrance.*

RASHID (*heading for the door*). Shit.

HASSAN. Rashid, hide.

RASHID. No, not now. We're together now. Eh, Hassan? Together.

ANTON *enters.*

ANTON. Well, what a happy sight. The whole family together. (*To* HASSAN.) I have a funny feeling you and me haven't really understood each other.

HASSAN. Plans have changed.

ANTON. Listen Mahomet, you can stick your fucking plans up your arse. Do I make myself clear?

RASHID. Get out of here.

ANTON. What?

ANTON *hits* RASHID *in the balls with his plaster.*

HASSAN. What are you doing? Do you want me to kill you?

ANTON. It's simple, isn't it? It's just there's some people only understand things when you beat it into them.

HASSAN. Get out of here. Go back to the shit you came from.

ANTON. I want that receipt. I want it now.

HASSAN. The receipt? I gave it to you.

ANTON. Give it me.

HASSAN. I don't have it.

ANTON. Now listen Mahomet, or you're going to get it as well.

HASSAN. What do you want? I told you I don't . . .

ANTON *hits* HASSAN *with the crutch.* HASSAN *falls.*

ANTON. Mahomet, you're lucky I'm in the state I'm in, because otherwise you'd be eating so much shit you wouldn't have any teeth left to chew it!

HASSAN *tries to get up but stays on his knees.*

ANTON. Mahomet, you'd better give me that fucking receipt before I lose patience. Mahomet, give me the receipt or I'll fucking lose my temper!

HASSAN. Ismi Hasan, machi Muhammad. (*My name's Hassan, not Muhammad.*)

ANTON. I think you owe me an apology.

HASSAN. Magadish nat'leb esmah. (*I'm not going to say I'm sorry.*)

ANTON. Listen, talk Christian or we're not going to understand each other.

HASSAN. I've spent my whole life saying I'm sorry. Magadish nat'leb esmah. (*I'm not going to say I'm sorry.*)

*ANTON hits a box next to HASSAN with his crutch.*

ANTON. You bastard give us that receipt!

*HASSAN slowly gets up. He takes the receipt from his djellaba pocket.*

ANTON. OK that's better. Think about how life is. I can smell guys like you from miles off. I know you, shit. I know shits like you. You give with one hand while you take with the other . . .

*Suddenly HASSAN puts the receipt in his mouth and chews it.*

Hey what are you doing, let go of that! Let go, shit! Give us the paper. Fucking shit!

*HASSAN has been quicker than him and has already swallowed it.*

ANTON. You swallowed it.

HASSAN. That's right.

ANTON. Holy shit.

*He knocks him to the floor with his crutch and hits him with it again and again.*

Who do you think you are…. Eh? Tell me who the fuck you think you are…Twenty five thousand, fifty thousand, five hundred thousand….Your mouth is full of shit. Belgium, Europe…. Where the fuck have you learnt to treat people like this? Let me tell you something: you are an ignorant son of a bitch. You think you know a lot but you haven't a clue… You think you can treat people as if they were electric fucking toasters, and you've got it really wrong… BECAUSE I AM NOT AN ELECTRIC TOASTER… you think because I've just broken my arm and you can treat me like shit … BUT I AM NOT SHIT…

HASSAN *doesn't move.* ANTON *looks at him, panting, and lets go of his crutch.*

Filthy son of a bitch. Swallowed the receipt. And you think I smell bad, you shit? You think I SMELL BAD. I'm going to shoot you, fucker. I'm going to shoot you in your Jewish Arab Moorish son of a shitty bitch head.

ANTON *picks up the price gun that fires little sticky labels with the prices on them. He goes back to* HASSAN.

And there you have it. the only language you understand. Let's have a look at the market price.

*He fires at* HASSAN's *forehead.*

ANTON. Mahomet you cunt you're worth two thousand one hundred and ninety five. That's cheap, cunt. That's a bargain.

RASHID *moves.* ANTON *looks at him. He bends over* HASSAN *for the last time.*

That's a knockdown price.

*He leaves.* RASHID *gets up and goes to* HASSAN.

RASHID. Hassan, Hassan.

HASSAN. Eh.

RASHID. Oh my God!

HASSAN. What is it?

RASHID. Nothing. Nothing at all. Don't worry.

HASSAN. Allah A Rabbi. (*Fuck. What a fright.*)

RASHID. It's OK, he's gone.

HASSAN. I'm cold. Uf, I'm frozen.

   RASHID *brings him a blanket..*

RASHID. Take my hand.

HASSAN. Ow.

RASHID. Sit up. Lean on this. That's it. Is that better?

HASSAN. Wily, wily . . . (*I've pissed myself.*)

RASHID. Are you sore?

HASSAN. I've pissed myself.

RASHID. I'm sorry, Hassan, I'm so sorry. Can you get up?

HASSAN. He wanted the receipt. I ate it.

RASHID. You ate the receipt?

HASSAN. I swear it. Wallah el aadim. (*I swear by God.*).
I swallowed it.

RASHID. Fuck, Hassan, he could have killed you.

HASSAN *tries to get up.*

Wait a minute, wait a minute. What are you doing?

HASSAN. The slippers . . .

RASHID. OK, wait a minute. Don't move. I'll get them.

RASHID *picks up the Arab slippers, which have been
thrown about the room. He goes to* HASSAN *and carefully
puts them on his feet.*

That's good. That's very good.

RASHID *takes* HASSAN *to a mirror.*

*Pause*

RASHID. Come and look.

RASHID *takes* HASSAN *to a mirror.*

There. What do you think?

HASSAN. Think of what?

RASHID. The djellaba. It really suits you.

HASSAN. Does it?

RASHID *puts on his slippers.*

RASHID. And African slippers. You should try them. They're
much more comfortable.

HASSAN. Do you think so?

HASSAN *looks at himself in the mirror. He thinks about it.*

*Fade to black.*

# BLEEDING HEART

## (*La Puñalá*)

*by*

## ANTONIO ONETTI

*translated by Oscar Ceballos and Mary Peate*

Antonio Onetti (born Seville 1962) began his theatrical
activities as an actor to later dedicate himself to direction and
playwriting. He has also taught at the Escuela Superior de Arte
Dramático in Seville and is a screenplay writer for film and
television. Since 1985 he has had a dozen plays produced,
nearly all of which were published including: *Los Peligros de
la Jungla* (1987), *La Chica de Cristal* (1987), *'Líbrame, Señor,
de mis cadenas'* (1989), *Marcado Por el Típex y La Diva al
Dente* (1990), *La Puñalá* (1991), *Salvia* (1993), *La Rumba del
Maletín* (1993) and *El Son Que Nos Tocan* (1995). *Purasangre*
and *Almasul y la Flauta de Plata* have also been published.
His most recent work, *Madre Caballo*, directed by Emilio
Hernández, was produced by the Centro Andaluz de Teatro in
October 1997, where he was writer in residence and toured all
over Spain to great acclaim throughout 1998. He won the
Marqués de Bradomín Prize in 1985 and 1988 and was the first
Spanish writer to attend the Royal Court International Summer
School in 1993.

BLEEDING HEART

WHOROSCOPE

*Bleeding Heart* (*La Puñalá*) was first performed in English as a rehearsed reading in the *Voices from Spain* season in the Theatre Upstairs on 11 April, 1997 with the following cast.

| | |
|---|---|
| SOURFACE | Tony Curran |
| LADY MARLBORO | Philip Voss |

*Director*   Jeremy Herrin
*Translators*   Oscar Ceballos and Mary Peate

**Characters**

SOURFACE

Nasty-looking thief, as the name suggests. Outside the law and out of luck, he makes his living however he can, mainly at the expense of tourists. He walks around a lot, stealing anything that comes his way and sleeping wherever night finds him. His criminal activity depends on his natural ability to charm people, but, watch out! He is a treacherous coward and he'll probably end up being Prime Minister of some South American country. Other features: allergy to flowers, particularly jasmine and smoking blonde tobacco (if it comes his way, of course).

LADY MARLBORO

Thick set transvestite in her fifties, proprietor of a trolley carrying tobacco, balloons and other knick knacks. He was quite a celebrity in his time, but these days he's reduced to talking about other people 'til the crack of dawn. Like any old-fashioned queen from Seville, he has a great passion for the Virgin Mary, particularly during Holy Week and the 'El Rocío' pilgrimage. So much so that he'll pay for it with his life. He still doesn't understand the meaning of AIDS and has no other vices than those which come naturally to him.

*The action, believe it or not, takes place in present day Seville.*

**Bleeding Heart**

*A small square in Seville during the early hours of Easter
Wednesday. A stone bench, a litter bin and a newspaper.*

SOURFACE *enters, hiding something under his jacket. He
rushes in and sits on the bench, out of breath. He looks
around. Once he's sure nobody has followed him, he calms
down a bit and gets out a woman's handbag, empties the
contents onto the bench, examines them and blows up.*

SOURFACE. You're cursed, Sourface! Sweet F A! Lipstick,
Tampax, some other bloody rubbish, a load of crap and
three credit cards . . . But not a penny of hard cash. Not one
penny! These tourists coming to Seville for the processions
are a right bunch of stingy bastards!

*He quickly puts everything back in the bag and throws it as
far as he can.*

Where are the spoils of tourism, the dollars, the foreign
currency? Stuck in banks and hotels because of those stupid
little cards. And for you, Sourface, nothing, not even a pack
of fags. Well there we are, another night sleeping out in the
streets like a tramp. And it's freezing cold and it stinks of
bloody jasmine everywhere.

*Resigned, he prepares his bed on the bench by covering
himself with sheets of newspaper.*

Would you believe it!? A good-looking bloke like me
without so much as a fiver in his pocket to pay for a hostel,
or a nice bird to cuddle up next to! All you need now is a
drunken penitent to have a go at you with his whip in the
middle of the night!

*As he's about to cover his face, a headline suddenly grabs
his attention.*

Fuck me! 'Sacrilegious plunder at the brotherhood of the Bleeding Heart'. What's this? 'Seville in shock. The holy image of Our Lady of the Sorrows, popularly known as Our Lady of the Bleeding Heart, adored by Seville's brotherhood of the Greatest Torment, last night suffered a sacrilegious theft, just two days before her procession on Good Thursday, which blah, blah, blah . . . so on and so forth . . . As well as the valuable gold dagger and the precious gems which the idol wore round her neck, the wicked thieves took her silver and ruby crown, her diamond necklaces, her emerald brooches, her rings and all the other jewelry adorning the Virgin, the value of all of which is thought to be incalculable . . . ' the rip-off of the century! What a genius! I bet he's got enough to get himself a bed for the night. ' . . . The crown, the necklaces, the dagger . . . ' With just one of those little rings I could live like the Maharaja Maharani for the rest of my life!

*He picks up a dog-end from the ground and lights it with a match.*

And to think of the times I've thought about doing the very same thing myself. Who hasn't! Well anyway, some smart arse got there first. And meanwhile, here you are, running around after tourists trying to grab their handbags. You're cursed, Sourface, and that's the truth! 'While the Brothers of the Bleeding Heart are holding a meeting to decide whether or not to cancel the procession due to the Confederation of Confederated Processions' call for a processional strike on Maundy Thursday in protest about ecclesiastical insecurity, police spokesmen have refused to comment as they so far lack any clues which would lead them to the criminals . . . 'Christ! Well if they don't hurry up they'll have to carry her round with a kitchen knife sticking out of her chest! That explains why Seville was in such a mess today with the filth turning the city upside down and locking people up if they so much as laughed in the street. It was impossible doing business today, even in the crowd in La Campana Square. Oh well! Maybe next time! Just go to sleep, you've got to work hard tomorrow if you want to take Mari Puri out for the night.

*He makes himself comfortable for sleep.*

Christ it's freezing! And what a stink! If only Our Lady of the Abandoned would come and get you out of this mess.

LADY MARLBORO *enters from behind him pushing a trolley full of cigarettes, sweets, balloons and other trash.*

LADY MARLBORO. Fear not, little thief.

SOURFACE *jumps, thinking it's an apparition, and doesn't dare turn round.*

SOURFACE. God, The Virgin heard my prayer! Forgive me Our Lady, I was only joking! And if you're here about the other day, I'm really sorry, I didn't mean to take the money from the poor box, the coins just stuck to my fingers! I'm really sorry, but I've already spent it all . . . !

LADY MARLBORO. So, now you're going round clearing out churches and taking the charity money, are you? I didn't know you were so holy.

SOURFACE. It's not what you think . . . !

*Realising his mistake.*

SOURFACE. Lady Marlboro it was you all the time.

LADY MARLBORO. Do I look like a Guardian Angel?

SOURFACE. (Great, just what I needed! This one clings like a limpet. We'll be here 'til Easter Sunday).

LADY MARLBORO. So, what's a big-shot like you doing sleeping out in the street? Doing penance for your sins?

SOURFACE. No Miss, I'm just making sure I've got a good spot to see the roman soldiers in the Macarena procession, 'cause I love them so much.

LADY MARLBORO *goes to sit down.*

LADY MARLBORO. Come on, shift your legs. I'm shattered after running round all night, and my bunions are black and blue from people standing on them. I'm sick of this trolley, sick of children, sick of balloons and sick of penitents!

LADY MARLBORO *sits down and takes her shoes off.*

SOURFACE. You must've done good business with all that walking?

LADY MARLBORO. Oh yes, a fortune! Enough to retire on!

SOURFACE. Be a good girl then and lend us a pack of fags, I'm sick of smoking dog-ends.

LADY MARLBORO. Poor Sourface! Are things that bad?

SOURFACE. I'm skint. Desperate. Ready to throw myself off the bridge.

LADY MARLBORO. And, if I were to advance you a pack, what would you give me in return . . . ?

SOURFACE. Many thanks and that's it.

LADY MARLBORO. Nothing else, darling . . . ?

LADY MARLBORO *slyly tries to touch him up.*

SOURFACE. Ehh! Hands off, let's not get into trouble here, OK!

LADY MARLBORO. Ooh, he's gone all macho suddenly!

SOURFACE. What d'you mean by that?

LADY MARLBORO. Well it's not how some wagging tongues would describe you.

SOURFACE. Which tongues would that be?

LADY MARLBORO. Tongues that swear they know you well. . . Well, tongues and other things . . .

SOURFACE. Lies, all lies.

LADY MARLBORO. Yeah, yeah . . . I know all about it.

SOURFACE. What do you know? Stop messing around and tell me which little queen's been telling you stories.

LADY MARLBORO. Someone . . .

SOURFACE. Fatima! I bet it was Fatima! I'll kill her when I find her!

LADY MARLBORO. Wrong, darling, it was Juanita Manicure . . .

SOURFACE. (Now I've put my foot in it). And what did that
waster tell you?

LADY MARLBORO. Nothing. I just saw her the other day
watching the procession of the little donkey and there she
was singing . . .

'My darling's got a rod
like a greasy flagpole . . . '

SOURFACE. What a bitch!

LADY MARLBORO. Well, we are very close, you know . . .

SOURFACE. You're cursed, Sourface! Wait 'til I catch that
little queen, I'll make mincemeat of her, I'll rip her tongue
out, I'll gnaw out her kidneys . . . ! What did she tell you?

LADY MARLBORO. I've told you, everything; the time in the
park, the time under the bridge, that time in the public
toilets . . .

SOURFACE. The fantasies of a dried-up slapper who has to
make it all up because she can't get a fuck!

LADY MARLBORO. Even that time with the yoghurt . . .

SOURFACE. The yoghurt as well? (I'm finished!)

LADY MARLBORO. It seems I'm the only one you haven't
invited to the party . . .

SOURFACE. Well, don't get your hopes up because all that's
over! (I knew this would happen sooner or later). And, of
course you've gone all round town telling everyone, you
little blabbermouth . . .

LADY MARLBORO. Me? No.

SOURFACE. Thank God!

LADY MARLBORO. Not . . . everyone.

SOURFACE. What d'you . . . ?

LADY MARLBORO. Go on, have one of these little darlings, and keep the pack.

*She takes a pack out of the trolley for him.*

SOURFACE. For me?

LADY MARLBORO. It's a present. You just relax, angel face, rose in bloom . . .

*She goes for him again.*

SOURFACE. OK, OK . . . Stop it now.

LADY MARLBORO. Aren't you going to be nice to your friend Lady Marlboro?

SOURFACE. Look, Stop fucking about, I'm not in the mood.

*He takes a cigarette and lights up, irritated and on edge.*

LADY MARLBORO. Ugh! So antisocial suddenly! Such ingratitude! And to think of all the smokes you've had off me . . .

SOURFACE *doesn't take any notice.*

LADY MARLBORO. By the way . . . How's that lovely girlfriend of yours? What was her name?

SOURFACE. Mari Puri? I walked her home just a while ago . . . Eh! Eeeeh! You wouldn't dare?

LADY MARLBORO. What a lovely little thing! So tall! Gorgeous figure! I wish I looked like that!

SOURFACE. Look Lady Marlboro, Mari Puri's a girl to love for good, not just to mess about with, if she found out, it'd be goodbye to this life, because without Mari Puri, I'm nothing.

LADY MARLBORO. Not a day goes by when she doesn't buy a pack of Fortuna from me.

SOURFACE. Don't do that to me, for God's sake! Don't! Especially not now she's going to get that job with the Council and take me away from all this.

LADY MARLBORO. What an imagination you've got, my morning star, my little sugar cube . . . !

SOURFACE. I'll do anything you want, but don't say a word to her!

LADY MARLBORO. Now you're talking, kid. I can't tell you how many times I've dreamt of those sweet lips, those little eyes of yours, that . . .

*He grabs his balls.*

SOURFACE. For fuck's sake, Lady Marlboro, not here, someone might see us!

LADY MARLBORO. There's nobody here! Don't be so uptight, sweet heart . . .

SOURFACE. OK. You win. But just a quickie, then you pay for my hostel bed and that's the end of it.

LADY MARLBORO. Tonight you shall stay at the Excelsior Hotel!

SOURFACE. And not a word to Mari Puri, or anyone else, 'cause if you tell Fatima, then she comes sniffing round, and then Juana Manicure, and then someone else, and then someone else . . . and there'll be no end to it . . . And it's one thing to get myself out of trouble, but another thing to end up enjoying it . . . !

LADY MARLBORO. Come here, I'm on fire, I'm overcome with love for you.

SOURFACE. (Agggh).

SOURFACE *goes to the bench and* LADY MARLBORO *jumps on him like a passionate young girl ready for anything, when suddenly,* SOURFACE *feels something very hard and very cold on* LADY MARLBORO's *chest.*

SOURFACE. Ow! What's that round your neck! It's all hard and cold!

LADY MARLBORO. What? It's nothing! My mother's crucifix!

SOURFACE. Well it's sticking in me. Take it off.

LADY MARLBORO. Let go!

SOURFACE. What a big crucifix!

*There's a scuffle and* SOURFACE *manages to grab it. Oh, surprise, it's the sacred dagger of the Virgin.*

This isn't a crucifix . . .

LADY MARLBORO. Just give it back. It's none of your business.

SOURFACE. It's a dagger encrusted with coloured stones . . .

LADY MARLBORO. Give it here, I said!

SOURFACE. But, Lady Marlboro . . . This is the dagger nicked from the Virgin!

LADY MARLBORO. No!

SOURFACE. It was you! Lady Marlboro, 'master criminal'!

LADY MARLBORO. Rubbish!. I found it in a bin, just by chance!

SOURFACE. You've kept quiet about this . . .

LADY MARLBORO *tries to take it from him.*

LADY MARLBORO. Give it to me right now or . . . !

SOURFACE. Or What? Are you still going to go telling tales to Mari Puri? What a fucked-up little hypocrite. You filthy bitch. And you were going to blackmail me with some story about yoghurt!

LADY MARLBORO *gets on her knees and prays to the heavens.*

LADY MARLBORO. I'm so ashamed, Our Lady! Forgive me! Remember what a good Catholic I am. Forgive me, and I promise I'll do a pilgrimage to Jerusalem, on my knees, with my arms up in a cross and a Bible in each hand.

SOURFACE. (Diamonds, rubies, emeralds . . . This little dagger's worth a fortune, if I find out where the rest of the treasure is . . . I'm saved . . . !)

LADY MARLBORO. Sourface. You've got to keep this a secret for me . . .

SOURFACE. Done.

LADY MARLBORO. 'Til I can put it back.

SOURFACE. Put it back?! Are you cracked or what?

LADY MARLBORO. Listen sweetie, it's not what you think. It wasn't really a robbery . . .

SOURFACE. Oh, really?

LADY MARLBORO. It wasn't. It was more of a delirium, a trance, it possessed me and . . . I just couldn't help it.

SOURFACE. A couple more attacks like that and I'd be freed of this curse of poverty!

LADY MARLBORO. Let me explain. I've always been a follower of Our Lady of the Bleeding Heart, and she knows it very well because she's seen me every year in her procession, following her, no matter how crowded it is, all the way from her chapel to the Cathedral and back again, walking right behind her, by her cloak. And every time I looked at that dagger stabbed in her bleeding heart my own heart was bleeding and it was as if I was floating just thinking how much that woman had suffered for our sins. But last Monday – I went to pray to her in her chapel – the devil possessed me and put the idea into my head that I had to feel the coldness of that dagger on my chest. Eventually, last night, I dressed up like a man, for the first time in forty years, so that nobody would recognise me. I filled a flask with coffee, sugar and a whole bottle of sleeping pills and headed towards her chapel. There she was with four brothers of the Greatest Torment guarding her. They all drank from my flask without suspecting a thing, and fell asleep in no time. I took the ladder, went up to her throne and with trembling hands I took the Holy Dagger from her chest. What a feeling! All that grace in my hands! I just wanted to hold it for a while and then put it back again, I swear, Sourface, but the sight of all that jewelry and shiny metal within my grasp . . . I went mad, I couldn't help

myself. And she seemed to be saying: 'Take it, Lady
Marlboro, It's no use to me . . . '

SOURFACE. I see, you took it to do her a favour . . .

LADY MARLBORO. It's the truth. May I be struck by lightning
if I'm lying!

SOURFACE. Don't tempt the heavens, they might strike you
down. You've looted the Virgin under cover of night with
malice aforethought.

LADY MARLBORO. No! No! No!

SOURFACE. . . . And in this story the only favour is the one
you're going to do me by making me a millionaire.

LADY MARLBORO. How?!

SOURFACE. By making me your partner and sharing the
treasure.

LADY MARLBORO. Never, Satan! I've got to take it back to
clear my conscience.

SOURFACE. Hypocrite! You want to keep it all for yourself.
Do you think I'm thick? But this dagger condemns you.
Either you share the stuff with me or I go to the filth and
you'll spend the rest of your life polishing the bars you're
behind.

LADY MARLBORO. You won't get a thing out of me. I'm not
scared of prison.

SOURFACE. We'll see about that.

LADY MARLBORO. Sourface, keep the trolley if you want.
I'll get you somewhere to live, I'll work for you, I'll be
your slave, but get this idea out of your head.

SOURFACE. No, Lady Marlboro! Think! Make the most of
this miracle. With what this merchandise is worth, you and
I could get off the streets . . . and live like kings!

LADY MARLBORO. You and me?

SOURFACE. Tell me where you've put it and I'll give you the
flagpole . . .

LADY MARLBORO. I don't trust you.

SOURFACE. Then I'll kill you, you witch!

LADY MARLBORO. You wouldn't dare.

SOURFACE. I'm running out of patience!

LADY MARLBORO. I'm not scared of dying!

SOURFACE. Really?

*Goes as if to finish her off.*

LADY MARLBORO. Oh yes I am!

SOURFACE. Well then, talk, or I'll slit your throat!

LADY MARLBORO. OK! Don't kill me! You win. Keep the dagger, it's worth a fortune and I'll take the rest of it back and then go into a convent.

SOURFACE. No deal.

LADY MARLBORO. Then what do you want?

SOURFACE. Fifty fifty.

LADY MARLBORO. Are you mad?

SOURFACE. You're driving me mad, that's my final offer. Just tell me where you've put the crown and we'll leave it at that.

LADY MARLBORO. But the crown's the most valuable thing!

SOURFACE. You can keep the rest, and if not . . .

LADY MARLBORO. All right, you bastard. But you're taking the light of day from me.

SOURFACE. Stop blabbering and spit it out.

LADY MARLBORO. The dagger first.

SOURFACE. What are you talking about! The crown first, then we'll see.

LADY MARLBORO. I hope you burn in hell!

SOURFACE. I hope so too.

LADY MARLBORO *opens a side door to the trolley and the crown and the rest of the treasure is shining inside.*

LADY MARLBORO. There it is.

SOURFACE. Wow! And you've been walking around Seville with all this?

LADY MARLBORO. I was out of my mind, I couldn't think of anywhere else.

SOURFACE. You thieving old witch! And you wanted to buy me for a few cigarettes!

LADY MARLBORO. Now you've got what you wanted. Give me the dagger and let's get it over with.

SOURFACE. You said it. Let's get it over with!

LADY MARLBORO. What are you looking at me like that for?

SOURFACE. You still want the dagger?

LADY MARLBORO. That was the deal.

SOURFACE. Here's the dagger . . . And here's the bleeding heart!

*He stabs her in the chest.* LADY MARLBORO *falls to her knees.*

LADY MARLBORO. Ah! Bastard! Murderer!

SOURFACE. You wanted to feel the cold dagger on your chest, didn't you? Well, there you are and I hope you enjoy it. Now you won't grass me up. Hasta la vista, arsehole. I'll see you in hell!

*He puts the jewels in the trolley and exits.*

LADY MARLBORO. Ah! Help! Police! He's killed me! I'm dying. Holy Virgin, please take me to your bosom. I repent all my sins.

LADY MARLBORO *dies, but with her last breath she has a hallucination and a dream about the music and the drums of Holy Week, very quiet at first, then growing to its apotheosis. The stage fills with smoke and a divine light appears. They are playing 'Campañilleros' for her. She also dreams of two archangels coming to her. One puts the cloak, the crown and the rosary around her shoulders, the other places a tray of church candles in front of her. As the dream goes on she feels infinitely happy and she forgets her tragedy.*

LADY MARLBORO. But . . . What am I hearing? Music! Drums! Which procession could be passing through here at this time of day? And those candles? And that smell of incense? My cloak! My crown! My rosary beads! And these archangels at my side! It can't be. Is it real or am I just dreaming? No, it's real. It is me they are carrying! And they're playing the Campañilleros march just for me! And this street? It's the Avenida! And that big church . . . It's the Cathedral! And all those people watching . . . ! Ah, What a moment of joy! This is what I always wanted! Me, carried aloft through the Cathedral doors! Thank you God! Thank you! Thank you! Thank you! (Aaah).

*Smiling from ear to ear, the Virgin Lady Marlboro expires and, in the darkness of death, she dreams of entering the chapel while the music reaches its climax . . .*

*The End.*

# ROUNDABOUT

## (*Rodeo*)

*by*

## LLUÏSA CUNILLÉ

*translated by Oscar Ceballos and Mary Peate*

Lluïsa Cunillé Salgado was born in Barcelona (Badalona) in 1961. She has studied with José Sanchis Sinisterra at the Sala Beckett's Writers' Programme in Barcelona. Her produced plays include: *Rodeo* (Calderón de la Barca prize, 1991), which was produced at the Mercat de les flors in Barcelona in 1993. Her other plays in Catalan include*: Molt Novembre* (1992), *Libración,* Barcelona Critics' Prize *(*1993), *La Festa* at the Romea Theatre in Barcelona (1994), *Jòquer* (1994), *Aigua, foc, terra i aire* (1994), *Accident* (1995), *La Venda* for the Grec Festival in 1997, *Privado* at the Sala Beckett (1998) and *Dotze Treballs* at the Sitges Festival and *Apocalipsi* at the Teatro Nacional de Catalunya in 1998. Many of these plays have been published. Her play *The Meeting* was performed at the Grec Festival in July 1999 and then in English at the Edinburgh Festival in August 1999.

*Roundabout* (*Rodeo*) was first performed in English as a
rehearsed reading in the *Voices from Spain* season in the
Theatre Upstairs on 11 April, 1997 with the following cast.

| | |
|---|---|
| SHE | Harriet Bagnall |
| FRIEND | Shaun Dingwall |
| WOMAN | Yolanda Vazquez |
| FATHER | Denys Hawthorne |
| BROTHER | Mark Strong |
| CLIENT / OTHER CLIENT | Nicholas Woodeson |

*Director*　Julie-Anne Robinson
*Translators*　Oscar Ceballos and Mary Peate

**Characters**

SHE
BROTHER
CLIENT
WOMAN
OTHER CLIENT
FRIEND
FATHER

## ACT ONE

SHE *is centre stage, sitting behind an office desk, typing on a swivel chair. At the edge of the stage there are some small steps leading towards the stalls. Upstage and on either side, three doors. The upstage door is different, wider and in better condition, next to it is a hat-stand with a black hat on it.*

*The* BROTHER *appears by the steps and goes towards the stage left door, he disappears. A short while later we hear a tap running, the sound stops, we see him again putting on a different jacket to the one he was wearing before. He sits in one of the two chairs in front of the desk, and takes out a packet of cigarettes.*

BROTHER. Is he here?

*Gestures stage right with his head.*

SHE (*while she keeps on writing*). No.

*The* BROTHER *offers the packet,* SHE *takes a cigarette, he lights his with a match, puts it out, then takes a second match and lights hers, and then puts the packet on the table.* SHE *gets an ashtray out of a drawer in the desk.*

BROTHER. I've had enough. (*Pause.*) What about you?

SHE (*still writing*). Me? (*Pause.*) I don't know.

BROTHER (*picks up the calendar on the desk*). October . . . a good month, an almost excellent month.

*They look at each other and smile for the first time.* SHE *takes the calendar from him, turns a few pages and shows him one of them as* SHE *speaks.*

SHE. April . . . almost as good as October.

*They smile again. Pause. The* BROTHER *stands up and walks to the upstage door.* SHE *talks without turning round while* SHE *types.*

There's nobody here.

BROTHER. Yes . . . , it's lunch time. (*He takes the hat from the hat-stand and puts it on.*) Why does he wear a hat? . . . it's ridiculous. (SHE *turns to look at him.*)

SHE. It's not his.

*Pause.*

BROTHER. Whose is it?

SHE *goes back to writing. The* BROTHER *takes the hat off and smoothes down his hair.*

Don't you want to tell me?

SHE. It belongs to someone who left it here.

*Stops writing and takes the sheet of paper off the typewriter.*

BROTHER. Is it really . . . someone's?

SHE. Yes, really.

*The* BROTHER *puts his cigarette out in the ashtray and sits down.*

BROTHER. I'm going bald, I'll have to buy a hat too.

SHE (*looking at a piece of paper*). Dad makes spelling mistakes and in the end I'm the one that gets confused. (SHE *corrects something with a ball-point pen.*)

*Pause.*

BROTHER. You do everything right.

SHE. Don't say that. (SHE *puts the typewriter to one side.*) Don't say that again.

*Pause.*

BROTHER (*takes a key ring out of one of his trouser pockets*). Present for you.

SHE. I don't want anything.

BROTHER. It's mine. I don't want anything either, I never accept anything. (*He puts the key ring away.*)

SHE. Sorry.

*The* BROTHER *stands up and disappears through the stage right door. There is a noise and he comes back with a desk drawer.*

BROTHER. Look . . . key rings, penknives, pens, even a ring . . . look . . .

SHE (*not looking*). I've already seen it. (*Pause.*) Some people are really careless.

BROTHER (*he starts laughing in a forced way*). Well look what I'm doing with all this . . .

*He throws everything in the bin next to the desk.*

SHE. Some of those things are his . . .

BROTHER. They're unrecognisable now . . . (*They both look at the bin for a while.*)

SHE. Some of those things were really nice.

*The* BROTHER *stands up, visibly depressed.*

BROTHER. I've had enough.

*Pause.*

SHE. I'm going on holiday.

BROTHER. Have you asked him yet?

SHE. I'm going anyway.

BROTHER. Where will you go?

SHE. To the mountains. I need to walk.

BROTHER. I wish I could go with you . . . If you go . . .

SHE. Come.

BROTHER. I can't.

SHE. We used to go everywhere together.

BROTHER. You mean before I got married?

SHE. I might not go on my own, anyway.

*Pause.*

BROTHER. Does he know yet?

SHE. What?

BROTHER. What you're doing.

SHE. Yes.

*By mistake, the* BROTHER *knocks over a box of paperclips with his arm. He gets on his knees to pick them up.*

BROTHER. Can you remember anyone in our family with a finger missing? (*Pause.*) No . . . well she insists it's my fault. She goes around like a madwoman, looking at old family photos trying to find someone with a missing finger.

SHE. If she's that set on it, she'll find someone.

BROTHER. But it's not that important . . . I've told her, if our son had a thumb missing, maybe then . . . And you should see how he manages with three fingers . . .

*Pause.*

SHE. I think I should visit you more often.

BROTHER. She'll end up giving him a complex.

*The telephone rings.* SHE *picks it up.*

SHE. Hello, can I . . . (*Hangs up.*) Same old joke.

BROTHER. I used to like going out at night, anywhere with a bit of life . . .

SHE. Before you got married?

BROTHER (*he sits forward*). Yes.

SHE. It's normal.

BROTHER. And then this job . . . I'm looking for something at the Council. It's a secret . . .

SHE. It won't be for long if it's at the Council.

BROTHER (*stands up*). Why do you dash all my hopes?

SHE. I deal with Council people every day and I hear about everything that goes on whether I want to or not.

BROTHER (*sits down*). But don't tell dad.

*Pause.*

SHE. You shouldn't have thrown his things away.

BROTHER. You're right.

*The* BROTHER *stands up, gets the drawer, retrieves all the things he threw away and exits through the stage right door. Pause. He enters again without the drawer and exits through the stage left door. Noise of water.* SHE *takes a book out of the drawer in her desk and begins to read.*

VOICE OF THE BROTHER. Aren't you going to have any lunch?

SHE. No.

*Pause.*

VOICE OF THE BROTHER. The towel needs changing. (*Pause. The* BROTHER *enters through the stage left door feeling his head.*) I'm going bald . . . (*He sits down.*) What does he look like? . . . Is he going bald too? (*Pause.*) Is he tall . . . is he short . . . Has he got a finger missing . . . ? (*Pause.*) We used to tell each other everything.

SHE. You never talked to me about your wife.

BROTHER. Are you thinking about marrying him? (*Pause.*) Don't do it. (*Pause.*) Go on, tell me what he's like, what his name is.

SHE. He's just a friend . . . Someone to pass the time with.

BROTHER. How much time? a lot of time . . . a bit of time . . . (*Pause.*) Or all eternity? (*Pause.*) No-one tells me anything. I've got no friends, I've lost them all since I got married. My wife, on the other hand, has kept all hers . . . ours, she says . . . but they're not. (*Pause.*) As soon as I get that job at the Council, I'll make new friends, it'll be easier. Because, tell me, how many friends have you got? . . . I bet it's not very many . . . tell me how many . . .

SHE (*without looking up from the book*). A few . . .

BROTHER. I don't know how you stay so calm, how you put up with all this, but I know you're about to explode, just like me.

SHE. I'm not about to explode.

BROTHER. Yes, you are . . . You've been reading the same book for a year now and it isn't even two hundred pages long, you think I hadn't noticed, that I don't notice what you do?

*Pause.*

SHE (*lifting her eyes from the book*). This is the third time I've read it, always at the same time, it's a book for this time of day. I read a paragraph carefully and sometimes I even learn it by heart. And when I go home, on the bus which is always full, standing there, I repeat one of the paragraphs to myself and then I think that nobody else on that bus, or even in the whole city, can be thinking what I'm thinking, reciting what I'm reciting for myself, just for myself, and that makes me feel . . . like nobody else in the city can be feeling at that precise moment. (SHE *goes back to her book.*)

*Pause.*

BROTHER. I don't know what this is all about, but believe me, it doesn't make me feel happy for you, quite the opposite in fact.

*Pause.* SHE *stands up and disappears through the stage left door which SHE closes behind her. The BROTHER stands up and picks up her handbag which is hanging on her chair. He takes out an address book and flicks through some pages, then he puts it back in the handbag and puts the handbag back where it was. SHE reappears, sits on the chair next to her BROTHER and looks him straight in the eyes.*

SHE. I promise if I find out about your job with the Council before it's official, I'll let you know immediately.

BROTHER. Official?

SHE. Yes, I imagine you've done some tests, filled in some questionnaires, been interviewed by someone . . .

*The* BROTHER *puts his hands over his ears and lowers his head.*

BROTHER. Why do you dash all my hopes?

SHE. Haven't you done any of those things?

BROTHER. I've got friends, I trust them.

SHE (*removes his hands from his face*). Didn't you just say you didn't have any . . .

BROTHER. Yes, I've still got a few.

*They look each other in the eyes, then* SHE *stands up, sits behind the desk again and looks at her book.*

Anyway you will tell me . . . won't you? . . . if you hear anything . . . if anyone on the phone . . . (*Pause.*) Answer me!

SHE. Yes, I'll tell you.

*Pause.*

BROTHER. Why do you reproach me for trying to improve myself? (*Pause.*) It's all very well all that about the bus, but have you considered the fact that, in the end, that thing you're thinking about that nobody else in the whole city is thinking about, isn't even yours? Have you . . . eh?

SHE. I can't understand how something so intelligent can suddenly occur to you, yet at the same time you can't understand that you'll never get that job at the council just by wishing for it.

BROTHER. You don't think I'm capable . . .

SHE. And I'm not capable of imagining anything that would be worth remembering on the bus.

*Pause.*

BROTHER. Why don't we both get a job at the Council?

SHE. I don't want to work there.

BROTHER. Don't tell me you prefer this.

SHE. I don't know what I prefer.

BROTHER. Well then ask yourself, instead of reading that book.

SHE. I will, don't worry. (*Carries on looking at her book.*)

*The* BROTHER *stands up and disappears through the upstage door and comes back with a flower in his lapel.*

BROTHER. D'you like it?

SHE (*smiles*). It suits you.

BROTHER. I'll wear it all evening and smile non-stop.

SHE. That'd make a change.

*He stares at her and then takes another flower out of his pocket.*

BROTHER. Look this one's for you. (*He puts it in her buttonhole.*) We look as if we're going to a wedding together. (SHE *looks at her watch.*) Don't look at your watch, are you scared? (*Pause.*) Have you got a mirror?

SHE. I think so . . . (*Opens a drawer.*) no . . .

BROTHER. Yes, you have . . . go on . . . give it to me . . .

SHE *closes the drawer, the* BROTHER *tries to open it, they fight, he finally manages to get the mirror and tries a few smiles into it.* SHE *smiles as well, he brings the mirror closer to his face, breathes deeply onto it and suddenly turns serious. Then he puts the mirror on the table and exits to the stage left room. Noise of water. A few seconds later he appears again drying his hands on a towel.*

SHE. You're ill. (*Puts the mirror away.*)

BROTHER. You, it's you who's ill if you go around using that mirror . . . (*Throws the towel into the stage left room.*)

SHE. For your information, this is the mirror that used to be in the bathroom.

BROTHER. You've had enough too. Come on, admit it.

SHE. Don't talk so loud.

BROTHER. Who's going to hear us? Who are we going to disturb?

SHE. Dad could turn up at any minute.

BROTHER. I'm not scared of him.

SHE. Well, you were in enough of a hurry to get 'his things' out of the bin . . .

BROTHER. I'll prove to you I'm not scared of him.

*He disappears through the stage right door, we hear noises, He appears again with the desk drawer and starts to throw all the objects back into the bin one by one.*

SHE (*lighting up a cigarette*). Let's see how long it takes you to get it all out again.

*After a little while the* CLIENT *appears from the proscenium steps.* SHE *and the* BROTHER *look to the front,* SHE *puts the cigarette out and puts the ashtray in the drawer. The* BROTHER *takes the flowers out of their buttonholes, and puts the cigarettes and matches in his pocket.*

CLIENT. Good afternoon.

SHE. Good afternoon.

*The* BROTHER *quickly collects the objects he had thrown in the bin and exits through the stage right door with the drawer and closes the door.* SHE *stands up and walks towards the upstage door.*

SHE. Would you like to go in? . . .

CLIENT. Do you mind if I stay here for a while . . . ? On this chair . . . if you don't mind . . .

SHE (*goes back to her desk*). No, have a seat. (*They both sit at the same time.* SHE *starts typing.*)

CLIENT. You just carry on as if I wasn't here.

*Pause. The* BROTHER *comes back from the stage right door and passes behind her to disappear again through the stage left door. Noise of water. He reappears again but wearing the same jacket as at the start. He walks towards the proscenium steps.*

BROTHER. Goodbye.

CLIENT. Goodbye.

*The* BROTHER *keeps looking at her until* SHE *looks at him, then raises his hand and hides a finger,* SHE *smiles putting her hand over her mouth so as not to show the* CLIENT *that* SHE*'s laughing. The* CLIENT *can't see the* BROTHER *as he's behind him. The* BROTHER *disappears by the proscenium steps. Pause.*

SHE. Just let me know when you're ready to go in . . .

CLIENT. Am I bothering you?

SHE. No, not at all.

CLIENT. I'd rather stay here a bit longer . . . it's so sudden walking straight in here from the street . . .

SHE. Of course.

*Pause.*

CLIENT. Can I go to the bathroom?

SHE. Yes, just a moment . . . (SHE *stands up, goes to the stage left door, disappears and reappears.*) You can go in now . . .

CLIENT (*stands up*). Thank you. (*He disappears through the stage left door. Noise of water. The* CLIENT *returns and sits in front of her again.*) I'm a bit nervous.

SHE. Yes, well, the first time . . . although you were here this morning, I think . . .

CLIENT. No, that was my brother.

SHE. Really?

CLIENT. Yes, everyone gets us confused, even though there are five years between us. That's his hat.

SHE. Yes, I was just telling my brother.

CLIENT. Your brother?

SHE. The one who left a minute ago.

CLIENT. That's your brother?

SHE. Yes.

CLIENT. He doesn't look like you. (*Pause.*) My brother's not as shy as me, less emotional . . . well, he's the eldest. (*Pause.*) I live on my own and I can't talk about things as soon as they happen. And gradually it gets you down, even more than personal misfortune . . . (*Pause.*) I used to have a cat, but he'd always escape through the window and come back all covered in bruises and scratches. He wouldn't let me take care of him, he just hid in the wardrobe and it was impossible to get him out. I had no option but to close the window, but he used to paw the glass, in the end I had to shut the door so I couldn't hear him. (*Pause.*) I miss him. (*Pause.*) But that wasn't the end of it . . . One day, walking past my neighbour's door, I saw him, he was just the same . . . covered in bruises and scratches, but looking a bit happier. (*Pause.*) I was happy for him. (*Pause.*) Your brother, now I think about it, he works here, doesn't he? (*Pause.*) How old would you say I am . . . ? Fifty? . . . That's my brother's age, I'm forty-five.

SHE*'s been typing the whole time.*

SHE (*takes the paper out of the typewriter*). Sorry . . . Could you sign here?

CLIENT. But hasn't my brother signed it yet?

SHE. No, he left before I could ask him.

CLIENT. I thought it'd been sorted out already.

SHE. We only need these two signatures.

CLIENT. He told me everything was sorted out . . . paid for . . .

SHE. Yes, it is paid for, we just need two relatives' signatures.

CLIENT. But I asked him twice and he insisted everything was done.

SHE. Yes, well, he might have thought so, but . . .

CLIENT. And he's left his hat . . . it's as if he was still here.

*Pause.*

SHE. Are you going to sign or not?

CLIENT. No, we'd better wait till he comes back.

SHE. Do you know if he's going to?

CLIENT. His hat's here . . .

SHE. Oh well, if he's going to come back . . .

*Pause.*

CLIENT. Are those two signatures very important?

SHE. They're . . . necessary.

CLIENT. Even more reason why he should take care of it.

SHE *goes back to her typing.*

CLIENT. He thinks things just get done by themselves . . . he's careless, and then you discover all these details which make everything so difficult, and they create embarrassing situations like this one now. You feel you're bothering me and I feel very embarrassed, but you must realise it's not your fault, or my fault, it's his fault, it's because he's so careless. The hat, for instance, he shouldn't have left it behind . . . I'm sure it's been a bother to you.

SHE (*stops typing*). The hat? No.

CLIENT. I'm sure it has.

SHE. My brother thought it was my father's hat.

CLIENT. I knew it . . .

SHE. But it hasn't bothered us at all.

CLIENT. You're very kind.

SHE *types again. Pause.*

SHE (*stops typing*). Are you sure you can't sign it?

CLIENT. No, please, don't insist, I can't. (*Stands up.*) Don't insist.

SHE. Sorry.

CLIENT. No need to apologise . . .

*The* CLIENT *walks towards the proscenium and stands there looking towards the audience a while.* SHE *stands up with a sheet of paper in her hand and disappears through the stage right door.*

CLIENT. Look at them, totally unaware of what's happening here, they walk right in front of us going God knows where . . . (*Pause.*) It's at these difficult moments that such thoughts get into your head, then time goes by, and I myself might walk by one day not thinking and someone in here will be thinking the same thing . . . How many times must it have happened already, do you know? (*He turns round.*)

SHE (*appearing through the stage right door without the papers*). No, I don't. (SHE *sits down and writes by hand. The* CLIENT *also sits.*)

CLIENT. I must seem very insensitive to you.

SHE. No, on the contrary.

CLIENT. Well, you can't be frank . . . not with me.

SHE (*stops writing*). Yes I can, and, in fact, there is some clear . . . evidence.

CLIENT. Evidence?

SHE. The signatures . . . your refusal to sign a simple piece of paper, as if you didn't want to put an end to something which is obviously painful . . .

CLIENT. Do you think so?

SHE. I'm sure so. It doesn't happen very often but it's not completely out of the ordinary.

CLIENT. Do you mean people sign no problem?

SHE. Yes, that's usually the way. (*Pause.*) On the other hand, you could interpret signing as an act of conviction, of strength.

*Pause.*

CLIENT. I suppose so.

SHE. It's not very common in the same day and less still in the same afternoon, to find both kinds of behaviour.

CLIENT. You mean to sign and not to sign?

SHE. Being sensitive and strong at the same time.

*Pause.*

CLIENT. No, it's up to my brother. He should've done it, I . . . can't. (*He stands up.*) I think I'm ready to go in.

SHE. Are you sure?

*Pause.*

CLIENT. Yes.

SHE *walks him to the upstage door, and they both disappear. Black.*

## ACT TWO

SHE *is discovered in profile, sitting at her desk. The door
which was upstage before is now stage right, and the one stage
left is now upstage, as if the room had turned ninety degrees to
the right. Stage left we can now see a large glass door with a
glass frame around it. It has horizontal stripes of smoked glass
through which we can distinguish the street where we can see
it's already late afternoon. The proscenium steps leading to the
stalls are still there. The hat-stand with the hat on it is next to
the stage right door. SHE is typing. A WOMAN appears
through the glass door.*

WOMAN. Good afternoon.

SHE (*stops typing*). My father isn't here yet.

WOMAN. We arranged to meet at this time . . .

SHE. I'm sorry. (*Pause.*) Please take a seat . . .

WOMAN (*sitting down*). It's not your fault.

SHE. He shouldn't be long . . . but I told you that yesterday.

WOMAN. And the day before yesterday . . . but don't worry . . .

SHE. That isn't his hat . . .

WOMAN. Yes, of course.

   SHE *starts typing again.*

WOMAN. It's a business matter.

SHE. Yes, you told me yesterday.

WOMAN (*takes out a card and gives it to her*). I'm not far
   from here. (SHE *tries to give it back to her.*) No, keep it.

   *Pause.*

SHE. Would you like a coffee?

WOMAN. No, thank you.

*Pause.*

WOMAN. I've got a feeling he won't come today either.

SHE. It's unforgivable.

*Pause.*

WOMAN. . . . Although I could tell you what I want, in case you haven't worked it out for yourself already . . .

SHE (*stops typing*). No I haven't, to be honest.

WOMAN. You're probably a bit too . . . cut off.

SHE. Yes, we probably are.

WOMAN. Not too much.

SHE. No.

*Pause. SHE starts typing again.*

WOMAN. Yes, I was intending to offer your father a deal, I think we'd all do well out of it.

SHE. I could talk to him if you like, I mean, if you're in a hurry, if you can't wait . . .

WOMAN. Can I have a look?

SHE (*stops typing*). A look? . . . Yes, I'll go with you if you like . . .

WOMAN. No, I don't want to bother you. (*Stands up.*) I won't go anywhere I shouldn't, don't worry.

*The WOMAN walks slowly towards stage right not opening any of the doors, comes back and sits where she was.*

WOMAN. People are strange.

SHE. What? (*Stops typing.*)

WOMAN. People are strange.

*They look each other in the eyes.*

SHE. Yes they are.

WOMAN. I've met lots of people, at their worst moments, at the most decisive moments, it's the nature of this business, and they never cease to amaze me.

*SHE starts typing again. Pause. The* WOMAN *picks up the book from the table, she opens it,* SHE *keeps typing but pays more attention to the* WOMAN, *who finally reads out:*

' . . . is very intelligent, or at least should be. People who passionately desire something should be rewarded with it.'

*She goes back to reading to herself again.* SHE *stops writing. The* WOMAN *puts the book on the table, stands up and walks to the glass door.*

It's a strange afternoon . . . (*She looks outside.*) A patisserie, a dry cleaners . . . what a strange combination. (*Pause.*) Sorry?

SHE. What?

WOMAN. Weren't you going to say something?

SHE. No.

WOMAN. Could I have a piece of paper?

*She goes to the table and notes something down on the piece of paper which* SHE *gives her, then she looks at what she's written, hesitates and tears it up keeping the bits of paper. She sits down.* SHE *starts typing again after putting the book away in the drawer.*

There's no doubt about it, your father is avoiding me.

SHE. He doesn't usually miss his appointments.

WOMAN. Do you agree with that idea?

SHE. What idea? . . .

WOMAN. That line in the book.

SHE. I can't remember it. (*Pause.*) It's only a line.

WOMAN. By the same token, someone who didn't passionately desire something shouldn't have it.

*Pause.* SHE *takes the sheet of paper off the typewriter and puts it on the table.*

SHE. If you'll excuse me . . .

SHE *stands up, disappears through the door at the back, we hear water,* SHE *comes back after a little while, sits in front of her desk, places another sheet of paper in the typewriter and starts writing. Pause.*

WOMAN. I would like not to have to do certain things, sometimes. People don't want to understand, people think a nice face should last forever . . . to go from the patisserie to the dry cleaners just like that.

SHE. Well, they're so close . . .

WOMAN. You've got a sense of humour . . .

SHE. Or at least I should have.

WOMAN. Are you upset?

SHE. No.

WOMAN. You mean yes, people say no when they mean yes.

SHE. People, people . . .

WOMAN. Me, you . . .

SHE *stops typing.*

SHE. You show up here every afternoon and put on this stupid pantomime. You must leave my father alone because he doesn't want to see you.

WOMAN. Did he tell you that?

SHE. No, he didn't, but if he wanted to see you he would've been here by now.

WOMAN. He will come, I'm sure he'll come, perhaps not today, or tomorrow, but one day . . .

SHE. But you can't come every afternoon . . . you can't!

WOMAN. I have no choice. I have to come. (*Pause.*) I know that deep down you understand me.

SHE. Because I'm very intelligent or at least I should be.

WOMAN. We should be friends, good friends, it would make these afternoons a lot more pleasant, and then your father might become less necessary, and it wouldn't be so important whether he came or not. And then he wouldn't be the main pretext for these visits which bother you so much.

SHE. I don't think that'd be possible.

WOMAN. Keeping in touch, daily contact . . . you must take that into account.

*Pause.*

SHE (*stands up*). You can wait for him in his office. In my father's office . . . (SHE *points to the proscenium steps.*)

WOMAN (*stands up*). If you like . . . (*Walks towards the steps.*)

SHE. Wait . . .

*The* WOMAN *stops. Pause. She comes back and looks straight at her.*

WOMAN. You don't hate me, maybe you did at first, but not anymore, you might even . . . be a bit fond of me. Someone who's not here for the usual, who says different things, who doesn't just pass through.

*Pause.*

SHE. Before you wouldn't even look at me, you used to just sit on that chair and not even look at me.

WOMAN. I did look at you, it was you who didn't look.

SHE. You wouldn't even talk to me, you sat on that chair and you wouldn't even talk to me.

WOMAN. I did talk to you, it was you that wouldn't listen.

*Pause.* SHE *sits down, and starts typing*

SHE. I suppose I'll have to get used to it.

WOMAN (*sits down*). Your father will see me in the end, I'm sure.

*Pause.*

SHE. Have you travelled? Since we have to talk we might as well find an interesting subject . . .

WOMAN. No, I've hardly travelled at all.

SHE. Me neither, but I have read a lot about travelling and travellers. And do you know what I miss? Details like what they've got in their suitcases, and things like that, which I find really intriguing. People leave so many things in their pockets, and many of them, with time, make holes in the lining and get lost . . . And then later, sometimes, they find them and they seem so strange to them that they become new again. To lose oneself in order to start again. (*Pause.*) Have you read the paper?

WOMAN. No, I haven't.

SHE. It doesn't say anything interesting . . . the adverts . . . some ridiculous advert, someone offering to look after old people by the hour, just like that, without any other information, without knowing them. I hardly understand anything else, well, I do, but I can't reach any conclusion like I can with the advert about the old people. Yes, things happen, nobody can doubt that, not even me, but they've already happened, if they really have happened like that. However the thing about the old people must happen or is happening at this moment. There's a difference. They've also called a bus strike, did you know that?

WOMAN. No, I didn't.

SHE. So I'll walk . . . Although three quarters of an hour . . . I like walking, but it'd be three quarters of an hour there and three quarters of an hour back. It seems a bit excessive . . . Sometimes I get off the bus a couple of stops early so I can stretch my legs. They're demanding a pay rise, and they want bus conductors back, someone to open and close the doors and sell tickets. They won't get what they want, there's a door mechanism installed at the front of the buses already . . . Do you know what that'd mean? How much does a bus cost . . . imagine changing the entire bus fleet so that the conductors can have their gadgets handy at the back of the bus, not to mention somewhere to sit, those new buses haven't got anywhere. They won't get what they want. I wonder how long the strike'll last . . . (*Pause.*) Haven't you got a cigarette? I smoke but I never have any cigarettes.

WOMAN. No, I don't smoke.

SHE. I've even got an ashtray but cigarettes . . . If I forget, I don't even smoke. Don't you think that's strange? You see, I've got no reason to smoke, that's what the doctor said about my case. Yes, as a matter of fact he said something else, but by that time I'd stopped listening to him. It was something to do with some scientific explanation which he was very pleased with, I could tell by the way he shook my hand at the end . . . as if he'd changed my life for me . . . I don't mind him having that impression, it tells you something about the character of a person . . . but it's not important either. (*Pause.*) Do you live in the city?

WOMAN. No, I don't.

SHE. You're lucky, you're a very fortunate person. People build dreams with their flower pots, their air fresheners, their music, even with animals, but the air, that certain feeling, it can't be disguised, it's to do with the limits, the straight lines, the indirect lights, the noises . . . too many things to be disguised all at the same time, and most people, of course, make the choice of surrendering to them, with abandon. There's nothing else they can do. (SHE *glances at her watch.*) Do you know what time it is? My watch has stopped . . .

WOMAN. No, I haven't got a watch.

SHE. The battery must've run out, I've had it for two years . . . and this is the first time it's stopped. I used to have one hanging on a chain round my neck, but it wasn't very practical, I can't remember how many times I had to disentangle it from this very typewriter, and eating . . . in the end I left it at home. I still wind it every evening, it's never stopped . . . it's almost a superstition, I have the feeling that if it stopped one day I'd stop with it . . . I know it's ridiculous, but that's what happens when you've had something so long. I only look at this one when it's absolutely necessary, and now it's stopped, I don't care, well, it's a bit annoying because right now I don't know what time it is exactly, but as the phone's so near I can find out immediately, by the way, hardly anyone's phoned this afternoon . . . In all the time you've been here the phone hasn't rung once, has it?

WOMAN. No, it hasn't.

SHE. It's a funny thing about phone calls . . . people's voices . . . how the same words are repeated . . . I'm lucky, when people phone here they're rather laconic, there isn't much to say, and I don't encourage them either, it wouldn't be right. Sometimes someone talks more than they should but the others make up for it . . . Yes, every now and then a joke. In bad taste. But I expect that now, one a day, two, if it's three it starts to get a bit much, it puts me in a bad mood and, since I can't unplug the phone . . . but on the whole it's not an enemy . . . the phone. Nor is it a friend, too many unknown voices. However, you can imagine so many things, of course there is no such thing as complete certainty, but who needs it? You only have to listen, that's all . . . (*Pause.*) Don't you think it's a bit chilly?

WOMAN. No, I don't think so.

SHE. I'm always cold, well, it's always a bit chilly here, I'm not complaining, with a jacket on it's not a problem but, after all, this is a warm country, or it was, we're a lot further south than most, a bit more heat shouldn't bother me . . . These days when the sun can't make its mind up have a special appeal, afternoons and mornings are easily confused, and then suddenly it's night, which there can be no doubt about . . . If I had to choose a moment in the day, I'd choose this one, although without a watch . . . I imagine it's . . . It doesn't matter, around this time, when the streets are almost in darkness. It's the time to check that you've done the most important things because you've got less time left . . . (*Pause.*) There's very little light, don't you think?

WOMAN. Yes, perhaps.

SHE *turns the lights on.*

SHE. That's better . . . (*Pause.*) Are you sure you don't want a coffee?

WOMAN. No, thank you.

SHE. I haven't made any, but it'd only take a moment . . . The coffee machine's in my father's office . . . (*Pause.*) To be honest, I'm glad you don't want any, the machine's a bit old and you have to give it a good thump to get it going. We need a new one, I never stop telling him but it doesn't do any good. And a coffee machine is indispensable in a place like this, people always welcome a coffee if you offer it nicely, it's a kind thought, as well as a . . . public service. And it's not that expensive, but he doesn't realise, he thinks it's superfluous, unnecessary. But whenever he feels like having a decent coffee he's in the café round the corner in no time . . . If you ask for him in there, they all know him, I'm sure they've even got a nickname for him. People like giving nicknames round here . . . (*Pause.*) Are you from round here?

WOMAN. No, I' m not.

SHE. But you've probably noticed. They pay a lot of attention to what happens in the street, any unusual noise, any noticeable murmur and they all come out to see what's happening . . . but no-one stays till the end . . . The other day, for instance, a woman was run over . . . yes, they all came out, but when they saw the woman was up on her feet, they went off without even asking her if she needed . . . help . . . or to be taken to hospital . . . Maybe one or two asked, but believe me, they didn't insist enough for the woman to accept the offer, and it was obvious she needed some assistance, she could have suffered internal wounds which, from the outside, . . . but they didn't insist, the poor thing just left on her own, talking to herself and feeling her left elbow . . . I could have asked her in but this place is in- timidating, as you know, and under the circumstances . . . it would've been rude even. (*Pause.*) I wonder if I'll be like them one day. It's a very common question, anyone could ask themselves, the difficult thing is to be completely sincere about the answer. Because you could leave it as a question, as if you were opening it, and leave it at that, without closing it, without answering, just leave it for tomorrow, for another day . . . (*The* WOMAN *interrupts her.*)

WOMAN. It's late. I must go. (*She stands up and walks to the glass door stage left. She stops.*) I'll come back tomorrow.

*The* WOMAN *exits through the glass door. Pause.* SHE *exhales deeply, then walks towards the glass door and stands there looking out attentively. Pause. The* CLIENT *enters through the stage right door, takes a handkerchief out of his pocket and dries his forehead, looks at the hat, then without making any noise he exits through the door at the back. Noise of water.* SHE *turns round, sits at her desk. Seconds later, the* CLIENT *appears again at the same time as* SHE *starts writing by hand.*

CLIENT (*wondering whether to take a seat*). Sorry, will you be here for long?

SHE. Yes, a while . . . but my father stays all night.

CLIENT. Ah . . .

SHE. Are you leaving now?

CLIENT. Yes, I think so. (*He sits down.*)

SHE. Are you all right?

CLIENT. Yes, yes.

*Pause.*

SHE. Your brother isn't here yet.

*Pause.*

CLIENT. Do you think it would be inappropriate if someone like me, in my circumstances, went to the theatre tonight?

SHE. Sorry?

CLIENT. You see, I've got two tickets for tonight . . . booked a couple of months ago. What do you think?

SHE. I don't know.

CLIENT. You're right, it's not very appropriate.

SHE. I didn't say that, go if you want to.

CLIENT. It's just that on my own . . . I don't dare ask anyone I
know . . . It makes me feel funny . . .

SHE. I understand.

*Pause.*

CLIENT. You wouldn't by any chance like to come to the
theatre this evening? It's only a play to while away the time,
it's not funny or anything like that, it's a serious drama . . .
a family drama. I've read the review and it sounds OK.
I know it's a bit sudden and we hardly know each other, but
I thought you might not have anything to do this evening
and you might fancy . . .

SHE. The thing is I don't know what time I'll be leaving, it
depends on my father and . . .

CLIENT. It doesn't matter, I understand, I shouldn't have
offered, it was stupid. What must you be thinking of me . . .

SHE. No, it's not a bad idea, honestly . . . (*Pause.*) What about
your brother? You could go with him.

CLIENT. With my brother? He doesn't like the theatre, and
anyway he wouldn't approve, he doesn't approve of anything I do or say, I'd rather take anyone but him . . . I don't
mean you because I already know you, it's just that . . .
I thought . . . God, what a fool I'm making of myself . . .

SHE. No, I understand . . .

CLIENT. It's very kind of you but I shouldn't have said
anything. Forget it, I probably won't go to the theatre, I'll
give the tickets away or I'll sell them. (*Pause.*) Please don't
tell anyone.

SHE. No, of course not.

CLIENT. And especially not my brother . . . He wouldn't
understand. (*Pause.*) I even know the plot of the play, it's
about a married couple going on a trip, but suddenly all
sorts of things start to happen so they can't go no matter

how hard they try, because the trip is very important for their relationship . . . told like that it sounds like a sitcom, but I assure you it's not. In the end, as you can imagine, there's no trip and they split up.

SHE. Sounds familiar.

CLIENT. Really?

SHE. Yes, I think I've read something . . .

CLIENT. Have you read the play?

SHE. No, the review, like you.

CLIENT. Ah . . .

*Pause.*

CLIENT. It's a pity to waste the tickets.

SHE. Someone'll use them.

CLIENT. How?

SHE. If you give them or sell them to someone . . .

CLIENT. Ah . . . (*Pause.*) I was thinking that you won't get your signatures if my brother doesn't turn up . . . and that would be terrible . . . I could phone him, but at this time . . . I feel responsible . . . I could take the hat myself but you wouldn't get your signatures . . . it wouldn't be fair . . . although if I signed . . .

SHE (*looks at him*). Do you think you could?

CLIENT. Well no, I don't feel strong enough.

SHE *keeps writing by hand.*

CLIENT. What a situation . . . you need two signatures and I need someone to go to the theatre with, it all comes down to two . . .

SHE. Two what?

CLIENT. Two things, two signatures, two tickets, two people . . .

*Pause.*

SHE. Your brother might still come.

*The* CLIENT *stands up.*

CLIENT. If you see him, please tell him . . . Don't tell him anything, he'll work it out.

SHE. Fine.

*The* CLIENT *walks towards the glass door.*

CLIENT (*stops*). If he doesn't come, you can phone me . . . I think you've got my number.

SHE. No, I've got your brother's.

*Pause.*

CLIENT. Well . . . goodbye.

SHE. Goodbye.

*The* CLIENT *disappears through the glass door.* SHE *looks in the direction he left while we go to black.*

## ACT THREE

*Night. The stage is empty. The room has been turned another
ninety degrees stage right so that the desk is now seen from
behind, the glass door is upstage, the two identical doors on
both sides and the hat-stand next to the steps leading to the
stalls. There is only one new element, leaning against the glass
door, on the floor, there is a funeral wreath of modest size.
After a while the* FRIEND *appears through the glass door with
a small bunch of flowers, he enters shyly, stays by the door,
and notices the wreath on the floor, then looks at his bunch of
flowers rather disconcertedly and immediately after we hear
the noise of water coming from the door stage right. Pause.*
SHE *appears through the stage right door.*

SHE (*surprised*). Hello . . .

FRIEND. Hello.

SHE *walks over to the desk and sits down.*

SHE (*after a pause*). Sit down, don't stand over there.

*The* FRIEND *moves towards her and offers her the bunch of
flowers.*

FRIEND. If I'd known there was a patisserie across the road, I
would have brought you a box of chocolates. (SHE *puts the
flowers on the desk and sits down.*) Do you mind me
coming here?

SHE. No.

FRIEND. I've spoken to your brother, he phoned me . . . he
seems like a . . . nice kid.

SHE. He's not a kid.

FRIEND. I wanted to give you a surprise.

SHE. Did he tell you he wanted a job at the Council as well?

FRIEND. Yes, I think he did . . . but he told me so many things
that . . .

*SHE looks at some papers with her back to the audience
while the FRIEND, at the other side of the desk, faces the
audience.*

Are you upset?

SHE. That's the second time today I've been asked that.

FRIEND. Are you?

SHE. No, I'm . . . surprised. (SHE *stands up and walks to the
glass door. He looks at his hands.*)

FRIEND. Do you mind if I wash my hands . . . ? The flowers
were wrapped in newspaper and they're covered in ink.

*He looks in her direction. SHE indicates the stage right
door with her extended arm. The FRIEND disappears.
Noise of water. SHE returns to the desk after a while, sits
down and sorts through a file. The FRIEND enters from the
stage right door and sits opposite her.*

FRIEND. I thought we could go to the pictures . . .

SHE. For one horrible moment I thought you were going to
say the theatre.

FRIEND. Why?

SHE. It doesn't matter.

*Pause.*

FRIEND. Why didn't you want me to find out where you
worked?

SHE. I think I told you at the start.

FRIEND. No, you didn't . . . or at least you weren't clear
enough for me to understand you.

SHE. I never am, you know that.

FRIEND. And that's why you asked your brother to tell me.

SHE (*stops working*). No, he did that on his own. (*Gets on with her work again.*) One of these days he'll invite you over to his house and he'll show you his son who has the strange feature of only having three fingers on one of his hands.

*Pause.*

FRIEND. Which one?

*They look at each other and start laughing.*

FRIEND. Will you be long?

SHE. I'm waiting for my father.

FRIEND. So I'll meet him.

SHE. No, it's better if you don't.

FRIEND. Do you want me to go before he gets here?

SHE. The thing is he doesn't like strangers.

FRIEND. I'm not a stranger.

SHE. He'll be tired . . .

FRIEND. We'll leave straight away. The last showing's at ten forty-five.

SHE (*stands up and sits down on the chair next to the FRIEND on the other side of the desk*). I don't feel like going to the pictures.

SHE *holds his hands.*

FRIEND. What do you feel like?

SHE *shrugs.*

FRIEND. The film sounds goood. It's about a woman who's just got divorced and goes to live in the country on her own, to a house where there was a terrible crime fifty years before . . . (*Pause.*) We could see a different film if you want . . .

SHE. Couldn't we go another day . . . ? Or you could go on your own . . .

FRIEND. On my own?

SHE. I'm a bit tired.

FRIEND. Well then we won't go to the pictures . . . (SHE *lets go of his hands.*)

SHE. We could go to my place.

FRIEND. All right, but we could go somewhere first . . .

SHE. Or to yours . . .

FRIEND. Of course, but . . . don't you fancy . . . I don't know . . . doing something?

SHE. Something? What do you mean by something?

FRIEND. Before we go to my place or yours.

SHE. We'll do something at my place or yours.

FRIEND. What's wrong?

SHE (*stands up*). Nothing's wrong. (*Walks towards the glass door.*)

FRIEND. You're angry I came here . . . I'm sorry, but I thought it'd make it easier. I don't mind you working here.

SHE. You don't mind?

FRIEND. It's just like any other job, also . . . you don't . . . I mean . . . you're in here . . .

SHE. Yes, I'm in here. And I hardly see them if that's what you mean.

FRIEND (*stands up*). It's stupid, let's stop talking about it.

SHE. But, we've hardly talked at all, we've hardly touched the subject.

FRIEND. There's no need.

SHE. Yes there is, it's why you came.

FRIEND. No, I came to take you to the pictures. (*Gets closer to her.*) What do you want to do?

SHE. Talk, can we talk?

FRIEND. We're already talking.

SHE. Let's carry on then.

FRIEND. What do you want to talk about? (*Goes behind her and puts his arms round her.*) It's late . . .

SHE. Yes, you're right, and I haven't done anything else all afternoon.

FRIEND. You see? (*Turns her round and kisses her.*) You're not angry anymore, are you? (*They kiss.*) I couldn't bear it if you left me.

SHE *pulls away.*

SHE. Why do you have to spoil everything?

FRIEND. What have I done?

SHE. It is not what you've done but what you've said . . . That you couldn't bear it . . .

FRIEND. Well, it's true . . .

SHE *walks to the typewriter and writes as she speaks.*

SHE. 'I couldn't bear it if you left me'. (*Takes the paper from the typewriter.*) Go on . . . sign it . . .

FRIEND. What?

SHE. Sign it.

*Pause.*

FRIEND. If you like . . . (*He signs.*)

SHE. You can't think of any other 'expressions'?

FRIEND. Why do you treat me like this?

SHE. That's what I'm talking about.

FRIEND. I don't understand you.

SHE. Carry on . . .

FRIEND. Don't you love me anymore?

SHE. Better and better . . .

FRIEND. What's wrong with you today?

SHE. I've heard that one before too.

FRIEND. Do you want me to go?

*Pause. The* FRIEND *puts the piece of paper in his pocket.*

SHE. Do you want to go?

FRIEND. I shouldn't have brought the flowers.

SHE. It's not that.

FRIEND. Tell me what I've done that's so terrible.

SHE. Sorry . . .

FRIEND. No, don't apologise now . . . tell me . . . (*Pause.*)
Don't you think it's worth it . . . that I won't understand?
(*He grabs her by the arm.*) Tell me . . . Do you think I'm
stupid . . . or what?

*Through the glass door we see the silhouette of a very tall
man, The* FRIEND *jumps back at the unexpected
apparition. The* OTHER CLIENT *enters.*

OTHER CLIENT. Good evening . . . (*To her.*) Do you
remember me?

SHE. Yes.

OTHER CLIENT. I came for my hat and, while I'm here, to
confirm tomorrow's appointment.

SHE. It's there . . . (*Points to the hat-stand.*)

OTHER CLIENT. Thank you.

*The* OTHER CLIENT *goes for the hat while* SHE *goes to
her desk to look at some papers.*

OTHER CLIENT. It is eleven o'clock, isn't it?

SHE (*looking at a sheet of paper*). Yes, eleven o'clock.

*The* OTHER CLIENT *brushes the hat with his hand as if to
knock the dust off it.*

OTHER CLIENT. Did my brother come?

SHE. Yes, this afternoon . . . ah, by the way, I need two signatures from you.

OTHER CLIENT (*looks at the* FRIEND *and then at her*). You want me to sign something?

SHE. Yes, I need them this evening or first thing in the morning.

*Pause.*

OTHER CLIENT. I'll sign now. (*While* SHE *gets the papers ready.*) My brother . . . did he stay very long?

SHE. Almost all afternoon.

OTHER CLIENT. Are you sure?

SHE. Yes. (*Pause.*) Here it is . . .

*The* OTHER CLIENT *takes his time to sign, he even sits down.* SHE *and the* FRIEND *look at each other for a few seconds.*

OTHER CLIENT. Anything else?

SHE. No, that's all.

OTHER CLIENT (*stands up*). In that case, I'll see you tomorrow.

SHE. Good-bye.

FRIEND. Good-bye.

*The* OTHER CLIENT *disappears through the glass door.*

FRIEND. What a sinister character.

SHE (*looking at the paper*). Look . . . the two signatures are different . . .

*The* FRIEND *gets closer and looks at the paper.*

FRIEND. He must've signed for his brother.

SHE *puts piece of paper away in a drawer. The* FRIEND *picks the flowers up.*

I'll take these ridiculous flowers away.

SHE. No, leave them.

FRIEND. No, I'll take them away . . .

SHE. Wait . . . (SHE *takes them from his hands and smells them.*) I don't know what's wrong with me today . . .

FRIEND. I can't leave you on your own.

SHE. I'm not on my own.

*Pause.*

FRIEND. Do you mean . . . ? (*He looks at the stalls.*) I don't know how you can joke about those things.

SHE. I'm not joking.

FRIEND. Really?

SHE. Listen . . . (*Looks at the stalls.*) Nothing. (*Pause.*) Why are you looking at me like that?

FRIEND. Are you all right?

SHE. You've been talking to my brother too much . . . (*Puts the flowers on the table.*) He thinks I should get a job at the Council with him.

FRIEND. It's not a bad idea.

SHE. But he'll never get a job there.

*Pause.*

FRIEND. We could get married . . .

SHE. Yes, one day.

FRIEND. I'm serious.

SHE. So am I.

FRIEND (*cheerful*). You could type it and I could sign it.

SHE. No . . .

FRIEND. Yes, like before . . .

SHE. Stop it.

FRIEND. I'll write it myself . . . (*Goes to the typewriter.*)

SHE (*moving it away*). No.

> *Pause.*

FRIEND. Well . . . I'd better go . . . I'll call you. (*He goes towards the door.*)

SHE. Will you pick me up tomorrow? I'll introduce you to my father. (*Pause.*) It's cold, wrap up warm.

> *The* FRIEND, *by the door, puts his collar up.*

> *Pause. He opens the door.*

FRIEND. Listen . . .

SHE. What . . .

FRIEND. I . . . (SHE *interrupts him.*)

SHE. Yes, me too.

FRIEND. What . . .

SHE. So do I.

> *Pause.*

FRIEND. Bye.

SHE. See you tomorrow.

> *The* FRIEND *disappears through the glass door. SHE sits down, types, moments later we hear the screech of car brakes, SHE continues typing for a little while, then SHE suddenly stops, gets up and walks to the glass door to look out. After a few seconds, The FATHER appears through the glass door.*

SHE. Are you all right?

FATHER. It was a woman . . . I think she's OK. (*They both look out.*)

SHE. D'you think?

FATHER. Yes, I saw it from a distance.

SHE. Didn't you go and see what had happened?

FATHER. No, some people had already come out . . .

SHE. It might've been serious.

FATHER. I don't think so, she got to her feet by herself.

*He walks to the hat-stand and hangs his hat up as he speaks.*

SHE. That doesn't mean much.

FATHER. What did you want me to do . . . ? There were already lots of people there . . . (*He disappears through the stage left door. Pause.* SHE *is still looking out.*) Who's been messing about in here . . . ? (*Pause. He appears through the stage left door.*) What's happening? (*He goes towards the glass door.*) You can't see a thing.

SHE. D'you think she's all right?

FATHER. How do you think I should know . . . (*They look at each other.*) Did you want me to bring her in here, or something . . . ? It would have been embarrassing, don't you think?

*Pause.*

SHE. You're right.

FATHER. Who's been messing about in the office?

SHE. Nobody.

FATHER. Nobody?

SHE. It might've been me, I had to find a piece of paper . . .

FATHER. And did you find it?

SHE. Yes.

FATHER (*ironically*). I am pleased. (*He disappears again through the stage left door. Pause.*) Did anyone call for me?

SHE. What?

VOICE OF THE FATHER. I asked if anyone had called for me . . .

SHE. No, no-one.

*Pause. The* FATHER *appears in the stage left doorway.*

FATHER. Aren't you going?

SHE. Yes, in a minute.

*The* FATHER *disappears through the stage left door.* SHE *sits at her desk and starts typing.*

VOICE OF THE FATHER. Can't you leave it 'til tomorrow? I've got a headache.

SHE *stops typing.* SHE *walks to the stage left door, disappears and shuts the door behind her. Long pause.* SHE *appears again, goes over to the desk and picks up some papers as* SHE *speaks.*

SHE. I don't think it's asking much . . .

FATHER. It's out of the question.

SHE. What if I find someone to stand in for me?

VOICE OF THE FATHER. Who . . . your brother?

SHE. No, someone else.

VOICE OF THE FATHER. A temp?

SHE. Yes, it'd only be for a few days . . .

*Pause. The* FATHER *appears in the stage left doorway.*

FATHER. Wait 'til summer like everyone else. There's always less work in the summer.

SHE. I've been telling you for months.

FATHER. It's not long . . .

SHE. I don't want to go in the summer, there are too many people everywhere.

*Pause.*

FATHER. Go whenever you want, go tonight if you like, but don't get anyone in, I'll manage on my own.

*He exits through the stage left door slamming it.* SHE *looks at the door, walks over there and opens it.*

SHE. It'll only be a week, you won't even notice.

VOICE OF THE FATHER. Don't be silly.

SHE *walks to the glass door. The* FATHER *appears in the stage left doorway.*

FATHER. I could give your brother a chance . . .

SHE. Yes, you could.

FATHER. But he's so useless . . .

*Pause.* SHE *goes back to her desk to carry on tidying up.*

FATHER. And you really can't wait 'til summer?

SHE. No.

FATHER. Do you know when was the last time I took a holiday?

SHE. Yes, I know. (*Pause.*) I'm going anyway.

*The* FATHER *disappears through the stage left door.*

VOICE OF THE FATHER. I can't find anything . . . I leave this place for a few hours . . .

SHE (*goes to the stage right doorway*). What're you looking for?

FATHER. Nothing.

*Pause.*

SHE. I'm going to walk.

VOICE OF THE FATHER. Well go then, go . . .

SHE. I'm going on holiday so I can go walking.

VOICE OF THE FATHER. You can do what you like on your holidays.

SHE. I just wanted you to know. (SHE *returns to her desk. The* FATHER *appears in the stage left doorway.*)

FATHER. And where are you going?

SHE. I don't know yet.

FATHER. Oh, you don't know . . .

SHE. No.

FATHER. Are you going with anyone?

SHE. I don't know that either.

*Pause.*

FATHER. It all seems rather up in the air.

SHE. I'm going.

FATHER. You're going. (*He disappears through the stage left door. Pause. She walks to the doorway.*)

SHE. I'll tell you the dates tomorrow. (*Pause.*) If you want me to I could find someone . . .

VOICE OF THE FATHER. No.

*Pause.*

SHE. I've also been thinking about getting married.

*Pause.*

VOICE OF THE FATHER. Are you going on holiday to get married?

SHE. No, I'm going so I can go walking.

VOICE OF THE FATHER. And who are you planning to marry?

SHE. You don't know him.

SHE *returns to her desk. Pause. The* FATHER *appears in the doorway.*

FATHER. Are you sure you want to get married?

SHE. No, I'm just thinking about it.

FATHER. What about him?

SHE. He's thinking about it too.

*Pause.*

FATHER. You'll let me know anything . . . definite.

*The* FATHER *disappears through the stage left door.*

SHE. Did you find what you were looking for?

VOICE OF THE FATHER. No.

*The telephone rings.*

VOICE OF THE FATHER. I'll get it. (*Closes the door.*)

*SHE walks to the desk, picks up the flowers, puts them back on the desk again, sits down. Pause. The FATHER appears through the stage left door.*

FATHER. You still here?

*He crosses and disappears through the stage right door. Noise of water. He opens the door and speaks from within the bathroom.*

The towel needs changing . . . (*Pause.*) Uh, what's wrong with this . . . ! (*The noise of water continues.*)

SHE. What's happening?

VOICE OF THE FATHER. I can't turn the tap off.

*SHE goes out through the stage right door.*

VOICE OF THE FATHER. It's broken . . .

HER VOICE. I'll close the stopcock.

*The noise of water can still be heard for a moment before it dies out.*

HER VOICE. I'll call a plumber tomorrow.

VOICE OF THE FATHER. No, your brother can do it . . .

HER VOICE. It'd be better to call a plumber.

VOICE OF THE FATHER. It's nothing . . .

HER VOICE. Get out, don't tread water everywhere . . .

*The FATHER appears through the stage right door.*

HER VOICE. It's been dripping for quite a while.

FATHER. Why didn't you tell me?

HER VOICE. I thought you'd noticed . . .

FATHER. I can't do everything. (*He moves stage left.*)

SHE (*appears through the stage right door*). The coffee machine's . . . broken.

FATHER. I know.

*He disappears through the stage left door and closes it. SHE goes to her desk to finish tidying the rest of the stuff while through the glass window we can see the BROTHER's silhouette. He stands still for a few seconds before entering. SHE turns round.*

SHE. What are you doing here?

BROTHER. Is he here . . . ? (*He looks stage left.*)

SHE. Yes.

BROTHER. Are you leaving already?

SHE. Is there something wrong?

BROTHER. Don't shout . . . (*Looks to the left.*) I don't want him to know I'm here. (*Sits on one of the chairs and covers his face with both his hands.*) I've done something terrible . . .

SHE. What are you talking about?

BROTHER. I didn't mean to, I swear . . .

SHE. But . . . What?

BROTHER. You must believe me.

SHE. What's happened?

*SHE sits in front of him. He speaks with his hands over his face and it's impossible to understand what he's saying.*

I can't hear you . . . (*He takes his hands from his face.*) What's happened?

BROTHER. Don't look at me like that . . . (*Pause.*) We argued again . . . like we always do, about something stupid, I can't even remember what . . . and then by accident . . . I shut the door just to slam it, I swear . . . you must believe me . . .

SHE. Which door?

BROTHER. Which door? . . . I don't know, a door . . . the
kitchen door . . . the sitting room door, the one between the
kitchen and the sitting room, and she was still there, next to
the door . . . because I shut it without looking, and then I
heard her fall and I, I . . .

SHE. You what?

BROTHER. I went out, I left, I couldn't . . .

SHE. You left her there on the floor?

BROTHER. Yes, yes . . .

SHE *stands up.*

SHE. Come on.

BROTHER. Where?

SHE. To your place.

BROTHER. No, not yet.

SHE. Come on . . . (*Takes him by the arm.*)

BROTHER. Wait . . . (*Pause.*) The thing is I didn't see her fall.

SHE. You didn't see her on the floor?

BROTHER. I only heard her.

SHE (*sits down*). You only heard her . . .

BROTHER. Yes, a solitary thud . . . I can still hear it . . . here . . .
(*He covers his ears. Pause.* SHE *picks up the phone.*) Who
are you phoning?

SHE. Who do you think?

BROTHER. The police?

SHE. Your house.

BROTHER. No, wait. (*Makes her replace the receiver.*) Wait a
moment . . . (*Stands up and walks from stage right to stage
left and back again looking down, he finally stops.*)

SHE. Can I ring now?

BROTHER. No, wait . . . (*He goes to the stage right door and disappears.*)

SHE. There's no water.

*The* BROTHER *appears again.*

BROTHER. What do you mean there's no water . . . ?

SHE. The tap's broken and I had to close the stopcock. (*Pause.*) Can I phone?

BROTHER. All right, go on . . . you're dying to do it. And, if you want to, you can tell him later. (*He points stage left.*)

SHE *phones, waits with the receiver next to her ear for a few seconds, then moves the receiver away from it.*

VOICE OF THE PHONE. Hello . . . hello . . . Who is it? . . .

*We hear them hang up.* SHE *holds the receiver up for a few seconds looking at the* BROTHER *and then hangs up.*

SHE. She's OK.

BROTHER. Are you sure you didn't dial the wrong number?

SHE. No . . . but if you want to phone . . .

BROTHER. Do you think it was her voice?

SHE. Yes.

BROTHER (*looking up*). Thank you, Lord . . . (*He sits down.*) Are you completely sure it was her voice?

SHE. Who else could it be?

BROTHER. I don't know, a friend.

SHE. No, it was her.

BROTHER. Thank you. (*He touches her hand.*)

SHE. Leave me alone. (SHE *stands up.*)

BROTHER. I'm sorry, it won't happen again, I won't argue anymore, I won't bother you with my problems anymore.

SHE. And you won't poke your nose into my business?

BROTHER. I swear. From now on I'll be a different person . . .
I'll make the most of this second chance . . . everything's
going to change . . . (*He stands up and walks towards the
glass door.*) I'll do anything, I'll leave all this behind,
tonight was a warning . . . it was the stress, really . . . (*He
turns to her.*) it's a warning for both of us, so that we both
change, don't you see?

SHE. I'm going on holiday next week.

BROTHER. Good, but it's not enough . . . I know, I'll find
something for you at the Council.

SHE. Forget it.

BROTHER. I owe it to you, I have to do something for you, let
me do it, please, let me . . .

SHE. All right, do something for me, something you can do
really well.

BROTHER. What? Just say it . . .

SHE. Take my place here while I am away, I won't be more
than a week . . .

BROTHER. Your place?

SHE. Yes, here, at my desk. I'll tell you what you have to do
before I go, you'll be fine. (*Pause.*) What's the matter?

BROTHER. I can't, I don't know anything about . . . all this.

SHE. I'll teach you.

BROTHER. Why do you have to go?

SHE. A minute ago you thought it was a good idea.

BROTHER. You just want to tie me here so I can't go to the
Council, you don't want a job there yourself and so you
don't want me to go either.

SHE. I just want to go on holiday.

BROTHER. I've still got opportunities. I'm not indispensable.
Anyone can do what I do . . .

SHE. All right, don't take my place for me, I'll find someone else.

BROTHER. Yes, that's a good idea, find someone else . . . Have you told him yet?

SHE. Do you care?

BROTHER. Well, I wouldn't want any last minute changes.

SHE. Me neither.

*Pause.*

BROTHER. Let's not argue. What I want is for us to get on well together, to be friends.

SHE. I think you'd better go home.

BROTHER. We can't leave it like this.

SHE. It's late.

BROTHER. Ask me for anything else.

SHE. I don't want anything.

BROTHER. You always ask me to do things I can't do.

SHE. You could do it perfectly well.

BROTHER. You see? That's how we started arguing at home, over nothing.

*Pause.*

SHE. Go on, go.

*Pause. He walks towards the glass door and stops.*

BROTHER. Would you go back home now?

SHE. Yes.

BROTHER. Do you want me to take you home first? I've got the car . . .

SHE. No, I'll take the bus.

BROTHER. As you wish . . . bye. (*He opens the glass door.*)

SHE. Wait . . . (SHE *takes the flowers and gives them to him.*)
You might need these.

BROTHER. You think so . . . ?

*He disappears through the glass door. SHE looks out for a while, then goes stage right, disappears and appears again putting on a coat. SHE gets her bag, goes stage left and opens the door.*

SHE. I'm off . . .

VOICE OF THE FATHER. What did he want?

SHE. What?

VOICE OF THE FATHER. I heard you.

SHE. Nothing . . .

VOICE OF THE FATHER. Are you sure?

SHE. Why didn't you come out if you were interested?

VOICE OF THE FATHER. Why didn't you call me?

SHE. I sorted it out on my own.

VOICE OF THE FATHER. That's what I thought.

SHE. All right . . . see you tomorrow.

VOICE OF THE FATHER. See you tomorrow.

*SHE walks to the glass door, stops there, goes back to the desk, gets the book from the drawer, puts it in her hand bag and then goes back to the glass door, and stops at the sight of her FATHER by the stage left doorway.*

FATHER. Go on holiday . . . and if you want to find someone for the mornings, I'll stay for the afternoons.

SHE. You?

FATHER. Yes, me.

SHE. I could find someone to stay all day and then you'd only have to come at night, like you do now.

FATHER. No, find someone just for the mornings.

SHE. It's too much, afternoons and nights . . .

FATHER. If it's only for a week, I'll manage.

SHE. But . . .

FATHER. Don't you think we're a bit cut off? (*Goes to the glass door.*) I've been thinking it might be time for a move. It'd have to be during the summer, of course . . .

SHE. Where to?

FATHER. The centre of town, where else . . . (*He looks out.*) It's a strange night.

SHE. Strange?

FATHER. When you come back I might have decided already . . . I might decide on one of those afternoons you're away walking. (*Pause.*) Go, it's late. (*He opens the glass door.*) Wrap up warm, it's cold.

SHE. Wouldn't it be better if . . . ?

FATHER. We'll talk tomorrow.

*Pause.*

SHE. Yes, we'll talk.

SHE *disappears through the glass door. The* FATHER *locks the door, picks up the funeral wreath and goes towards the proscenium steps while we go to black.*

# WOLF KISSES

*by*

## PALOMA PEDRERO

*translated by Roxana Silbert*

Paloma Pedrero was born in Madrid in 1957. She is an actress, a director and a playwright. Her produced plays include: *La llamada de Lauren* (1984), *Resguardo personal* (1985), *El color de Agosto* (1987), *Besos de Lobo* (1986), *Las fresas mágicas* (1988), *Noches de amor efímero* (1989), *Una Estrella* (1990), *Aliento de Equilibrista* (1993), *Locas de amar* (1994), *La Noche que ilumina* (1995), and *En el tunel un pájaro* (1997). Her plays have been translated into English, French, Portuguese, Catalan, Polish, German and Italian. She has had work produced in France, the U.S., Brazil, Argentina, Cuba, Chile and Germany. She has been awarded several prizes, including the Tirso de Molina. She writes for various publications, and she is a member of the editorial team of the magazine *Primer Acto*. She also runs directing and playwriting workshops.

*Wolf Kisses (Besos de Lobo)* was first performed in English as a rehearsed reading in the *Voices from Spain* season in the Theatre Upstairs on 12 April, 1997 with the following cast.

| | |
|---|---|
| LUCIANO | Russell Barr |
| ANA | Iona Carbarns |
| RAUL | Kenny Doughty |
| AGUSTIN | Roy Hanlon |
| CAMILO | Kenneth Bryans |

*Director*   Philip Howard
*Translator*   Roxana Silbert

**Characters**

ANA

LUCIANO, *her friend*

CAMILO, *her suitor*

AGUSTIN, *her father*

RAUL, *her fiancé*

*The action takes place in Jara, an imaginary small Spanish town at the beginning of the 1970s.*

## ACT ONE

### Scene One

*The railway station in Jara, a Spanish town. LUCIANO a sickly and effeminate looking boy of about seventeen is sitting on a bench. He holds a shoe box on his lap. CAMILO, a robust man, comes out of his office. He wears a station master's uniform.*

CAMILO. Hello. What's happening? Why are you here so early?

LUCIANO (*shyly*). I came to show you my worms. Do you want to see them?

CAMILO. Well . . .

LUCIANO. I've got four cocoons and three butterflies. Look.

CAMILO. Wow! An impressive collection of insects.

LUCIANO. Do you want a couple?

CAMILO. No. No, it's OK. Don't . . .

LUCIANO. Have you got any woodbines?

CAMILO (*producing a packet*). Why don't you buy your own tobacco.

LUCIANO (*takes out his lighter*). Like it?

CAMILO. It's all right.

LUCIANO. I'll swap it for your cap.

CAMILO. My cap?

LUCIANO. Yes. I like that cap.

CAMILO. I can't give you this. It's the only one I've got.

LUCIANO. Oh.

CAMILO. When I get another one you can have it, OK?

CAMILO *starts to go.*

LUCIANO. Wait! (*Holds up the lighter.*) So you like it?

CAMILO. I've already told you I like it.

LUCIANO. It's yours.

CAMILO. What . . . ? Give it back to your dad.

LUCIANO. It's mine. He gave it to me.

CAMILO. Keep it then. At least you can give a light after scrounging a cigarette.

LUCIANO. Right. OK.

CAMILO. I'm going in . . .

LUCIANO. Do you know who's arriving?

CAMILO (*patiently*). Who?

LUCIANO. Anita. Agustin's Anita. She's coming back.

CAMILO. What? Ana's coming back?

LUCIANO. Yes.

CAMILO. How do you know?

LUCIANO. I heard. There was a lot of shouting at Paulina's house yesterday. I stopped at the gate to listen and overheard everything. She was asking why Ana had to return now. And Agustin replied that Ana was his daughter after all, with more rights to him than Paulina. Mother says Ana couldn't stand her aunt and they sent her to the convent after Agustin was widowed so she wouldn't make a fuss about . . . that business.

CAMILO. When's she arriving?

LUCIANO. On the ten o'clock Express.

CAMILO. What, now?

LUCIANO. Yes. They said tomorrow yesterday and tomorrow is today, right?

CAMILO. She must have finished her studies.

LUCIANO. Studies? Mother says the nuns kept her on as the school cleaner. If she's studied on her own, that's another story.

CAMILO. Is she coming to stay?

LUCIANO. How should I know?

CAMILO. You know everything else. You sound like a news bulletin.

LUCIANO *(hurt)*. I only told you what I heard.

*Enter* AGUSTIN, ANA*'s father. A rustic-looking man in his fifties. Out of breath.*

AGUSTIN. Good morning.

CAMILO. Good morning Agustin.

AGUSTIN. The Express isn't running late, is it?

CAMILO. No, I don't think so; it's usually punctual. Do you want a drink? You look out of breath.

LUCIANO. I'll go! *(Enters the office.)*

AGUSTIN. I thought I was late . . *(Nervously.)* My Ana's coming home. Imagine! After all these years . . . Oh my God my stomach's churning . . .

*LUCIANO returns with a bottle of wine and gives it to* AGUSTIN.

AGUSTIN. Thanks boy. *(Drinks.)*

CAMILO. Staying long? Ana I mean?

AGUSTIN. No, I don't think so. She's ill. Did you know?

CAMILO *(alarmed)*. Ill. What's wrong with her?

AGUSTIN. Well . . . Pneumonia or something like that.

CAMILO. Is it serious?

AGUSTIN. No. But she needs time to recover and there's no place like home.

CAMILO. She must be grown up.

AGUSTIN. A young woman. She's eighteen already.

CAMILO. I thought she'd put Jara behind her. Seeing as she never visited. Not even in the holidays . . .

AGUSTIN. Needs must. What I mean is . . . bronchial complaints are unpleasant. So . . .

CAMILO. Of course. Of course.

AGUSTIN. She wrote to say she was coming back and . . . nothing really, that she'll be staying with us. (*Agitated*.) It must be just about to arrive.

CAMILO. I'll go and see. (*Enters his office*.)

LUCIANO. Could I have a cigarette please Agustin?

AGUSTIN. Yes, here.

LUCIANO *lights the cigarettes*. AGUSTIN *smokes nervously*.

LUCIANO. You didn't come to the card game yesterday.

AGUSTIN. No.

LUCIANO. You won't come today either obviously.

AGUSTIN. I don't know.

LUCIANO. Because you wouldn't leave Ana alone on her first day.

AGUSTIN. Sorry?

LUCIANO. You won't be coming to the game today either. Right? Yesterday Tinin fell out with José and refused to buy his round of drinks. He threw down his cards and . . . (*Sound of train whistle*.)

AGUSTIN. Quiet, quiet, it's here.

*A moment of suspense. The sound of the train crescendos until it crosses the empty stage. Blackout. The sound of*

*voices and background noises. The train pulls away. The*
*station re-appears. ANA is there with her suitcase,*
*embracing her father. She is a tall, slim woman with big*
*eyes that appear to want to see further into the horizon.*

AGUSTIN. My God . . . ! How you've grown! (*Pause.*) How
are you?

ANA. Much better. (*Coughs.*)

AGUSTIN. Too thin. Thin and pale like an asparagus. But in a
few days you'll . . .

ANA (*interrupting him*). Did you get my letter?

AGUSTIN. Why else would I be here?

ANA. You didn't reply.

AGUSTIN. You wrote to me last minute. You didn't give me a
chance to reply. Anyway how was your journey?

ANA. Fine. Short.

*ANA looks at LUCIANO who is in the conversation.*

AGUSTIN. Do you remember Luciano? Señora Venancia's
son?

ANA. Oh yes. You're much older now.

*LUCIANA carefully and seriously takes ANA's hand and
kisses it reverently.*

ANA. Why did you do that?

LUCIANO (*blushing*). Didn't . . . didn't . . . didn't you like it?
I thought a lady . . .

AGUSTIN *gestures to ANA that LUCIANO is a bit slow.
ANA smiles for the first time and speaks to LUCIANO
amiably.*

ANA. Yes of course I liked it, it's a nice gesture.

*CAMILO approaches from the office door from where he
has been observing ANA intently.*

AGUSTIN. And this is Camilin. Do you remember Camilin?
He's the station master now.

ANA *nods and stretches out her hand.* CAMILO *shakes it affectionately.*

CAMILO. Welcome to town. How are you?

ANA. Well. And you?

CAMILO. Not as well as you. You look wonderful. (ANA *looks away.*)

ANA (*to her father*). Let's go. I'm tired. (*Coughs.*) And I have to take my medication.

CAMILO. Give me a few minutes and I'll drive you.

AGUSTIN. Don't worry son, I've brought the tractor.

ANA. The tractor?

AGUSTIN. Yes, she's running nicely. A leisurely way for you to see how things have changed.

CAMILO. No, no. I can take you in a flash.

ANA (*to CAMILO*). Thanks. I'd rather travel in the tractor.

AGUSTIN. Let's go. (*Takes the suitcase.*) This is very heavy.

ANA. It's full of books, novels . . .

AGUSTIN. You'll never have time to read all these. (*To the men.*) See you later.

*They walk towards the door.* AGUSTIN *exits first. As* ANA *is about to exit,* CAMILO *calls her.*

CAMILO. Ana! (ANA *turns around.* CAMILO *approaches her.*) It's . . . Just . . . There's a dance this evening, if you like . . . I could take you . . .

ANA. I can't go to the dance. My fiancé is working in Paris and in a few months' time he's coming to get me and we'll be married.

CAMILO (*embarrassed*). I'm sorry. I didn't know.

ANA. You know now. Goodbye. (*To* LUCIANO *who has approached them smiling.*) See you soon Luciano.

CAMILO *and* LUCIANO *bid her farewell.* ANA *exits.*

CAMILO (*a bit absent-minded*). She's like a painting.

LUCIANO. She's a stuck-up superwoman from the city.

CAMILO. What do you know?

LUCIANO. And she's got a boyfriend.

CAMILO. Yes. (*Becomes pensive.*) She said he would be away for a few months. In a few months I . . .

LUCIANO. You what?

CAMILO. What's it to you? Go on! Get lost! I've got work to do. (*Goes to his office.*)

LUCIANO (*takes out his lighter*). Do you want it or not?

CAMILO *doesn't turn back.*

LUCIANO. I'd rather give you a light anyway.

CAMILO (*without looking at him*). OK. (*Enters his office.*)

LUCIANO *is left staring at the door for a minute. Then he picks up his box of worms and exits running.*

*Blackout.*

**Scene Two**

AGUSTIN*'s kitchen in Jara.* ANA *dances in the half light. She is wearing a large cape and an old hat made of feathers.* LUCIANO *sings and sometimes plays his flute.*

ANA. Stop! You're singing really badly. (*Takes off her hat and cape and puts them away in a small tea-chest.*) My father might turn up at any moment and he's had it in for me these past days. OK tell me your secret and go.

LUCIANO. I can't today. I have to go to confession first. My secret is a sin.

ANA. Even better; that makes it more interesting. Come on.

LUCIANO. It's just that . . . I don't know.

ANA. Is it an old secret or a new one?

LUCIANO. The day before yesterday. I committed it the day before yesterday and . . . I enjoyed it.

ANA. You enjoyed it? You mean it was pleasurable? (LUCIANO *nods.*) Do you regret it?

LUCIANO (*thinks it over*). No.

ANA. So why go to confession? You're better off telling me.

LUCIANO. It's just that . . .

ANA. Are you going to tell me or not?

LUCIANO. It's a bit embarrassing.

ANA. If you don't tell me we'll break our pact.

LUCIANO. No. No. I'll tell you. (*Pause . . . breathes in.*) The day before yesterday I fucked a sheep belonging to the shepherd from Cañizo.

ANA. Which one?

LUCIANO. Does it matter?

ANA. Of course it matters. We have to slaughter her immediately. Imagine if she's pregnant; she would give birth to a freak . . .

LUCIANO. That's impossible.

ANA. There have been such cases. I've read about them in books. She might have a baby with a tail or a unicorn or . . .

LUCIANO. What's that?

ANA. Never mind. Which sheep was it? Could you identify her?

LUCIANO (*hurt*). Of course I could. But I assure you nothing will happen.

ANA. Men! Your pleasure is always at someone else's expense. Poor little sheep! We have to help her.

LUCIANO. Ana you're babbling. I shouldn't have told you. I thought you'd understand. Do you think the shepherd never does it.

ANA. I'm surprised at you Luciano.

LUCIANO. I'm very lonely.

ANA. So am I but I don't abuse anyone.

LUCIANO. So what do you do?

ANA. I sin alone and I don't need the help of a single photograph. It's easy; I can even be thinking about something else. It's almost magic.

LUCIANO (*with considerable interest*). Magic?

ANA. Yes, I've got a magic button.

LUCIANO. Where?

ANA. You're so stupid sometimes Luciano! I'll explain another day. Right now we need to think about that poor animal. Anyway, if something happens to her who do you think will get the blame?

LUCIANO. Nothing can happen, trust me.

ANA. Really? Oh really? You know more than me now do you?

LUCIANO. No. It's not that. I didn't tell you the whole truth. It wasn't, it wasn't, it wasn't just a sheep. It was, it was, it was . . .

ANA. What?

LUCIANO. A ram.

ANA. A ram? Oh thank goodness. What a relief. (*Sounds outside.*) Father! Put the light on. Quick! It's him.

ANA *puts a ludo board on the table and they both quickly begin to play. Enter* AGUSTIN *holding a bottle of wine.*

ANA. What are you doing? (*To* LUCIANO.) Still here? Your mother is looking for you.

LUCIANO (*gets up scared*). Mother? I was just going. See you tomorrow.

AGUSTIN. God bless.

ANA. Bye. (LUCIANO *exits.*)

ANA (*putting away the board*). You're early today. Do you want dinner now?

AGUSTIN. I'm not hungry. Pass me a glass.

ANA. You should eat something. Your face is turning yellow.

AGUSTIN (*pouring himself some wine*). Sit down.

ANA. Shall I heat up some beans?

AGUSTIN. No. Sit down, I need to talk to you.

ANA. Or would you prefer fried eggs?

AGUSTIN. I don't want any dinner!

ANA. OK . . . I was just going to bed. I don't feel well and . . .

LUCIANO. Ana!

ANA. Look, I'm coming out in a rash and I need to rest. (*Goes to the door.*)

AGUSTIN (*gets up, grabs her and sits her down on a chair*). I told you to sit down!

ANA. You're hurting my arm.

AGUSTIN. You're hurting my soul and I don't complain. (*Pause.*) Time goes by and there's no sign of your Frenchman. I wouldn't mind if you did something useful but what do you do? Eh? What do you do? You lock yourself up indoors and . . . play Ludo with that . . . retard. Camilo dotes on you but you won't as much as look at him. You're not on speaking terms with your aunt. Paulina's such a good woman, always worrying about you . . . (ANA *begins to shake her head and show the whites of her eyes.*) Don't start . . . ! Don't start your nonsense, my nerves are already on edge!

ANA. Water . . . ! Water . . . ! I feel feverish. I'm dizzy. I'm going to faint.

AGUSTIN (*shaking her*). Stop messing about! Come on now. Sit properly. I've got good news.

ANA (*recovering*). Good news? Oh! I'm going blind!

AGUSTIN. Do you remember Don Miguel?

ANA. The doctor?

AGUSTIN. Yes. He's working in the city and lives in a nice house. Your poor aunt, who only has your best interests at heart, got in touch with him to see if he could find you a position. (*Takes off his beret and wipes the sweat from his brow.*) Don Miguel needs a maid and has agreed to give you a job. (*Pause.*) What do you think?

ANA (*alarmed*). Father I can't leave here. I'm waiting for my fiancé.

AGUSTIN. If he turns up, I'll give him directions and send him to you.

ANA. No! He wouldn't come! He told me to wait at home. He writes to me here.

AGUSTIN. He doesn't write to you anywhere!

ANA. Here! This is where he thinks I am and where he'll find me.

AGUSTIN. If he turns up I'll bring him to you.

ANA. But . . . I can't go to the city! I'll fall ill again! The doctor advised the countryside. I could die in the city. I feel dizzy! (*Coughs.*)

AGUSTIN. You're healthy now Ana. Don't make me say things I'll regret. Your aunt says you'll live like royalty. You won't be a servant, you'll be a maid; you'll be a maid with white gloves. It's a chance to straighten out your life. You can't carry on like this!

ANA. Father, I beg you, don't send me back to the city. You can't imagine what it's like. It's an inferno.

AGUSTIN (*after a moment*). What about your aunt? If you stay will you love her?

ANA. No. I can't. Don't ask that of me. That woman has poisoned you against me.

AGUSTIN. She is your dead mother's sister.

ANA. She's a black shadow separating us.

AGUSTIN. She's given me an ultimatum: you or her. She wants us to marry. Paulina has always been very good to me. You won't understand that.

ANA. My fever! Water, father. Touch me. I'm burning. Ahh . . . !

AGUSTIN. Don't lie to me any more Ana. I know all about your fevers.

ANA. What do you know?

AGUSTIN. They expelled you from school . . .

ANA. No!

AGUSTIN. All these years I've never uttered a word. Not to you, not to anyone. But I know everything; the nuns told me.

ANA. What did they tell you?

AGUSTIN. That that bastard made you pregnant.

ANA. No! No! They're lying. They're all lying. He never touched me. I had terrible fevers that seized my heart. (*She cries.*) I was very ill . . . (*Pause.*) Isn't that right? Say yes. Say yes.

AGUSTIN. Lifetimes are long daughter and you can start again. You've got a long road still ahead of you. I haven't. I'm old and I want to spend the last years of my life peacefully with your aunt.

ANA (*looking at him with hatred*). If you marry her I'll denounce you to the police.

AGUSTIN. What?

ANA. Yes, I'll denounce you to headquarters and they'll put you in prison.

AGUSTIN (*laughs*). What for?

ANA. One night Mother was screaming with pain and nobody was responding. I got up to look for you. You weren't in the

house. So I went in to the yard. All the hens were scattered
outside their coop. Then I saw you. You were with her . . .
I watched you writhe and pant. It was years before I realised
what you were doing. But that night I understood the
meaning of death and despair.

AGUSTIN (*drinking nervously*). That was a bad dream.

ANA. That was adultery. And that is forbidden by law. Mother
died very shortly afterwards.

AGUSTIN. Your mother was ill in the head. We did everything
we could to save her. Ask Don Miguel. She was incurable.

ANA. Did she know? Did she know you cheated on her?

AGUSTIN (*banging the table*). No! No! No!

ANA. Are you admitting you cheated on her?

AGUSTIN (*trying to calm himself down*). I did everything in
my power and spent every last penny on medicines for her.
Let's be clear about that Ana. But she was ill for many
years, almost since your birth. We never slept together. I'm
a man for God's sake! Not a saint! (*Drinks.*)

ANA. Couldn't you wait? Of course not, men don't know how
to wait.

AGUSTIN. You've got to forget everything and rebuild your
life Ana. (ANA *begins to tidy the kitchen like a robot.*)
There's a lot of people in the city and you can be just
another face there. That isn't possible here any more.

ANA. OK I'll go and work as a servant. So you two can feel
free again.

AGUSTIN. A maid.

ANA. I'll fall ill and die in three days.

AGUSTIN. You'll live like a princess . . .

ANA. But it doesn't matter. My only wish is to be buried here.
In my town.

AGUSTIN. Don't talk rubbish.

ANA. In the soil. Bury me next to Mother. And don't leave me alone on the first night.

AGUSTIN. You'll earn a good wage and you'll be able to marry in style.

ANA. Flowers. White flowers. Lay white flowers on my grave.

AGUSTIN. Ana!

ANA. Don't worry. My death won't be your fault. It's my destiny.

AGUSTIN. You'll drive me insane. Insane!

ANA. I leave my tea-chest to Luciano in my will. Go ahead: get married and live happily . . . (*She looks into his eyes distracted.*) You don't have much time. When Raúl arrives tell him I was true to him.

*Her father looks at her; not knowing what to say. Drinks desperately.*

ANA. I hadn't predicted you'd get me out of the way again. I'm going to bed.

*Goes to the door and faints at the threshold.*

AGUSTIN. That's enough! You're the one who's going to kill me! (*Tries to sit her up on the chair. Shakes her.*) Ana! That's enough! (*Picks her up in his arms and takes her to the bedroom.*) Anita; I know I'm a bad father, I know, but then you're not very understanding. Right now we're both going to bed; you can think things over and I'm going to sleep this off. And tomorrow we'll talk again. We both have things to be sorry for. Agreed? (ANA *is still unconscious.*) Ana if you want to stay . . . you'll stay. (*Sighs.*) You stay.

*Blackout.*

**Scene Three**

AGUSTIN's *kitchen.* AGUSTIN *and* CAMILO *are chatting and drinking wine.*

CAMILO. Yes I'm building myself a little house near the station. So I don't have to drive in every day.

AGUSTIN. I hear it's a splendid house.

CAMILO. Not really. It's small but welcoming. There's a small piece of land and a workshop.

AGUSTIN. Things aren't going badly for you then?

CAMILO. I can't complain . . .

AGUSTIN. What's next? Do you think about settling down?

CAMILO (*smiling*). Not really. It hadn't crossed my mind.

AGUSTIN. You can say that because you're young but the years flash by like lightning, and when you're old, as the storm clouds clear, you'll find you're missing something. I'm living proof of that.

CAMILO. I've heard your news. I think it's a good idea Agustin.

AGUSTIN. The first time you get married in white. The second: in black.

CAMILO. It's the wanting to that's important.

AGUSTIN. That's what I believe. I'm not short of desire. I feel I've been given a new lease of life, Camilin. You mustn't let cowardice get in the way; if it has to be fought, fight it. Anyway, I'm not the first widower to try again.

CAMILO. That's true.

AGUSTIN. And old ships can't sink any deeper. More wine?

CAMILO (*restless*). Well . . . I think I should be on my way.

AGUSTIN. Wait, I'll see if . . . she's stubborn. She hasn't changed at all since she was a girl. I don't need to tell you that. The day I took her to the station she threw a packet at me through the window; you saw her. Insisted she wouldn't take her aunt's sausages and, can you believe this, threw them at me as the train pulled away.

CAMILO. She looked beautiful that day.

AGUSTIN. Furious you mean.

CAMILO. Both.

AGUSTIN. Wait a moment . . . She told me she had six pages left. She loves novels. She doesn't do anything else. Try and persuade her to go out. She takes no notice of me.

CAMILO. She won't take any . . .

AGUSTIN. Of course she will. Deep down she likes you. She never stopped when she was little 'Camilin this' and 'Camilin that'.

CAMILO. That was a long time ago . . . Lots has happened since then.

AGUSTIN. Nothing, nothing ever happens. You think life is teaching you something but nah . . . We're born fools. We die fools.

CAMILO. But we lose our innocence on the way.

AGUSTIN (*after a while. Seriously*). Innocence lives in the heart. Nowhere else.

CAMILO (*in the same cordial tone*). That's true Agustin.

AGUSTIN. This girl, this girl . . . I'll go and see if . . .

AGUSTIN *goes towards the door as* ANA *appears. She is subtly made up.* CAMILO *stands.*

AGUSTIN. Ah Ana. Was the ending that interesting?

ANA. Hello Camilo. Sit down please. (*Gives him her hand.*)

CAMILO. How are you?

ANA. Fine, fine.

AGUSTIN. What would you like to drink?

ANA (*surprised*). Me?

AGUSTIN. Tell me what you want and I'll go to the bar.

ANA. Thank you father but please don't worry.

AGUSTIN (*to* CAMILO). She doesn't like wine. But Anita dear it's no trouble. I need to stretch my legs. (*He walks towards the door.*) And a bite to eat? Something tasty? (*Goes to exit.*)

ANA. Father! (AGUSTIN *returns.*) We don't need anything.

AGUSTIN (*ignoring her*). What do you mean? The aperitifs are on me. I'll be right back. (*Exits.*)

    ANA *and* CAMILO *are left alone, not knowing what to say to each other. Tense silence.*

CAMILO (*looking round*). I haven't been here for years.

ANA. Since I left?

CAMILO. Before then.

ANA. A long time.

CAMILO. I'd join you at tea-time and your mother would feed us bread and quince.

ANA. But you grew up faster than me and you stopped joining us for tea.

CAMILO. I'm still older than you; three years and three days. What were you reading?

ANA (*shows him the book*). A novel.

CAMILO (*flicks through it*). Any good?

ANA. Passionate.

CAMILO. You must lend it to me.

ANA (*surprised*). Do you read?

CAMILO. Sometimes. I get a lot of spare time at the station so when I get bored of carving . . .

ANA. Do you still carve? (CAMILO *nods.*) You were always stripping branches as a boy.

CAMILO. I made you this.

    *Brings out a figure carved from wood.*

ANA. Thank you. It's beautiful.

> ANA *examines the figure.* CAMILO *observes* ANA. *At one point their gazes meet and they both look down.*

ANA. Who is it?

CAMILO. Isis, an Egyptian Goddess. Goddess of life.

ANA (*looks at the base*). You haven't signed it.

CAMILO. Should I?

ANA. Artists always sign their works.

CAMILO (*takes out his knife*). Right. (*Begins to carve his name.*)

ANA. Why life?

CAMILO. She represents Love faithful beyond the grave. According to legend, Osiris, Isis' husband, was betrayed by his brother and murdered. Isis gathered her husband's body and breathed life into him, 'phoo', resuscitating him for a few seconds. Later she was able to give birth to the dead God's son. That's why she's always suckling a baby. What's wrong? Don't you like it?

ANA. Yes, it's . . . a lovely story. Why are you here?

CAMILO. Your father invited me.

ANA. I know. (*Laughs.*) What an absurd situation. Both of us sitting here, staring at each other. Not knowing why.

CAMILO. I know why.

ANA. Please tell me. I am living in a dream world.

CAMILO. That's just it. I've come to wake you up.

ANA. Why? I don't know what you see in me.

CAMILO. Nor do I.

ANA. It must be because you're a bit mad – like me. I know people round here think I'm a crazy . . . (*She laughs.*)

CAMILO. They don't know what they're saying.

ANA. Do you know me?

CAMILO. I would like to get to know you.

ANA (*shaking her head*). It's too late Camilo.

CAMILO. Ana, let's go to the dance together on Saturday night. I'll invite you.

ANA. You don't know anything about me.

CAMILO. I don't care. And I don't care what people say about you.

ANA. What do you care about?

CAMILO. Getting you out of here, for better or worse.

ANA. Getting me out of my own home?

CAMILO. And out of my head.

ANA. Then there isn't a problem. We won't be seeing each other again.

CAMILO. Why not? Tell me why not?

ANA. I'm waiting for someone.

CAMILO. You're not waiting at all. Nobody can be faithful to a phantom! Ana.

*He takes one of her hands. ANA is momentarily paralysed, disturbed. Then snatches her hand away brusquely.*

ANA. No, don't touch me, I can't stand you touching me. Oh God . . . hands, kisses, bodies. That's all it's about.

CAMILO. That's not what it's about. I can get that whenever I want.

ANA. Listen Camilo, I'm here because I promised my father I'd come down and talk to you. It was a deal.

CAMILO (*refuting*). That's not true.

ANA. How would you know?

CAMILO. You're wearing lipstick.

ANA (*wiping it off*). No.

CAMILO. And eye shadow.

ANA. This is my natural colouring!

CAMILO. And you've perfumed your hair.

ANA. None of this is for you! None! (*Tense silence.* ANA
*relaxes and changes her tone.*) Yesterday, only yesterday I
got a letter from him. He's saving up and he'll be here soon.

CAMILO. You're lying. I know from Luciano that you invent
those letters.

ANA. What? What has Luciano said?

CAMILO. Luciano hasn't actually said anything but the
postman never comes here.

ANA (*absent minded*). The postman . . . the postman . . . the
postman . . . Where's my father? Where's my father gone?
Go Camilo. I need to be alone.

CAMILO. OK. (*He gets up. Tries again on his way out.*) Can I
visit you again?

ANA. No.

CAMILO. All right. But once, a long time ago, at Jara station,
a little girl left town and the last thing she did was kiss the
station porter. Why?

ANA. Just go Camilo. Leave me alone please.

CAMILO *leaves.* ANA *realises he's forgotten his knife and
goes to call him but changes her mind. She picks up the
knife and the figure and with the knife traces over*
CAMILO's *name where he's carved it.* AGUSTIN *enters
carrying bottles.*

AGUSTIN. What did you say to him?

ANA. What could I say to him father? I told him the truth; I'm
waiting for Raúl, he mustn't visit again. (AGUSTIN
*crumples into a chair.*)

*Blackout.*

## Scene Four

ANA *is reading in the kitchen.* LUCIANO *enters.*

ANA (*speaking quietly*). You're early.

LUCIANO. Hasn't your aunt left yet?

ANA. She's getting ready.

LUCIANO. So . . . Shall we play?

ANA. Of course.

> *Takes out the ludo board and counters and puts them on the table.*

LUCIANO (*raising his voice*). I bagsy red and yellow.

ANA. Don't even think about it. I'm having red and yellow.

LUCIANO. No way!

ANA (*whispering*). Louder!

LUCIANO (*almost shouting*). Red and yellow are mine!

ANA (*giving him the counters*). You can have red and blue, I'll have yellow and green. Your throw!

> *They play. All the dialogue referring to the game is spoken very loudly.*

LUCIANO. Five! (*Whispering.*) When is she leaving?

ANA. Three! Any minute now. She's going to seven o'clock Mass.

LUCIANO. One! Have you got a letter for today?

ANA. Six! I get another go! No, he's written me a poem. Five! Your throw!

LUCIANO. Two! I was in the Bar with Camilo. He bought me a beer.

ANA. Really? Four! Did you give him the calendar?

LUCIANO. Five! No there were too many people around. I've decided not to give it to him. I'm fed up of people laughing at me. It's in my bag. I've brought my flute as well.

ANA. Wait!

LUCIANO (*startled*). Got you! I've got you!

ANA *gestures for him to be quiet. Both of them listen attentively until they hear the front door shut.*

ANA. Uf . . . I thought she'd never go. (*Tidies away the board.*)

LUCIANO. It's much more difficult since your father got re-married. Look he hasn't shut the larder. Give me a bit of chocolate.

ANA (*gives him half a pound of chocolate*). I've got to keep an eye on the rice. Remind me to switch it off in six minutes. (LUCIANO *gets the flute out of his bag.*) I've got a marvellous poem for today.

LUCIANO. Ana, it's my turn to start. Yesterday I didn't get a go because you wrote yourself such a long letter.

ANA (*gives him a fixed stare*). He wrote to me! Look at me! (LUCIANO *looks at her.*) He wrote to me. (LUCIANO *nods.*) Go on then you start. He bought you a drink?

LUCIANO. Yes and some stuffed gherkins. Then we played snap and he won.

ANA. Really? But you're an invincible snap player.

LUCIANO (*coquettishly*). I always let Camilo win.

ANA. Why?

LUCIANO. To make him feel more manly.

ANA. Ah . . . ! And then?

LUCIANO. He gave me another note to pass to you. (*Gives it to her.*)

ANA. Rip it up.

LUCIANO. Aren't you going to read it?

ANA. No. OK. Yes. Give it to me. (ANA *opens the envelope reads the letter and tears it into little pieces.*)

LUCIANO. What did it say? Did he mention me?

ANA. Have we started yet?

LUCIANO. Yes, from now.

ANA. Then light the candles. I can't tell lies in all this light.

LUCIANO *lights the candles and switches off the light.*

LUCIANO (*with feeling*). What did he say about me?

ANA. Well . . . erm . . . you're a good card player.

LUCIANO. What else?

ANA. Well that . . . oh I don't know! I'm not inspired today. Why haven't you given him the calendar?

LUCIANO. I didn't want him to laugh at me. (*Takes it out of his bag.*) Or worse; punch me. Take it, keep it in your tea-chest.

ANA (*looking through it*). I don't know how you can fancy these men?

LUCIANO (*reading*). They're body builders.

ANA. They're just muscle. You only have to take one look to see they don't have a brain cell between them.

LUCIANO. If you're going to nag me I'm leaving.

ANA. I'm sorry, don't go. Let's carry on.

LUCIANO. You mean let's start don't you? Today's not your day . . . eh?

ANA. OK! What would you like us to do? I'll let you choose.

LUCIANO. I want you to find something out. (ANA *nods.*) Ana, do you think I'm retarded?

ANA. No!

LUCIANO. Use your special powers.

ANA. I don't need to. It's obvious you're not.

LUCIANO. People aren't nice to me.

ANA. They're not nice to me either.

LUCIANO. That's because you're a bit of a . . . witch.

ANA. And you're a bit of a poufter.

LUCIANO. I'm not a poufter! I'm an . . . homosexual, that's how you explained it.

ANA. Exactly.

LUCIANO. You said there are a lot in the city and many more in Paris, which means I'm not that unusual.

ANA. No you're not. But we live in Jara. And here being different is the same as being mad or retarded. (*She laughs.*)

LUCIANO (*also laughing*). I'm not retarded but sometimes I pretend to be. Take Camilo.

ANA. What about him?

LUCIANO. He's mad about you. But I don't mind because I know that deep down . . . in your heart of hearts, you scorn men.

ANA. I'm waiting for Raúl.

LUCIANO. Yes I . . . (*Pause.*) I'd like to be normal, like everyone else.

ANA (*brusquely*). What for? Normal for what?

LUCIANO. For lots of reasons. No-one's ever opened a door for me Ana. I've never been able to . . .

ANA. Oh shut up! You can't want those trappings – invented by people who want to feel big, important, powerful. All that means nothing.

LUCIANO (*after a moment. Conceding*). OK, you choose what to do. I feel melancholy today.

ANA (*animated*). Do you want to be Raúl? Raúl likes women a lot.

LUCIANO. Pass me that poem, you just wait. (ANA *passes it to him.* LUCIANO *makes a musical entrance playing the flute. Then he begins to read.*) 'Though you may be far, your laughter is hidden in my hat. And without . . .'

ANA (*interrupting him*). Wait. I was just wondering . . .
 Luciano have you ever been with a girl?

LUCIANO. Me? No!

ANA. So, how do you know you don't like them?

LUCIANO. They don't turn me on.

ANA. How can you be sure if you haven't tried? Want to try
 with me?

LUCIANO (*scared*). With you? What for?

ANA. You might find it works. Come on.

LUCIANO. I don't know, it's not right.

ANA. It doesn't bother me. Come on, touch me a bit.

LUCIANO (*retreating*). I don't want to.

ANA. Aren't you Raúl?

LUCIANO. What did Raúl do to you?

ANA. Nothing! He never did anything to me.

LUCIANO (*happily*). Then nor will I.

ANA. Weren't we playing?

LUCIANO. Yes of course. And I wasn't me.

ANA. Nor me, me.

LUCIANO (*looks at her for a moment*). I'd prefer to read you
 the poem OK?

ANA. Fine. I was doing it for you. (*Gets up and puts on her
 hat and cape.*) Begin.

LUCIANO. Shall I play it again?

ANA (*curtsies*). Delighted.

 LUCIANO *plays a musical preamble and begin to read.
 Moves around the room playing out the situations.*

LUCIANO.
 'Although you are far, your laughter is hidden in my hat.
 I may not see you but I always carry your eyes in my luggage.

You are a moon that lights up my nights as I walk.
You are the droplet that colours my sadness an olive green.
And it is so beautiful! And it is so lovely!
That I live only to hold you.' Raúl.

LUCIANO *takes the flute and starts to play again. Suddenly stops and begins to sniff.*

LUCIANO. Ana can you smell something strange?

ANA. The rice! Oh God I forgot to switch it off. The witch will kill me!

ANA *turns off the fire, stirs the rice.* LUCIANO *looks at her and moves to her.*

LUCIANO. Let me try it.

ANA. No don't, my aunt will notice. It's all burnt.

LUCIANO. I mean . . . I'd like to touch you. To see if . . .

ANA. Now? OK but hurry up. (*Looks at her watch.*) We don't have much time left. (LUCIANO *doesn't move.*) Come on . . . (*Since* LUCIANO *is hesitating,* ANA *grabs his hands and puts them on her breasts.* LUCIANO *tenses up.*) Well? What? Hurry. My aunt might arrive any minute now. (*A paralysed* LUCIANO *doesn't reply.*) Can you feel anything? Do you like it?

LUCIANO. I don't think so.

ANA (*sighs with relief*). Thank God. Nothing's changed then.

LUCIANO. Since when?

ANA. A minute ago. Always. You've passed the baptism of fire. You've proved you're not like the rest. (*Kisses him.*) Friend. Now, get lost. She's about to arrive. (*Switches on the lights and puts away the cape and hat.*) Tomorrow at seven?

LUCIANO. Let's dream for real tomorrow. Today was a fiasco.

ANA. D'accorde mon cheri. Oh God the rice!

LUCIANO *exits.*

*Blackout.*

*End of Act One.*

**ACT TWO**

**Scene Five**

*Many years later.* ANA *sings while she does the housework.*
AGUSTIN *enters dragging his legs. He has aged a great deal.*

AGUSTIN. Where's your aunt?

ANA. In town.

AGUSTIN. Why didn't you go with her?

ANA. I never go with her. Have you taken your medicine?

AGUSTIN. Yes.

ANA. With wine or water? (AGUSTIN *doesn't reply.*) Have
you eaten?

AGUSTIN. I'm not hungry.

ANA. You won't flesh out this way! (ANA *continues singing.*
AGUSTIN *walks from one side of the kitchen to the other.*)
Stop pacing. I can't . . . What are you looking for?

AGUSTIN. Nothing.

ANA. Good. Because you may look but you won't find . . .

*The father sighs and sits on the chair.* ANA *continues
working and singing.*

AGUSTIN. There's a dance on this afternoon. Why don't you
go?

ANA (*looks at him in surprise*). What do you mean?

AGUSTIN (*impulsively*). I mean you are going to the dance
this afternoon because I say so.

ANA. Don't spoil my day father. I'm happy. (*Continues to work.*)

AGUSTIN. What will become of you if I die Ana? You can't
let me pass away in dread.

ANA (*stops what she's doing*). You have to do something for
me Father. You've never done much and you owe it to me;
don't die until I've left home.

AGUSTIN. That's not up to me. (*Points upwards.*) He who
commands, commands.

ANA. Stop drinking and God will help you. If you abandon me
before I leave, you'll die a sinner.

AGUSTIN. If I could . . . if I could see you settled. If only
you'd listen to me for once. Why do you think Camilo
hasn't married?

ANA. He doesn't want to.

AGUSTIN. Wrong. I know it's because he couldn't have the
woman he loved. Believe me.

ANA. Nonsense. There's plenty of women in the world. You of
all people know that.

AGUSTIN. Then why hasn't he got married?

ANA. Maybe there's something wrong with him.

AGUSTIN. Like what?

ANA. I don't know. Each of us is ill in our individual way.

AGUSTIN. He's always been there for you.

ANA. Was there. Not now.

AGUSTIN. You didn't give him a chance. But he's never
married . . .

ANA (*interrupting him*). No, I didn't want to see him. I never
want to see him.

AGUSTIN. But why?

ANA. I had a premonition this morning. My moment is near
Father. Very soon I will cease to wait.

AGUSTIN. Good. Can you start today?

ANA. Don't tease me. I won't need to wait because he'll arrive.

AGUSTIN. We'll see . . . How can you be so sure after all these years?

ANA. He loved me.

AGUSTIN. He loved you? He loved you! He had a strange way of proving it.

ANA. He's also a coward.

AGUSTIN. And?

ANA. He's indebted to me. His conscience is troubling him. One day, when he finds himself alone, he'll understand the reality of life and return for me.

AGUSTIN. That is an absurd idea, a fantasy . . . (*She coughs.*)

ANA. Stop it Father. Don't upset me.

AGUSTIN. Why don't you react for God's sake? Why did I have to end up with a daughter like you? Why?

ANA. Because you're a man of no faith.

AGUSTIN. What's wrong with the others? Won't any of them do?

ANA. I'm not in love with the others.

AGUSTIN. Only your bloody Frenchman. Right? God, you don't live in this world. Don't you realise that your ship is sinking. Look at yourself in the mirror. You're not a fresh faced girl any more. It won't be long before no-one will want you.

ANA. Nobody wants me now. Can't you see that? The only person who comes here is Luciano and he gets badly punished for it. What do the rest say about me? Tell me what they say?

AGUSTIN. People don't know what they're talking about. You've got to be seen out on the streets, make them realise

you're still the brightest. You've . . . you've made yourself
ill locked up here in the dark. The humidity in the walls has
affected your nervous system . . .

ANA. I'm not disturbed. I'm waiting for a man!

AGUSTIN. You're torturing me . . . ! torturing me . . . ! Why
has God punished me like this? I never hurt a fly.

ANA. Are you sure?

AGUSTIN. Don't answer back. I am still your father. It's not
my fault you're here. (*Building up steam.*) And you've
behaved like a tart!

ANA. Don't call me that . . . ! Not that . . . ! Not that . . . !
(*She starts to show the white of her eyes.*) Oh . . .

AGUSTIN (*regretting his outburst*). No Ana, don't be a pain in
the neck. Come on now, don't upset me . . . (*Shakes her.
Suddenly he doubles up in pain.*)

ANA (*reacts on seeing him*). What's wrong?

AGUSTIN. Nothing, I'm fine now . . .

ANA (*touching him*). Where does it hurt?

AGUSTIN. It was just a little stab. It's gone now . . . (*Pause.*)
Ana I've got a confession to make. You mustn't tell anyone.
What I mean is your aunt mustn't find out. My business
went well in its last years and I managed to save a bit of
money. It's not much but if anything should happen to me
I want you to know where it is. It's not in the safe so that
your aunt won't find it. I want the money to be for you.
It's . . . it's 1,000,000 pesetas . . .

ANA. But Father . . .

AGUSTIN. Be quiet. It's under the fifth floor tile before you
get to your bedroom. It's stuck down at the moment and I
want you to promise me you'll only lift it off after I have
gone.

ANA. Why are you telling me this?

AGUSTIN. I think my batteries are running out.

ANA. Don't say that. You can't die now. You have to wait for me to leave first. (*She gives him a fixed stare.*) If you betray me now, there will be no going back.

AGUSTIN. I only want you to know the money is yours.

ANA. Father promise me you'll stop drinking. There's still time to sort things out.

AGUSTIN. I can't make promises at my age.

ANA. Use your will power. You have to change your habits.

AGUSTIN. No-one changes at my age.

ANA. For no-one.

AGUSTIN (*after a moment*). For no-one.

ANA (*moves away from him and with a far away look*). Then I prophesy the worst of deaths for you. Yes I see it in your eyes. You will die in terrible agony. Delirious and in pain.

AGUSTIN. How can you say such horrible things!

ANA. You'll turn completely yellow and lose your sight.

AGUSTIN. Shut up! Shut up!

ANA. While your second wife lifts up all the tiles in the house. Plaf . . . ! Plaf . . . ! Plaf . . . !

AGUSTIN (*slaps her*). That's enough! You're mad!

ANA (*after a moment. Bursts into tears*). Sorry father. It's not what I want. (*Approaches him and touches him.*) I see it in your eyes. You have such a sad look . . . dilated pupils. Your eyes are becoming translucent. I loved you the way you were. Strong and proud. Like an oak tree. Don't betray me. Don't die. Now we have got used to each other. Now I don't get in your way any more . . .

AGUSTIN (*wiping away her tears*). You have your Mother's eyes.

ANA. The eyes you like best. Right father?

AGUSTIN. Oh Anita those eyes . . . those eyes reflect all my guilt. And you are sending me to my grave with them engraved on my heart. (*Goes to the larder and looks for something.*) I'm going out.

ANA. Where?

AGUSTIN. Don't worry. I hardly touch a drop these days. But I like holding the glass. It gives me . . . some peace.

AGUSTIN *exits slowly.* ANA *looks at him sadly. Afterwards she goes to her tea-chest, opens it with a key and takes out some old envelopes. She takes out a pencil and paper and writes a letter. Enter* LUCIANO.

LUCIANO. May I?

ANA. Luciano.

LUCIANO. I had to come now. I have something urgent to tell you.

ANA. Can't it wait until seven o'clock?

LUCIANO. No, that's the point. I can't come this evening.

ANA. Why not?

AGUSTIN. Mother said if I come here again she'll tie me to a chair.

ANA. So? She's always threatening you.

LUCIANO. This time she means it. She says you're poisoning me and filling my head with evil thoughts.

ANA. Have you said something? What have you told her?

LUCIANO. Mother has been talking to Fernando, Tomasita's father and they want to marry us.

ANA. But Tomasita's retarded!

LUCIANO. Exactly. I've refused and threatened them with a hunger strike.

ANA. What did they say?

LUCIANO. Nothing. Mother grabbed my sideburns and pulled until I confessed.

ANA. What did you confess? What did you confess?

LUCIANO. What I am.

ANA. You told your parents you're queer!

LUCIANO. No. I told them I'm an homosexual.

ANA. And what did they say?

LUCIANO. They didn't understand what I was talking about at first but then Father marched over to the vet's house and looked it up in the dictionary.

ANA. Oh my God Luciano! You shouldn't have done that!

LUCIANO. Now they blame you. They say you're driving me mad and they want me to take some medicine.

ANA. Medicine? What for?

LUCIANO. I don't know. But I'm not taking their medicine or marrying Tomasa. She is, by the way, very happy with the news.

ANA. What is this parental obsession today with getting us married?

LUCIANO. Yours as well? (ANA *nods*.) They're just passing the buck.

ANA. You've learnt a lot haven't you?

LUCIANO. I'm not getting married. No way.

ANA. That's what I like to hear!

LUCIANO. I'll go on hunger strike!

ANA. You won't be able to do your milk round or visit me.

LUCIANO. Why?

ANA. You'll be too weak.

LUCIANO. I'll eat in secret.

ANA. That's not honest. You'll just have to be brave.

LUCIANO. But I don't want to die.

ANA. Why not? It would be a beautiful gesture.

LUCIANO. Come on. I don't want to overdo it.

ANA. In that case you need a different course of action. Come at seven and we'll plan. OK?

LUCIANO. No, not this evening. It's too difficult. It might be better if I don't come for a while and then . . .

ANA. Are you serious?

LUCIANO. I have no choice . . .

ANA. Don't you believe in me either?

LUCIANO. Yes.

ANA. Then be strong Luciano. You have your reasons. What's a beating? There are worse kinds of pain. You can't stop visiting me now. We've got so much to do . . . Raúl will be arriving soon and I'll take you to Paris with me.

LUCIANO. What about Mother?

ANA. What about your mother?

LUCIANO. Can she come?

ANA. Are you really stupid or just pretending? How can you escape from your mother if you take her with you?

LUCIANO. You're right. She has to see it from my point of view. I can explain myself properly now. Can't I Ana? Now I know a lot more words. (*Resolute.*) I'm going home.

ANA. Do me a favour. (*Puts the letter in the envelope.*) Take this, put a stamp on it and post it. It has to go urgently.

LUCIANO (*reads the envelope*). Are you sure you want me to send it?

ANA. Yes. This time yes. It's got to go today. (*Voices outside.*) What's that?

LUCIANO (*frightened*). Mother!

AGUSTIN *enters.*

AGUSTIN (*to* LUCIANO). Outside. I don't want any trouble.

LUCIANO (*to* ANA). I've had it!

ANA. You have your reasons remember.

LUCIANO. But . . .

ANA. Come on. It was so clear in your mind. Forward!

LUCIANO. I'm in serious trouble.

*Pounding on the door.*

AGUSTIN. Go! I don't want any fighting in my house.

LUCIANO *looks at* ANA *in desperation.*

ANA. Sometimes you need to confront things.

LUCIANO (*squeezing strength from every pore in his skinny body*). Yes; yes I have my reasons and I won't let anyone lay a finger on me. (*Goes towards the door.*)

ANA. Goodbye.

AGUSTIN. He won't be back.

LUCIANO *exits. Outside we hear* LUCIANO*'s cries of 'ay' as he is beaten.* ANA *covers her ears with her hands so as not to hear.*

*Blackout.*


**Scene Six**

AGUSTIN*'s wake. A coffin surrounded by lit candles.* ANA *enters slowly, approaches the coffin, observes her dead father.*

ANA. Alone at last . . . They've all gone to bed. People are so two-faced, Father; they were all here while there was an atmosphere and anise: twenty, forty of them. Now, in the dead of night, they've ended their duty. No, no I'm not saying they don't care; don't be offended, they loved you. You were a drunk but a good man . . . Are you looking at me? (*Gets nearer him.*) No, you've only got one eye open. That brute Paulina kissed you so hard she opened one of

your eyes. Even 'though you don't want to look at me I
know you can hear me. Did you like what people said about
you? I didn't leave my room during the party but I could
still hear them. You've never been kissed so many times in
one day, have you? Not even when you married Mother.
People kiss the dead to bid farewell to Death: ciao, au
revoir, good riddance . . . Do you know what they're
saying? That I cast the evil eye on you. They say I practise
Black Magic, that I bring bad luck. More than one Believer
bathed himself in Holy Water before entering our house.
Oh yes. Fools! If it were up to me Father you would still
be strong and upright. Don't wink at me! This is no time to
be genial. I know you died to avenge me. Father you have
betrayed me by abandoning me and you punish me with
your silence. Can I still hope? You don't have much time
left . . . They want to bury you at ten tomorrow morning.
Open your other eye! Do it for me! Please! I asked you to
wait so many times and . . . nothing. Nothing! Father, if you
have any feeling for me, any little bit, open your other eye.
(*Looks closely at his face.*) Don't you want to? Do you like
being dead? Do you know something? You . . . you look
handsome. Yes, sober. You're looking . . . I don't know, very
dignified. You look like a normal man. If you would only
say 'Ana!' I would forgive everything and we could start
again. Say it: 'Ana' Quietly Father. Move your lips. let me
see . . . ? A-n-a, A-n-a, A-n-a. Come on Father 'Ana . . . '
(*A noise.*)

LUCIANO (*offstage*). Ana.

ANA *stifles a scream and doubles up. A frightened*
LUCIANO *appears in half light at the door.*

ANA. What are you looking for?

LUCIANO (*gasping for breath*). He . . . He's here.

ANA. You frightened me. What are you doing here at this time
of night?

LUCIANO. Mother wouldn't let me come. But she's fallen
asleep so . . . I've escaped.

ANA. You didn't need to come.

LUCIANO. I brought him these flowers.

ANA. Give them to him and goodbye.

LUCIANO. Here, you arrange them for him.

ANA *takes the flowers and puts them at her father's feet.*

ANA. Goodbye Luciano. My aunt might wake up.

LUCIANO. I . . . I wanted to share in your grief.

ANA. You can't; my grief is galloping at top speed.

LUCIANO. I just wanted to say if . . . if you need anything . . .

ANA. You've become very courteous since you stopped
     visiting.

LUCIANO. I mean it. I haven't forgotten you.

ANA. That's why I've seen so much of you this year.

LUCIANO. Mother . . .

ANA (*covering her ears*). Yes, yes; I know.

LUCIANO. How are you?

ANA. Do you care?

LUCIANO. Yes.

ANA *looks at him momentarily.*

ANA. Move. (*They move away from the coffin.*) He can
     overhear us.

LUCIANO. Overhear us?

ANA. I'm getting married in a few months.

LUCIANO (*with a knowing smile*). Congratulations.

ANA. He replied. He replied with a letter full of feeling.
     Memories are powerful Luciano.

LUCIANO. When is he arriving?

ANA. Soon. He's sorting out some important matters.

LUCIANO. Will he come in the grey Jaguar?

ANA. Maybe . . . He said he'll bring me a French wedding dress, like one a Parisian bride would wear.

LUCIANO. And I'll play the wedding march on my flute.

ANA. Yes.

LUCIANO. In the . . . cathedral.

ANA. Yes.

LUCIANO. It will be the best wedding Jara's ever seen.

ANA. Yes and Father will walk me down the aisle. Father . . . Father will be on my arm . . . I'll be on his arm . . .

*Begins laughing and ends up crying inconsolably.*

LUCIANO. Are you crying? What's the matter?

ANA. Luciano I want to die.

LUCIANO. Don't cry Ana; it upsets me.

ANA. Shut my eyes and gently disappear into the wind like a dandelion. Then they'd kiss me too; my body's empty of kisses. (*Dries her eyes and looks at* LUCIANO.) Luciano, do you care about me?

LUCIANO. Of course I do.

ANA. Would you do something for me?

LUCIANO. Yes.

ANA. Whatever I want?

LUCIANO. Whatever you want.

ANA (*smiling at him*). Wait here a minute. (*Returns with a packet.*) Look.

LUCIANO. Holy Mother of God! I've never seen so much money in one place.

ANA. It's for you. Father left it to me and I'm giving it to you so you can save yourself. Or if you don't, at least buy yourself a new van or a pearl necklace for your mother. And if you want to leave town . . . you could . . .

LUCIANO. But this is yours. Why are you giving it to me?

ANA. I won't be needing it.

LUCIANO. How come?

ANA. You promised to do whatever I asked. (LUCIANO *nods. ANA takes out* CAMILO's *knife.*) Cut me here. (*Shows him her wrists.*) Then leave quietly. Tomorrow I'll join Father.

LUCIANO (*with a nervous giggle*). You're not serious?

ANA. Yes. (LUCIANO *begins to shake his head.*) No I'm not serious. It's another game Luciano. Take it. (*Gives him the knife.*) Do it quickly. A sharp cut. (LUCIANO *looks at her uncertainly. ANA smiles at him.*) Please Luciano; it'll be the best thing you've ever done for me. (*Offers her wrists.*) Here.

LUCIANO. Here?

ANA. Yes across my veins. It's got to be very quick. (*Strokes his hair.*) Very quick.

ANA *shuts her eyes.* LUCIANO *puts the knife to* ANA's *wrists. Looks at her and smiles. Quickly turns the knife round and presses* ANA's *veins with the handle.*

LUCIANO. Zap! Done!

ANA *opens her eyes. She looks at her wrists and looks at* LUCIANO *with an air of desolation.*

ANA. You didn't cut me.

LUCIANO. How could I cut you . . . we were playing.

ANA. No, no; I'm not playing. I want you to slit my wrists.

LUCIANO (*tensely*). I don't understand.

ANA. We're not playing now. Look at me. I'm talking to you seriously. This is different. This time it's for real.

LUCIANO (*scared*). But . . . you're asking me to kill you.

ANA. God sent you here to do this.

LUCIANO. No, I only came to express my condolences.

ANA. Listen. I want us to share one secret for all eternity.
Even 'though no-one will ever discover it, you'll feel proud
to have done this. Do you understand?

LUCIANO. Not really . . .

ANA. It's very simple. Do the same as before but this time use
the blade.

LUCIANO (*his fear increasing*). No, no, no.

ANA. Yes. I am begging you. From the bottom of my heart.
Pick up the knife.

LUCIANO. No, no, no . . .

ANA. If you don't . . . (*Fixes her eyes on him.*)

LUCIANO (*terrified*). Don't look at me like that . . . (*Retreats.*)

ANA. If you don't Luciano . . .

LUCIANO (*covers his face with his hands*). No. not the evil
eye. Not the evil eye!

ANA *remains paralysed. The knife falls from her hands.*
*Weakly.*

ANA. You poor boy. Not dying alone takes too much effort. It's
impossible. Our friendship will sleep . . . sleep irremediably.

LUCIANO. You're ill. Ill in the head.

LUCIANO *exits running.* ANA *dazed picks up the knife and*
*looks at it.*

ANA. You don't want to either do you little knife? (*Approaches*
*her father.*) Father he . . . he also says I'm ill in the head.
(*Touches her head.*) Am I ill? (*Picks up the flowers.*) Look
how pretty these are. Poor Luciano brought them for you.
(*Gets closer to his face.*) Father you've shut your other
eye. Why? You've shut your eyes on my darkness. Traitor,
traitor . . .

*Blackout.*

## Final Scene

*Jara's railway station. Springtime. An aged and corpulent Camilo talks to a smartly dressed* LUCIANO. *The station clock marks approximately 5.30pm.*

CAMILO. You're getting married . . . well . . . well . . .

LUCIANO (*restless*). Hmm. . . about time isn't it? Do you think it's a bad idea?

CAMILO. Do I? It's nothing to do with me.

LUCIANO. We're going to live with Mother, and . . . I will carry on life as usual. What about you?

CAMILO. What about me?

LUCIANO. Seeing anybody?

CAMILO. As many as I can! (*He laughs.*)

LUCIANO. And . . . ?

CAMILO. Get married?! Not me! I'm still young.

LUCIANO (*impulsively*). I prefer you single. (*Backtracking.*) I mean . . . you're better off alone. I mean, what I mean is strong-minded men can do it. Bah, I'm talking rubbish . . .

CAMILO. Nerves. Getting married is a serious business.

LUCIANO. True. (*Pause.*) You never gave me the cap.

CAMILO. What cap?

LUCIANO. That one. Your one. You promised it to me once. When I was a kid. Remember?

CAMILO. No.

LUCIANO. I've never had a uniform. I don't like all uniforms, but . . . I like that one. I'd like to get married in that uniform.

CAMILO. A Railways uniform? You're joking . . .

LUCIANO (*touching the uniform*). No, this one.

CAMILO (*moves away and starts to laugh*). You want me to lend you my uniform to get married in. You're mad.

LUCIANO (*seriously*). I don't see what's so funny?

CAMILO (*teasing*). You've come to ask me for my uniform?

LUCIANO. No, I didn't. (*Annoyed.*) Can't you take a joke? I don't like people laughing at me.

CAMILO. Don't get angry. It amused me. Here. Take this. Smoke it.

LUCIANO. You treat me like shit. You don't do it to anyone else. Why?

CAMILO (*surprised*). I don't like the way you look at me sometimes . . . That's all.

LUCIANO. I'll go if I upset you.

CAMILO. What's the matter with you?

LUCIANO. Nothing. (*Kicks the ground.*) I'd like to beat you to a pulp.

CAMILO (*laughing*). OK . . . OK . . . You're really worked up. Go home and have a drink.

LUCIANO (*firmly*). Yes, I'm going.

CAMILO. Look, if it's about the cap . . .

LUCIANO. No, no; forget it.

CAMILO. Luciano, I've heard that trains won't stop at Jara soon. I'll give you everything when the station shuts down. OK?

LUCIANO. No. (*Walks away.*) Well OK. Do whatever you want.

CAMILO. We're not going to come to blows over a cap are we?

LUCIANO. You're a shit.

CAMILO. I need all my patience for you.

LUCIANO. Me too. See you tomorrow. (*Exits.*)

CAMILO *goes into his office. A train goes by at top speed. Doesn't stop. The station is empty again.* ANA *enters and sits on a bench. She looks serene. Her face is made up. She is dressed in white and carries a straw hat which she rests at her side.* CAMILO *enters. He is surprised to see her and, still standing, exchanges a long look with her. Then he smiles timidly and approaches her.*

CAMILO. Hello Ana. What . . . what a surprise . . .

ANA. Didn't you expect me?

CAMILO. Expect you? Why would I?

ANA. Of course, why would you?

CAMILO. I thought . . . I thought you never left the house.

ANA. Today's the first day I've come out.

CAMILO. I'm glad you have. And, most of all, I'm very happy your first visit is to the station.

ANA. Why?

CAMILO (*blushing*). Because . . . well because I'm still here.

ANA. Is the six o'clock Express late?

CAMILO. No, why? Are you expecting someone?

ANA. Raúl's arriving; yes the Frenchman. It's a shame he didn't get here before. Father won't meet him. (CAMILO *stares at her, incredulous.*) It's all happened very fast. A few letters, the strength of the past . . . Yesterday I received a telegram: Arriving tomorrow, on the six o'clock Express. Stop. Wait for me. Stop. Raúl. And at that moment I began to see everything. The letters danced in my head as if they were moving to music, drum music. Each note, a blow, each blow a year. Until nothingness, until the moment of departure.

CAMILO. Ana are you feeling all right?

ANA. I've never felt better. Things have never been clearer to me. (*Looks at him tenderly.*) You look old.

CAMILO. I'm overcome by your honesty.

ANA. You are my mirror. I didn't realise how much time had slipped by until I saw you a moment ago.

CAMILO. When I saw you on the other hand I felt young.

ANA. Really? Why?

CAMILO. A very strong feeling stirred in me. A feeling that has always lived here.

ANA. What do you mean?

CAMILO (*lowering his gaze*). Nothing.

ANA. Is that feeling still there?

CAMILO (*nodding*). You're an obsession. You haunt me. Many evenings, after I leave here, I walk into the town so I can gaze at your house, see your shadow in the window . . . At first it seemed like a nightmare but afterwards . . .

ANA. And now? What am I to you right now?

CAMILO. Whatever you want to be.

ANA. Perhaps we could still . . .

CAMILO. What?

ANA. After I read the telegram yesterday I thought about you. I thought about you a lot. I said to myself: God, it was so close! I only had to open the window and breathe and you would have heard. Instead . . .

CAMILO. Yes?

ANA. I only had to hear your name and I'd tremble with fear. But not now. I'm not scared anymore.

CAMILO. So we could . . .

ANA. Yes?

CAMILO. Try . . . I don't give a fuck what people say. Be my partner at the dance.

ANA. Here? (CAMILO *nods*.) Not here.

CAMILO. Wherever you want.

ANA. Somewhere by the sea.

CAMILO. By the sea? The sea's a long way off.

ANA. By the sea.

CAMILO. Agreed. When?

ANA. Now. We have to get the six o'clock train. (CAMILO *looks at her disconcerted*.) I'm getting on it; you're welcome to join me.

CAMILO. Now?

ANA. Now or never.

CAMILO. Why the urgency?

ANA. I've told you. The telegram yesterday woke me up. It arrived full of light. I don't want to be a prisoner a day longer. And Raúl's arriving and I'd rather not see him. I didn't have time to stop him coming. Only urgency wakes sleeping souls.

CAMILO. I don't understand . . .

ANA. Maybe it's because you don't believe me. Can you love someone and not believe them?

CAMILO. What about you? What do you feel?

ANA. I feel you; I feel you for the first time. (*Takes his hand*.)

CAMILO (*happily*). I can't believe you're here by my side.

ANA. Let's leave here Camilo. The train will be here in a few minutes. One of the last. What will you do when the station closes down?

CAMILO. We need to talk. Time to plan properly.

ANA. More time? No, no; we've lost so much already . . .

CAMILO. I should arrange . . .

ANA. There's nothing to arrange. What for? I've got money.

CAMILO. Ana, why make things difficult for ourselves?

ANA. Difficult? It's so easy . . . The train stops and, at that moment without hesitating, we jump on the last carriage. (*She laughs.*) No-one will ask us for a ticket. Not with you in that uniform.

CAMILO (*also laughing*). When will you stop playing?

ANA *unexpectedly takes hold of* CAMILO*'s head and kisses him on the mouth. A train simultaneously whistles in the distance.*

CAMILO (*starting*). The Express!

ANA. The Express!

CAMILO. I've got to go to my office.

ANA. What for? We need to be quick. The train won't stop here for long.

CAMILO. Come with me Ana. We'll talk calmly afterwards.

ANA (*fixes him with a stare*). I'm getting on that train.

CAMILO. Don't be silly . . . we've got a lot to do before . . . come with me.

ANA. No.

CAMILO. Fine. Then wait here. I'll be back.

ANA. When?

CAMILO. Right away. As soon as the Express has left.

ANA *nods mechanically.* CAMILO *goes into his office happily and hastily. The train arrives. Blackout. The train pulls away. There is now an elegantly dressed man carrying a suitcase on the platform, searching with his eyes.* ANA *has gone.* CAMILO *comes out of his office and sees the man. He also searches round.* ANA *has gone.* RAUL *nervously approaches* CAMILO.

RAUL. Excuse me. Do you know a young lady called Ana Ramirez?

CAMILO *perplexed nods.*

RAUL. I thought she'd be here to meet me . . . strange . . .

CAMILO (*coming to*). Are . . . you the Frenchman?

RAUL (*surprised*). My name is Raúl . . . Raúl Mendez.

CAMILO. I'm . . . the station master . . .

RAUL. I can see that. What about Ana? Has she been here?

CAMILO. She came. Yes she came; but I don't see her now.

RAUL. So she was here?

*They both look round.*

CAMILO. Wait.

*On a bench he sees the figure of Isis he'd given her; there's an envelope on top of it. He picks up the figure and reads the envelope. Suddenly he looks up and out into the horizon. RAUL approaches him.*

RAUL. Is something wrong?

CAMILO (*handing him the letter*). She left on the train you arrived on. She left you this.

*RAUL opens the letter and reads it. His composure gradually crumbles.*

RAUL (*almost rhetorically*). Has she gone? (CAMILO *nods. Silence.*) When does the next train go?

CAMILO. Where?

RAUL. Wherever.

CAMILO. In six hours.

RAUL. Thank you.

*Picks up his suitcase and sits on a bench. Reads the letter again. Suddenly begins to laugh hysterically. CAMILO approaches him.*

CAMILO. Are you all right?

RAUL. She says she's sorry, sorry she couldn't let me know sooner . . . and goodbye. (*Laughs bitterly.*) Do you know what else? She's in love with another man. She realised yesterday she was in love with another man. Another man . . . (*Sadly.*) Eh? Doesn't it make you laugh?

CAMILO (*shaking his head*). Sometimes you just get there too late . . . too late.

*Throws his cap angrily to the ground. The two men look at each other momentarily in silence as the lights dim.*

*Blackout.*

*The End.*